PALESTINE

Isa Khalil Sabbagh, the author's father, left Palestine
for Britain in the 1930s and made a career in the
West when he was not allowed to return to Israel.

PALESTINE

A Personal History

...

KARL SABBAGH

Atlantic Books
LONDON

First published in Great Britain in 2006
by Atlantic Books, an imprint of Grove Atlantic Ltd

1 2 3 4 5 6 7 8 9

A CIP catalogue record for this book is available
from the British Library.

ISBN 1 84354 344 3

Printed in Great Britain by
CPD, Ebbw Vale, Wales

Atlantic Books
An imprint of Grove Atlantic Ltd
Ormond House
26–27 Boswell Street
London WC1N 3JZ

THE PLEA

To find me you must stop the noise:
silence the guns and the tanks,
the shouted orders
and the shouts of defiance,
screaming and weeping,
and listen.

My voice is very weak.
You must try to hear it.
You will have to come close
and pick away the tumbled stones
carefully, gently.

When you find me, lift me out,
help me to breathe;
set my broken limbs
but don't think it's enough
to give me back a fragile existence.

I need food and water,
I need a home that will last,
health and hope and work to do.
I need love.

You must embrace me
and take me to your heart.
My name is Peace.

Sue Sabbagh, June 2002

CONTENTS

ILLUSTRATIONS

The author and publishers are grateful to the following for permission to reproduce illustrations: 6, 8, 63, 87, 93, 107, 120, 126, 127, 134, 158, 166, 172, 175, 185, 191, 249, 254, 273, G. Eric and Edith Matson

Photograph Collection, Prints and Photographs Division, Library of Congress, Washington, D.C.; 27, © Ziad Daher, Nazareth 1999; 291, Getty Images. All other images from the author's personal collection.

Every effort has been made to contact all copyright holders. The publishers will be glad to make good in future editions any errors or omissions brought to their attention.

ACKNOWLEDGEMENTS

Many people have helped me shape my ideas for this book by providing information and encouragement in the research and writing process, but the person whose inspiration and example have been most before me at every stage is Edward Said, the Palestinian intellectual and writer, and my dear friend. In his own writings he marshalled a huge amount of evidence of the injustices done to the Palestinians and wrote about the topic unapologetically, in spite of continual attempts to silence any presentation of the Palestinian case. I, too, am unapologetic, and I have no doubt that this book too will generate hostility from those who would prefer Palestinians to stay silent and accept their fate. Since Edward's death, his wife Mariam and his children, Wadie and Najla, have continued to be supportive of my work and I owe them thanks.

A number of members of my own family have been very helpful in sharing their memories and their comments. They include Ulla Sabbagh, Ghassan Khalil Sabbagh, Aleef Sabbagh, Hasib Sabbagh and Elias Sabbagh. It is unfortunate – and a sign of the depth of fear that exists nearly sixty years after 1948 – that other relatives who experienced the events surrounding the expulsion of Palestinians from their homes are still reluctant to talk about it. On my mother's side of the family I am grateful to my uncle, Peter Graydon, for sharing his memories of wartime years in London.

I would like to thank a number of people who have been helpful in various ways, from reading drafts of the text and giving me their comments to supplying hospitality and information. They include Ilan Pappe, Nur Masalha, Elfi Pallis, Avi Shlaim, Afif and Christ'l

Safieh, Mahmoud Hawari, Raymonda Tawil and Hala Taweel, Hanna and Tania Nasir, Vera Tamari, Nadia Abu-el-Haj, Leila Tannous, Karma Nabulsi, Ghada Karmi, Diana Allan, Sasha Hoffman, Tim Rothermel, Iain Chalmers, Philip Davies, Diana Allen, Fergus Bordewich, and Duaibis and Maha Abboud Ashkar.

David Ben Shimon was an excellent guide to Safad in my search for traces of my family there, and I was able to explore most of the sites connected with Daher al-Omar thanks to an *Ancient and Modern* travel grant.

Peter Oppenheimer at the Oxford Centre for Hebrew and Jewish Studies encouraged me to use his excellent library, and the meetings and archives at the Middle East Centre at St Antony's College, Oxford, provided valuable background material.

My wife, Sue, has encouraged and supported my work in many different ways, and I am grateful in particular for her poem of hope with which the book begins.

Finally, at Atlantic Books I have received much encouragement and guidance from Toby Mundy, Clara Farmer and Bonnie Chiang, and efficient editing from Ian Pindar and Jane Robertson.

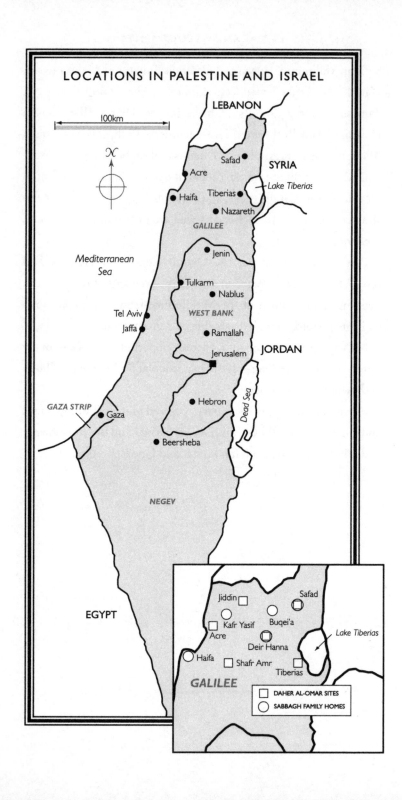

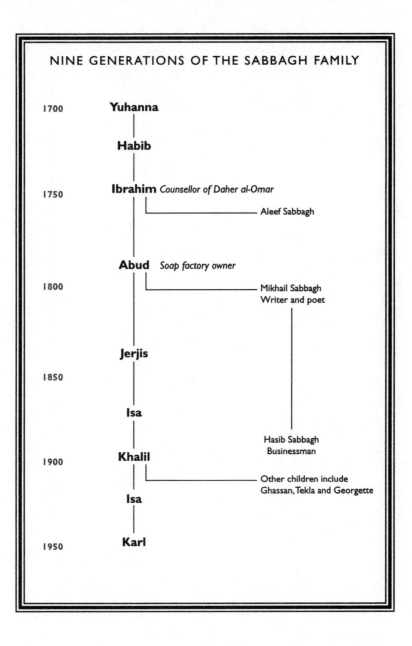

NINE GENERATIONS OF THE SABBAGH FAMILY

1700 · **Yuhanna**

Habib

1750 · **Ibrahim** *Counsellor of Daher al-Omar*
└─────── Aleef Sabbagh

Abud *Soap factory owner*
1800 ·
└─── Mikhail Sabbagh
Writer and poet

Jerjis

1850 ·

Isa

Hasib Sabbagh
Businessman
1900 · **Khalil**
└─── Other children include
Ghassan, Tekla and Georgette

Isa

1950 · **Karl**

PROLOGUE

I am the son of a Palestinian father, but I am endowed with few
of the characteristics associated in the popular mind with
Palestinians or Arabs. I am not poor, unshaven or a speaker of
broken English. I do not know how to use a gun or manufacture a
bomb. I have had little to do with camels, sand or palm trees. But I
both sympathize and identify with the Palestinian people.
Interestingly, the sympathy was formed in my early years when I
knew little about my own family connections with Palestine, raised
as I was by an English mother in south London. But I could read
about history and about the way in which a group of Jews called
Zionists set themselves the task of turning an Arab country into a
Jewish homeland, against the will of the majority of the inhabitants
who had themselves been promised independence and self-
government after the First World War.

A few years ago I came across an article by Freya Stark, traveller
in the Middle East, published in *The Times* in 1940. It was headed
'Wireless in Arabia' and described a scene in a village square on the
Arabian peninsula, as the inhabitants sat around listening to
Arabic music on the radio:

> The square, though subdued, is full of listening ears, but
> it is the power of these pastoral melodies that they carry
> their own loneliness with them and bring into their notes
> the quiet horizons, the long days of sea-faring on
> mountain pastures, the empty, easy hours of noonday
> when they were first conceived. It is pleasant to have this
> calm contrasting picture to the European news. This now

comes, dropping slowly in tempered accents: we are lucky to have an announcer with a beautiful voice. He picks out every syllable, giving it full value in a way that Arabs, who all adore their language, appreciate and understand ...

I like to think that 'beautiful voice' belonged to my father, Isa Khalil Sabbagh. Stark was writing at about the time my father, working for the BBC, had become one of the most popular Arabic announcers and presenters on the radio, when there were no national broadcasters to be trusted in the Middle East and the whole Arab world turned to the BBC for objective accounts of what was going on in the world war raging around them.

My father had come from Palestine to Britain in the 1930s, after graduating from the Government Arab College in Jerusalem. He was still in his teens but he lied about his age in order to enter a British university to study history. When the BBC advertised for staff for its new Arabic Service, he applied and was appointed. He

As one of the Arab world's most popular broadcasters during the Second World War, Isa Khalil Sabbagh produced programmes and was also a war correspondent for a time.

became an announcer, a newsreader and then a programme producer and presenter.

At the beginning of the war, fearful of being put out of action by German bombing, the BBC evacuated some of its departments to a large country house near Evesham in Worcestershire. One of these was the Variety Department, where my mother worked as a secretary. Another was the News and Programmes section of the Arabic Service, where my father was making his name as a newsreader and presenter. One department produced programmes with titles like *Ack-Ack Beer-Beer*, *Variety Bandbox* and *Workers' Playtime*; the other was responsible for daily readings from the Koran and a regular series called *Ala Hamish al-Akhbar (On the Margin of the News)*, known to the British engineering staff as 'The Hamish'.

My mother, a citizen of Great Britain, a country that had initiated the disastrous change in fortunes for Palestine and Palestinians, knew nothing about the Middle East. Indeed, for her entire life she was unable to pronounce my father's Arabic

Isa Sabbagh wrote and directed radio plays in the Arabic Service of the BBC in the 1940s.

Christian name. But he was handsome, she was beautiful, and at a time when no one knew how long the war would last or what would be the final result, it seemed a good idea to marry. I was the result. Within a couple of years of my birth, my parents divorced, although my father stayed in Britain and continued to broadcast for the BBC Arabic Service.

When my father left Palestine to study abroad, he expected to return regularly to the country his family had lived in for generations. Since the end of the First World War Palestine had been governed by Great Britain, charged by the League of Nations with bringing the country eventually to self-government. At the time this task was given to Britain the population of Palestine was more than 90 per cent Arab, and so, like most Palestinians, my father expected one day to be a citizen of a largely Arab and independent Palestine.

But in 1947 he was sent by the BBC to report on a UN vote that decided, after a lot of partisan pressure on the members of the General Assembly, that the majority population of Palestine should hand over more than 50 per cent of its land to the minority of Palestinian Jews. The result of this vote, resisted by the Arabs, was a war in 1948 that ended in the establishment of the Jewish State of Israel in Palestine and a ban on Palestinians, like my father, from returning to their homes. Two years later my father left Britain for America to start the *Voice of America* Arabic Service and a few years after that he became an American citizen and began a life-long career in the American State Department.

I often wonder what 'Palestine' meant to my mother and others of her class, which I suppose we would call lower middle. Today, for most people, the Israel–Arab dispute is defined by headlines about bombings, political assassinations, the Wall, settlements and illegal occupation, all of which are far from the cause of the problem. In the same way in the 1940s, when people were pre-occupied with the Second World War, their only awareness of Palestine would be framed by terrorist attacks (this time by Jews) against British soldiers, illegal immigration into Palestine, and riots by Jews and Arabs. Then, as now, the day-to-day events in the conflict conveyed little or nothing about the roots of the dispute, and I'm sure my mother was only dimly aware of the historical steps that led to her former husband having no home to return to.

I shared in that ignorance for most of my childhood. I later realized that for centuries there have been peculiarly narrow limits to British understanding of Palestine. The British view has been determined either by the Bible or by a specifically Jewish perception of the land. The Arab population has always suffered from being perceived as 'natives', a view that was promoted to the British by those European Jews who wanted to capitalize on the colonialism that was inherent in British government at a time when the Empire still made a major contribution to British identity. Nowadays, of course, to be a native means little more than to be an indigenous inhabitant of a country, and the idea that 'natives' should govern themselves is seen as a right, rather than as a privilege to be earned. But in the corridors of power in early twentieth-century Britain, the politicians were perfectly happy to go along with the idea that the natives of Palestine would be incapable of self-government.

As one of those natives my father knew better. He was from a society with a long tradition of local self-government, through village leaders and town mayors, a self-supporting agriculture-based economy, and a culture that was founded on Islam and Christianity, with an educated middle class. But Palestinian history was of no interest to the nations of the West. Just as today 'Western-style

Many photographs of nineteenth- and twentieth-century Palestine focused on the stereotype of the Arab peasant in the landscape, often with biblical overtones.

democracy' is seen as the highest ideal a nation can attain, so then men in top hats and morning coats in Whitehall could not conceive of any merit in a culture they knew only from figures in Victorian watercolours of the Holy Land or naive accounts of horseback rides across biblical terrain. Since that time, understanding of Palestinian history and culture has not really improved outside the Middle East. In fact, today, the activities of Israel on the world stage, supported by the United States, are sometimes accompanied by the denial that there *is* a history of Palestine.

In this book I propose to show that the foundation of the State of Israel perpetrated an enormous injustice against the Palestinians. This injustice was achieved by promulgating a series of institution-alized lies to the rest of the world – a process that continues today. There was a slick slogan – 'A land without people for people without a land' – invented by the Zionist Israel Zangwill, which has the power to stick in people's minds, and serves the useful purpose of implanting the false impression that Palestine was uninhabited when Jews decided to agitate for it to become their state. As Alexis de Toqueville said: 'It is easier for the world to accept a simple lie than a complex truth.' Golda Meir, an Israeli Prime Minister, said in 1970: 'There is no such thing as a Palestinian people.' Just as Dr Johnson refuted Bishop Berkeley's claim that we can't know the existence of anything, by kicking a large stone,[1] the Palestinian people – who apparently don't exist – have amply refuted Golda Meir's claim since 1970, often in tragic ways.

The following are typical of the sort of remarks you can find in discussions of Middle East affairs on the websites of supporters of Israel:

> '... the concept of "Palestinians" is one that did not exist until about 1948, when the Arab inhabitants, of what until then was Palestine, wished to differentiate themselves from the Jews. Until then, the Jews were the Palestinians.'

> 'The Arabs who now call themselves "Palestinians" do so in order to persuade a misinformed world that they are a distinct nationality and that "Palestine" is their ancestral homeland.'

> '... many of the "Palestinians", or their immediate ancestors, came to the area attracted by the prosperity created by the Jews, in what previously had been pretty much of a wasteland.'

> 'The nationhood of the "Palestinians" is a myth.'

In contradiction to these erroneous statements, this book will show that Palestine and the Palestinians do exist and have done for centuries. From the beginning of recorded population statistics in the area, until 1948, Palestinian Arabs formed a significant majority of the population of Palestine, for most of the time about 90 per cent. Most of the Jewish people who demanded to rule over the territory of Palestine in the twentieth century had no connection with that territory other than through a religion whose adherents had ruled a part of the area for a period about 2–3,000 years ago. Hostility between Jews and Arabs in Palestine today is largely a product of the events of the last eighty years, rather than being a traditional enmity. In order to create a state with the smallest possible population of non-Jews, Jewish forces deliberately expelled many Palestinian Arabs from their homes in 1947 and 1948. Today, to conceal the injustice done to the Palestinians, Israel continues to present false accounts of their history.

Some readers may already feel that this list of claims reads too much like 'PLO propaganda'. In a sense, in that these are claims that the PLO (among others) has been trying to propagate over the years, this is true. But judgements about the truth of such statements have to be made on the basis of evidence not prejudice.

A rare archive image of Palestinians in a twentieth-century occupation.

Palestinian writers are often accused of dwelling too much on history. 'What's past is past. Even if injustices were done to the Palestinians, we have to move on.'[2] But of course, the people who complain about retelling the history of the last hundred years base their support of Israel on a mythical history that is far older. What's past is indeed past.

There are two other stories to mention – one which will be in the book, the other which will not. As I investigated my own family's history in Palestine it turned out to impinge at various points on the wider historical picture and so I have used what I have discovered to personalize the history of the Palestinian people as well as to show the long and intimate associations Palestinians have with their land.

What will not be in the book is much about the period after 1948. I have not dealt with the early years of Israeli interactions with Palestinians both inside and outside Israel, nor with the various wars fought between Israel and the Arabs, nor with peace talks, Palestinian terrorism, Israel's targeted assassinations, 'one state or two?', the demographic problem, Gaza, the West Bank, or the so-called security fence. We read about these in our daily newspapers and there are documentaries about them on television. They are all the consequences of the massive injustice done to the Palestinians in the first half of the twentieth century, which is the subject of the book.

Neither do I offer a comprehensive solution to the Palestinian–Israeli problem. But I do believe that pressure on Israel to agree to a just solution will grow with public understanding of the circumstances that led to the establishment of Israel in 1948. And that is also what this book is about.

Karl Sabbagh, April 2005

I

ANCIENT PALESTINE

• • •

Aleef Sabbagh, a cousin I had known for less than twenty-four hours, stretched his arms wide in an olive grove in the Galilee. He was showing me the width of the trunk of one of his family's olive trees, wider than he could spread his arms. 'Eight hundred years old,' he said, with pride and a little exaggeration. The gnarled and twisted tree still bore a rich crop of olives each year. It was coming up to harvest time, and soon Aleef, his brothers, their wives, children and cousins would be in this grove picking the olives as he and our family had done for hundreds of years.

Where should one begin in assessing the competing claims of Arabs and Jews to Palestine? How far back in history should a claim be allowed legitimacy? There are fully fledged nations in existence today, members of the United Nations, which not only did not exist a hundred years ago but whose people had no national identity at that time. There are other peoples, the Armenians or the Kurds, for example, who have existed with a cultural and social unity for a thousand years or more, yet do not have independent nationhood free from the control of a superior power.

It sometimes seems that the argument between the Israelis and the Palestinians is fought on the basis that the further back in

history either side can show residence in the area, the more entitled they are to the land today.

'The key to understanding Israel,' says a modern tourist guide to
Israel, 'is to understand that it was created as the modern reincar-
nation of an ancient Jewish state. Israel was the Promised Land of
Abraham and Moses, the Israelite kingdom of David and Solomon,
and the home of Jesus of Nazareth and the Jewish Talmudic sages.
Although the Jewish presence in the country has been unbroken
for more than 3,000 years, several massive exiles – first by the
Babylonians in 586 BC and then by the Romans in AD 70 – created a
diaspora, a dispersion of the Jewish people throughout the world.'[1]
Or, to take a different view, 'Jewish tenure of Palestine, in any real
sense of the word "Palestine", was never complete and it only
lasted continuously, within its limits, for seventy years. It lasted,
this vaunted possession, for no longer than the lifetime of one man,
and that was three thousand years ago.'[2] (This refers to the time of
David and Solomon, from about 1016 BCE.)

The land of Palestine is a small territory in the eastern
Mediterranean, about 250 miles from north to south and 70 miles
at its widest from east to west. The southernmost third of the
country, stretching down to the Red Sea, is largely desert, but the
northern two thirds is dominated by a fertile plateau, separated
from the Mediterranean by a coastal plain. Over the centuries it
has changed from being a focus of world attention, a crossroads of
great power conflict in pre-Christian times, to a backwater in the
heyday of the Ottoman Empire, when the Turks ruled over the
Middle East and parts of Eastern Europe.

In the north, the hilly region of Galilee stretches from the ports
of Haifa and Acre to the beautiful town of Safad, where my family
originated, and to Lake Tiberias, the New Testament Sea of
Galilee. In the middle of the country, Tel Aviv and Jaffa are on the

Aleef Sabbagh in the Galilee landscape his family has inhabited for many generations.

coast and forty miles south-east is the hill city of Jerusalem. Further east the hills drop steeply to the Jordan valley, the town of Jericho, and the Dead Sea. In the southern part of Palestine, the Mediterranean coast curves round towards Egypt, and a little way inland is the city of Gaza, while stretching further southwards towards the Red Sea is the Negev desert. Scattered throughout the 10,000 square miles of Palestine are ancient towns and villages, organized over the centuries into traditional allegiances and rivalries, with larger towns forming regional capitals and centres of trade and culture for the surrounding villages.

Many different 'peoples' have lived in Palestine over the centuries. I say 'peoples' in quotes because there is no really accurate way to determine from historical texts and excavations the precise connections or ethnicities of the groups who have left traces of their presence. A name given to one group may imply that its members are different from a group with another name, but in fact a combination of intermarriage, religious conversion and adoption of foreign customs and styles may mean that some groups with different names were ethnically identical.

Five thousand years ago, a succession of population groups migrated north from the Arabian peninsula into areas of the Middle East. These people are labelled together as Semites because their languages were all related and presumed to be derived from a common tongue. These groups were organized into tribes and founded civilizations in territories that stretched in a broad band across the modern states of Iraq, Jordan, Israel, Syria and Egypt. The group that populated the area of Palestine became known as Canaanites. Another group of Semites left the Arabian peninsula, arrived in Egypt and then, two thousand years after the Canaanites, travelled to Palestine, where they became known as Hebrews (from the word 'habiru' meaning 'nomad'). Here they started out by adopting many of the characteristics of the Canaanites, including their culture, traditions and dialects and their polytheistic religion. But at some point the Hebrews adopted monotheism, an idea they had come across in Egypt, and the precursor of the Jewish religion was born.

Since the 1970s, on the basis of surveys by Israeli archaeologists in the West Bank, it has been concluded by most experts that the first communities that were to form the ancient states of Israel and Judah settled in the central highlands of Palestine in the late thirteenth or early twelfth century. Some elements of these people may have come from elsewhere in Palestine, some from just over the Jordan; but they were local indigenous people. Whether some group joined them that had recently been in Egypt is an open question: there is absolutely no material proof of this, and the culture of these hill farmers was entirely 'Canaanite'. It was to be a couple of centuries at least before these farming communities coagulated into a 'nation' and formed a political state.

In considerable detail, the Old Testament describes a series of events, some of them said to be divinely caused, from the birth of

Abraham in 2050 BCE, through the Jews' period of slavery in Egypt, entry into the 'Promised Land', reigns of various kings, including David and Solomon, over an area of Palestine they called Israel, and division of this area into two 'kingdoms', Judah and Israel. The books go on to describe how these two kingdoms met different fates, one falling to the Assyrians and the other to the Babylonians, who destroyed the temple in Jerusalem and shipped the people of the kingdom off to Babylon. These last events were said to have taken place between 720 and 586 BCE. After returning from exile, a group of Jews rebuilt their temple and continued to live and worship in the area. A priestly family known as the Maccabees or the Hasmoneans established an autonomous kingdom in the second century BCE which was, in one researcher's words, 'the nearest that Judah ever approached to the ideal enshrined in its literature, a monarchic state stretching over most of Palestine'.[3] During many of the political upheavals, some Jews stayed on in their territory, which was under occupation by the Persians, then, after the conquests of Alexander the Great, by successive kingdoms based in Egypt and in Syria. Eventually, after a brief period of Jewish independence (c. 150–66 BCE), Palestine came under Roman rule, and the single Jewish state was broken up into several different territories. This was the case when Jesus of Nazareth was born.

What we are told today about the history of the period, and particularly the early history of the Jews, usually comes from biblical texts written centuries later, describing 'kingdoms', 'empires', 'battles' and 'temples' that may conjure up in the modern mind much grander events than were really the case. One researcher has described Palestine three to four thousand years ago as 'an Egyptian province ruled by local princes who looked upon themselves as faithful vassals of their patron, the Pharaoh.'[4] He goes on to describe these princes as more akin to 'mayors' of cities, instead of being the imposing monarchs we read about in the Bible. And since the descendants of the other inhabitants of the land – the Canaanites, the Phoenicians, the Philistines, the Aramaeans, the Edomites – have not left voluminous accounts of *their* kings and kingdoms, priests and prophets, it's easy to believe, as many people do, that the whole area was dominated for a thousand years or more by Jews.

Over the centuries and up until the present day, many people have seen the presence of the 'Israelites' in Palestine, and the part they played in local history, as the predominant factor in determining modern claims to Palestine. Not only do they base this on the claims of the Old Testament, but also on prayer books and sacred writings, which tell in some detail of a 'restoration' of modern Jewry to 'the Land of Israel' after the arrival of a Messiah, a 'promised one' who will rebuild the kingdom. 'An eighteenth-century story tells of a certain Rabbi Yitzhak of Berdichev in Poland who sent out invitations to his daughter's wedding: "It will take place next Tuesday in the Holy City of Jerusalem. If, God forbid, the Messiah has not arrived by then, it will take place in the village square."'[5]

To me and, I suspect, to many uncommitted people, using the map of the world as it might have been three or four or six thousand years ago is not a very appropriate basis for granting sovereignty in the modern world. It is difficult to think of a nation that exists today that would bear any similarity in borders or demography to the entity that existed on its territory three thousand years ago. The activities of neolithic farmers in Ireland, for example, contribute very little to an understanding of the conflict in Northern Ireland today.

And the situation is even more confusing when one takes into account the way in which names of groups and places change over centuries and across languages. Modern accounts of the history of the Jews and of where they lived in the past often blur the edges between places called 'Israel', people called 'Israelites' and an ethnic group called Jews. There are even doubts about whether there is any ethnic continuity between most Jews today and the Hebrews of the Old Testament. Philip Davies points out that the Bible describes a kingdom called Israel, some of whose inhabitants worship Yahweh, or Jehovah, and some who don't, and where there is no ethnic correspondence to cultural affiliation and no *ethnic* reason for differentiating between Canaanites and Israelites. Indeed, some Canaanites also worship Yahweh. Israel was a culture and not an ethnicity. There's some evidence that even in biblical times, many Jews did not see Palestine as their homeland. At the opening of the Christian era, there were nearly five million Jews in the Roman Empire, of which only 700,000, less than 15 per cent, were in Palestine.

One of the problems that obscures the truths about people and places in history is that names and historical identities are sometimes only tenuously related. The people that Scotland takes its name from are today's Irish; the Scots themselves are descended from a people called the Picts. The British today are not descended from the British who were encountered by the Romans. *Those* British fled to Wales and Cornwall and were replaced by Angles and Saxons who came from Germany.[6]

From time to time even the history of the name 'Palestine' – which is now associated with Palestinian Arabs – is questioned. Some academics trace it back at least two thousand years: 'That grand old man of Greek history, Herodotus, had already used the expression Syria Palestine for the whole coastal region from Lebanon to Egypt, and it was taken over by the Roman emperors as a new name for Judea in the second century. Two centuries later,

Palestine became an even more comprehensive designation. The Byzantine rulers had three Palestines, of which the Second was the northernmost, occupying the territory south of Lebanon around Haifa. The region around Jerusalem was named First Palestine, while Third Palestine incorporated a large piece of old Arabia – the Sinai, Negev, and the eastern bank of contemporary Jordan south of Amman. The term Palestine accordingly evokes an ancient geographical and administrative coherence, and for later antiquity it represents an even more unified pattern than the province of Arabia.'[7]

Golda Meir, Prime Minister of Israel from 1969 to 1974, disagreed. 'There is no such thing as a Palestinian Arab nation,' she said. 'Palestine is a name the Romans gave to Eretz Yisrael with the express purpose of infuriating the Jews ... Why should we use the spiteful name meant to humiliate us? The British chose to call the land they mandated Palestine, and the Arabs picked it up as their nation's supposed ancient name, though they couldn't even pronounce it correctly and turned it into Falastin, a fictional entity.'[8]

In fact there hasn't been a period in the last two thousand years when the Arab inhabitants of the area, and those who came in contact with them, didn't know their territory by the name 'Palestine'. 'Palestine became a predominately Arab and Islamic country by the end of the seventh century,' writes Edward Said. 'Almost immediately thereafter its boundaries and its characteristics – including its name in Arabic, Filastin – became known to the entire Islamic world, as much for its fertility and beauty as for its religious significance. In the late tenth century, for example, we find this passage in Arabic:[9]

Filastin is the westernmost of the provinces of Syria.
In its greatest length from Rafah to the boundary of Al

Lajjun (Legio) it would take a rider two days to travel
over; and the like time to cross the province in its breadth
from Yafa (Jaffa) to Riha (Jericho).... Filastin is watered
by the rains and the dew. Its trees and its ploughed lands
do not need artificial irrigation; and it is only in Nablus
that you find the running waters applied to this purpose.
Filastin is the most fertile of the Syrian provinces. Its
capital and largest town is Ar Ramlah, but the Holy
City (of Jerusalem) comes very near this last in size.
In the province of Filastin, despite its small extent
there are about twenty mosques, with pulpits for the
Friday prayer.[10]

Sixty per cent of the population in the tenth century was in agriculture and all of them believed themselves to belong in a land
called Palestine.

Haim Gerber, a professor at the Hebrew University of Jerusalem,
would also disagree with Golda Meir that 'the Arabs picked up
[Palestine] as their nation's supposed ancient name' from the
British in the twentieth century. In his paper 'Palestine and Other
Territorial Concepts in the 17th Century' Gerber provides a wealth
of detail from seventeenth-century legal documents to show that
there existed what he called 'embryonic territorial awareness' that
went beyond mere naming of the place of one's birth or home.[11]

In the seventeenth and eighteenth centuries people travelled
from the west to 'Palestine' and wrote about it. The Turks conquered 'Palestine' along with Syria and then, a few years later,
according to the historian Mosshe Sharon, 'joined Palestine to the
province of Syria, whose capital was Damascus. Palestine itself
was divided into five districts, or Sanjaks, each named after its
capital ... Gaza ... Jerusalem ... Nablus ... Lajjun ... and Safed.'[12]

A sixteenth-century map of Palestine

One legal text studied by Gerber deals with cases like 'a man from a village of the villages of Palestine' who swore an oath of divorce, and asks 'What if a year later he travelled outside of Palestine … was he to be clear of his oath?' Indeed, Gerber quotes another authority describing the author of the legal text as 'the great scholar of Palestine'.

A modern Palestinian historian has written: 'The idea [of "Palestine"] … had regional and local roots. It was not a coincidence, for example, that the central Ottoman government established an administrative entity with borders practically identical to those of Mandate Palestine on three brief occasions during the nineteenth century: 1830, 1840 and 1872. Moreover, local economic networks that integrated the cities with their hinterlands, peasant mobility and clan relations; and commonly shared cultural practices, such as the annual Nabi Musa pilgrimage that enjoyed "national" participation, were some of the factors that contributed to a shared collective historical memory and sense of identity.'[13]

At least, then, Palestinians believed they were living in Palestine even if others might now doubt it. But of course, in a literal sense there was no state of Palestine until the twentieth century. In fact there was no state, either, of Jordan, Syria, Egypt, Saudi Arabia, or indeed Israel. The modern idea of a state with internationally recognized borders, a head of state aided by an administration and people with passports or identity cards and so on, applied to very few political entities before the nineteenth century. But this does not destroy the argument propounded by nationalists throughout Europe in the great upheaval after the First World War, that people who could demonstrate continuity of habitation in a particular territory should be granted independence and self-rule.

I will deal mainly in this book with the history of the last four hundred years, a period for which documented evidence proves a continuing presence of Palestinian Arabs – including members of my family – as a large majority in the territory of Palestine. Although people of Arab origin have lived in Palestine for thousands of years, as one goes back further in time it is increasingly difficult to argue that descendants of earlier peoples who lived in the land should have priority over its surviving inhabitants – even if such descent could be proved for certain groups of either Arabs or Jews. The United States has very strong arguments for not handing over its sovereignty to native Americans; Brazil for not abdicating power to its indigenous inhabitants; and Belgium for resisting any claims on its territory – should they come – from the Netherlands and France.

The history of Palestine since the seventeenth century proves that Arabs always formed a substantial majority of the population during that time, and it is likely that they have done so for the last thousand years or more. These Arabs, furthermore, are people with an identity and a culture that is distinctly Palestinian, as opposed to

Egyptian, Arabian or Iraqi. It is certainly true that there were other groups who also lived in the territory. One of the most significant of those were the Jews, although to say, as one internet source – called misleadingly 'Palestine Facts' – says, that Palestine was 'virtually empty' except for its Jewish communities is nonsense.[14]

There are tremendous disparities in figures between those who support the Zionist case for ruling Palestine and more neutral observers and academics. Some of the disparity is due to the fact that population figures are not easy to estimate with any great certainty. The further back in time you go, the less reliable they are (although there is now a pretty good understanding of the system the Ottoman Turks used to assess the population of their empire, which included Palestine). But no quibble between academic demographers can bridge the gap between the meaning of the phrase 'virtually empty' and the authenticated figures available for the populations of major Palestinian cities and towns.

In the light of this, I will try wherever possible to use Jewish sources – both Zionist and uncommitted – to supply evidence for the predominance of Arabs in Palestine, in the belief that they will be less susceptible to arguments of bias. For example, in 1837 Moses Montefiore, the Victorian Jewish philanthropist, made a trip to Palestine and came back estimating that there were 'about 8,000 Jews [in the whole of Palestine] living principally in Jerusalem, Safad, Tiberias, and Hebron.'[15] As this is the same as the number of Arabs living in Jerusalem at the time, the Jews were clearly not numerically dominant in the country.[16]

There are few firm data from the period before the Ottoman conquest of the area that can be used to assess the question of the Palestinian Arabs' claim to Palestine. It was only in the years after 1516, when the Ottoman Turks conquered Syria and Palestine, that we begin to find evidence of a particular identification of different groups within the empire with the territories in which they live. Just as the Arab world today is not an amorphous mass of interchangeable Arabs, it was not the case that the imposition of Turkish rule made everyone Ottoman citizens in anything other than name. An Arab (or a Jew) who lived in Safad, a hill town in northern Galilee, did not abandon his affection for his home town, his relatives in nearby streets and villages, his particular dialect of the language of his parents, or the food he ate on feast days, because the Sultan Selim was now his sovereign. The Sultan may have conquered Syria and Palestine, but he was also six hundred miles away.

For the Ottoman rulers, Palestine was more than just another province in an empire that stretched from Hungary to Yemen and Algeria to the Caspian Sea. The Ottomans were Muslims, and Palestine was on the pilgrimage route from Turkey to Mecca and Medina in Arabia, and housed a number of sites sacred to Muslims. It was also the focus for Christian and Jewish travellers visiting their own religious sites and therefore a potential source of friction between the Ottoman Empire and other countries. The Sultan's government took special care to ensure law and order in these provinces, since both the Muslim pilgrims and the foreign visitors were likely to be attractive to bands of robbers.

We know quite a lot about the population of Palestine once it came under Ottoman control in the sixteenth century because of the regular censuses the government instituted. According to the results of these censuses – five of them in fifty years – Palestine had about 300,000 inhabitants, 90 per cent of them Muslim Arabs. The other 10 per cent were mainly either Christians (who were also principally Arabs) or Jews.

Palestinians are often assumed to be Muslim, although in fact Christianity began in Palestine. Some Christian families among

Palestinian Arabs today are probably descended from the first Christians, though many were later converts. The Sabbaghs were Christian Arabs and my family tree goes back at least to 1700. When the Ottomans conquered Palestine they treated the Christians and Jews in a different way from the mainly Muslim population. Because they were known as 'People of the Book' – belonging to religions that shared prophets with Islam – the Sultan, as head of the Muslim faith, was required to protect their lives and properties. In return for this protection they were subjected to special rules relating to marriage, taxation and so on. Nevertheless, to the ordinary population they were seen as infidels and at various times suffered from abuse. Their affairs were regulated by the Ottoman government through their religious leaders who were based in Constantinople. However, some Christians claimed European nationality, thereby gaining the protection of the consuls of European countries that had diplomatic relations with the Turks.

Although treated differently from the majority, the Jews living in Palestine were able to maintain and expand traditional communities in towns such as Safad, Jerusalem and Tiberias. In spite of the fact that there were barriers to Jews and Christians taking up senior posts in the Ottoman government, many Jews participated in the financial administration of areas of the empire. Some Jews (and Christians) who agreed to convert to Islam rose to the highest administrative posts in the land. The post of Grand Vizier, the Sultan's chief minister, was held by nine men between 1520 and 1566, and only one of them was of Muslim birth.[17]

The task of maintaining law and order in its provinces was a constant headache for the Turks, mainly because they lacked soldiers to police their empire. Their armies were fighting wars on two fronts, east and west, for long periods. In addition to facing widespread criminal activity, the Ottoman rulers in Constantinople had another problem: collecting taxes from farmers, merchants and village leaders. The Ottoman Empire could not function without regular funds. In especially troublesome regions the Ottomans appointed local rulers, often Bedouin sheikhs from territories on the edge of the Empire. One of these rulers became so powerful in the eighteenth century that he became known generations later as the 'First King of Palestine'. He also benefited from the cunning and greed of one of my ancestors.

2

'THE FIRST KING OF PALESTINE'

• • •

In autumn 2003 I drove around northern Israel. Starting in Tiberias, on the western shore of Lake Tiberias (the Sea of Galilee), I visited towns, villages and deserted hillsides, looking for what was left of the eighteenth-century 'kingdom' of a Palestinian sheikh.

I first heard of Daher al-Omar al-Zaydani* over lunch with friends in Nazareth. One cannot have a 'normal' conversation in an Arab home in Israel or Palestine, a conversation about books or films or nuclear war or cloning. From soup to nuts the conversation is always about the Israelis and the Palestinians. On this occasion, I was talking to a Coptic historian, who turned to me during a discussion about the history of the Palestinians and said: 'You know, there was a state of Palestine in the eighteenth century. It lasted for over thirty years, and was so well run that the Ottomans allowed the Palestinians self-rule. And one of your relatives had an important role in the story.'

States, as we know them today, were not a feature of the Middle East in the eighteenth century. The whole area from Albania to

---

* Also found with variant spellings: 'Zahir', owing to the fact that the first letter of the name in Arabic sounds midway between z and d; 'Umar' sometimes used instead of 'Omar'.

A painting by a modern Palestinian artist of the 'first king of Palestine', Daher al-Omar, imagined in his citadel overlooking the port of Acre.

Egypt was under Turkish control. No stable boundaries in the Ottoman Empire divided one 'nation' from another. There were provinces and sub-divisions of provinces, but the Ottoman rulers often changed these boundaries. If a local governor fell into disgrace, his province would be divided among neighbouring governors. Or a leader would need to be rewarded, so territories would be amalgamated to satisfy him. Nevertheless, for a considerable period of time Daher al-Omar, of Bedouin stock, ruled over an area covering what is now northern Israel and southern Lebanon, and sometimes as far south as Gaza.

The Ottoman government left him alone because he achieved a level of relative peace, financial prosperity, fair tax-collecting and freedom from crime. It was easier than trying to impose direct rule from Constantinople. Daher also valued good international relations, both for security and for commercial reasons. Northern Palestine was a productive cotton-growing area and he acquired a monopoly from the farmers in his jurisdiction. Then he traded with European merchants, notably the French, who reluctantly agreed to pay his high prices.

As a consequence, we know about Daher's activities from French and English travellers. Daher also had two Arab biographers, both Sabbaghs: Abud was my great-great-great-grandfather; Mikhail was his nephew. However, by far the liveliest account of Daher's reign, if not always the most accurate, comes from Count Constantine de Volney. He travelled in the Middle East between 1783 and 1785, about eight years after the death of Daher and describes him in glowing terms:

> It is long since Syria has beheld among her chiefs so great a character. In military affairs, no man possessed more courage, activity, coolness, or resources. In politics, the noble frankness of his mind was not diminished even by his ambition. He was fond only of brave and open measures. And heroically preferred the dangers of the field to the wily intrigues of the cabinet. He preserved the simplicity of [Bedouin] customs and manners. His table was not different from that of a rich farmer; the utmost luxury of his dress never exceeded a few cloaks, and he never wore any trinkets. The greatest expense he incurred was in blood mares, for some of which he even paid as high as twenty thousand livres (eight hundred and twenty-five pounds.*) He likewise loved women; but was so jealous of decency and decorum, that he ordered that every one taken in an act of gallantry,† or offering insult to a woman, should suffer death; he had, in short, attained the difficult medium between prodigality and avarice, and was at once generous and economical.[1]

---

* Late eighteenth-century sterling equivalent.
† One eighteenth-century meaning of 'gallantry' was 'amorous intercourse or intrigue'.

I was pleased to discover that my ancestor Ibrahim Sabbagh was Daher's vizier or chief minister. Ibrahim was a Christian Arab with some kind of medical training and he was Daher's doctor as well as his minister of finance. Was Daher's saintly nature, perhaps, attributable to the wise counsel of my ancestor, I asked myself.

No, was the answer. Ibrahim was a nasty piece of work, although his worst excesses go unmentioned by the Sabbaghs who became Daher's biographers. But I must tell the truth. My great-great-great-great-grandfather was, among other things, a miser and an embezzler.

Daher al-Omar was probably a camel driver in his youth. He came from Bedouin tribes that never settled but roamed around northern Palestine, southern Syria and other parts of the Ottoman Empire. The Zaydani (Daher's family name) camped on the banks of the Jordan in the area of the Sea of Galilee.[2] The Bedouin were sometimes regarded as inferior by the more settled Arabs who farmed or traded. Volney describes the effect on the townspeople of Acre when some Bedouin visited. They came from the faraway Arabian desert, so they were a rare sight.

> When, in the time of Shaik Daher, some of their
> horsemen came as far as Acre, they excited the same
> curiosity there, as a visit from the savages of America
> would among us. Everyone viewed with surprise these
> men, who were more diminutive, meagre, and swarthy,
> than any of the known Bedouins. Their withered legs
> had no calves, and appeared to consist merely of tendons.
> Their bellies seemed shrunk to their backs, and their hair
> was frizzled almost as much as that of the negroes. They
> on the other hand were no less astonished at everything
> they saw; they could neither conceive how the houses

and minarets could stand erect, nor how men ventured
to dwell beneath them, and always on the same spot;
but above all, they were in an ecstasy at beholding the
sea, nor could they comprehend what that *desert of water*
could be.[3]

By the middle of the seventeenth century Daher's family had
abandoned their nomadic habits and settled down in northern
Palestine between Tiberias and Safad. Daher's father and grandfather had been tax collectors for the Ottoman government. The
'tax-farming' system allowed specific individuals in a community to
collect taxes for the Ottoman government from peasants and
farmers, taking a proportion of the tax as reward for doing the job.
Often tax-farmers extorted the maximum they could and passed
on the minimum.

Daher inherited the right to collect taxes in the region and soon
established a reputation as a fighter and a man of commerce. His
first settled base was the hill town of Safad, where my family come
from. He acquired a succession of wives, partly to cement rela-
tionships with important families in the region and partly, as
Volney points out, 'because he loved women a lot'. The village of
Nazareth was under Daher's rule and its inhabitants 'were obliged
to make a present [of a thousand piastres] to every wife [Daher]
married, and he took great care to marry almost every week'.[4]

In the 1730s and 1740s Daher extended his influence over a vast
region, through tribal alliances and skilful negotiation. By forging a
bond with the unruly Beni Saqr tribe, he took over the sizeable
town of Tiberias, his first power base. Before long Daher invited
Jewish families from Damascus to come and settle in the town,
including bankers and merchants whose contacts helped develop
the area. More Jews moved into Daher's territories as word spread

of the stability and lack of crime. Soon Jews arrived from more distant parts of the Ottoman Empire, including Smyrna, Aleppo and Cyprus.

Daher was visited in 1737 by the British traveller Richard Pococke, on a journey through the area. 'When I came near Tiberias I sent a man before with a letter from the consul to the sheik who, having much company with him, ordered his steward to entertain me at his house, and provisions were sent from the sheik's kitchin.' Pococke was well treated by Daher, who obviously enjoyed meeting visitors from the West, but he found it difficult to get a decent night's sleep. 'They drive their cattle within the walls every night, lest they should be stolen,' he wrote, 'so that the place abounds with vermin, and as they have a great number of asses as well as other cattle we were frequently disturbed with their noise.'

Daher had to take precautions to protect himself from the hostility of the pasha of Damascus, the nearest provincial ruler in the Ottoman hierarchy. This pasha was not always well disposed to a sheikh who posed a potential threat. 'When I was at Tiberias,' Pococke wrote, 'they were very busy in making a fort on the height of the north of the town, and in strengthening the old walls with

Tiberias, one of Daher al-Omar's capitals, showing the mosque he built in the eighteenth century.

Daher al-Omar's mosque in modern Tiberias, hemmed in
by concrete malls and housing.

buttresses on the inside, the sheik having a dispute with the pasha
of Damascus; who after this took his brother in a skirmish, and
caused him to be publicly hanged in that city, but the pasha being
soon after removed, they were freed from their apprehension on
that account.'[5] In 1742, another pasha, Soliman el-Adm, besieged
Daher in Tiberias and bombarded the town, 'to the great astonish-
ment of all Syria, where bombs are but little known, even at
present', noted Volney.[6]

The citadel Daher built in the centre of Tiberias is now derelict.
Nearby, within a few yards of the shore of the Sea of Galilee, Daher
constructed a stocky, stone mosque, with a tower or minaret on the
eastern corner, and an exterior with a pattern of alternating dark
and light stones, a recognizable feature of other buildings constructed during his control of Palestine. The mosque has been
neglected since 1948, when Tiberias became entirely Jewish. A
concrete shopping centre was built around it – the usual mix of
hairdressing salons, gift shops, clothes shops and cafés. When I
visited the town in 2004 some of the shops were closed, the café

was deserted and the steps and dais of the mosque were littered with old shopping trolleys and discarded bottles. Standing on an abandoned dining chair I peered through the window bars into the mosque's interior. Rubble, plaster and stones had fallen from the ceiling. The steps to the minbar (or pulpit) were cracked and waterstained and people had thrown household refuse through the window on to the floor where Daher, his family and the community had once prayed.

Most of the time the Ottoman government – the 'Porte', as it was called – accepted the taxes Daher raised and left him alone, but when the local pasha of Damascus took against him, it usually meant trouble. Damascus was only hours away from Tiberias and after his headquarters were attacked Daher began looking for a base that was further away and had access to the Mediterranean. In the 1740s he captured the harbour of Acre, a port on the northern Mediterranean coast of Palestine governed by an Ottoman official from Sidon. Volney described Acre as 'a heap of ruins, a miserable open village without defence'.[7] The Governor of Sidon had stationed a representative (or Aga) there, but when Daher sent a message that he was on his way to take over the port the Aga fled. Daher and his soldiers rode into Acre and the village was his. The Governor of Sidon didn't seem to mind. He knew Daher would continue to pass on the taxes and he recognized his reputation for good government and preserving law and order.

With much of northern Galilee under his rule, Daher could control the production and sales of agricultural products in the region: wheat, barley and citrus fruit, as well as olives, the basis of a significant soap industry. But cotton was the most important crop. There was a growing market in Europe and Daher established contact with French merchants and created links with Malta, Cyprus and Livorno.[8] He had a monopoly of Galilean cotton and told the French they had to pay his high prices. It didn't always work. When the French refused to pay, Daher broke off relations, but he failed to find any other buyers so he came to a compromise. The French still found it advantageous to trade through Daher, because of his skill and fairness in commercial transactions.

These growing trade links meant that Acre expanded. There were new shops and warehouses and a cotton market, a long elegant arched arcade that still stands.

Before the rise of Daher, roaming Bedouin tribes would ransack villages, rob farmers, and terrorize the highways, all of which stifled trade. It was said to be impossible to travel without the protection of fifty armed cavalrymen. Daher improved the situation by requiring the head man of each village and town to guarantee security in his area, and to compensate victims from his own pocket. By 1746, Mikhail Sabbagh reports, 'An old woman with gold in her hand could travel from one place to another without fear or danger.'[9] Daher devised a cunning means of crime prevention. He sent 'decoy' women to travel the roads of the area and he put about the message that anyone who accosted them would be captured and executed. Around this time the French consul in Sidon reported that Daher 'speaks and acts as though he were the master of all Galilee.'[10]

Like most Palestinian Arabs at the time Daher was a Muslim. But a small percentage of them were Christians, many of them Melkites (a Christian sect following the Byzantine rite but in Arabic). Like the Jews, the Melkites were attracted to Daher's Palestine as a haven from the persecution they faced in Aleppo and other Syrian towns. Daher's tolerance of different religious groups led to close friendships with Christian merchants, one of whom, Yusuf Qissis, became his scribe and counsellor.

In 1757 Daher fell ill and in spite of the efforts of his personal physician, he failed to recover. Then Qissis brought a Christian friend of his, who was also a doctor, to see if he could help. In those days there was little a doctor could do with a seriously ill patient except take the credit if the patient happened to get better. Fortunately for Ibrahim Sabbagh, this is exactly what happened, and he therefore replaced Daher's regular doctor. It was the beginning of a twenty-year relationship. Ibrahim began as a friend and doctor, then took over from Qissis as counsellor when he fell from favour.

An uncle of mine living in Beirut told me a story about Ibrahim that he had heard from an old priest in the mountains of Lebanon. I'm not sure how reliable it is, but I offer it here as the earliest account of my branch of the family tree.

Some time in the late seventeenth century a man called Yuhanna lived in the Syrian town of Shweir and married a princess from the religious sect known as the Druzes (an offshoot of Islam dating back to the tenth century AD). He was probably called Yuhanna Shoueri, after the town he lived in. Yuhanna had four sons, Abud, Habib, Mikhail and Yusuf. Abud, the eldest, went to Sidon and set up business as a dyer (*sabbagh* in Arabic). His family thus became known as 'Beit Sabbagh', the house or family of the dyer.

One of Abud's brothers, Habib, married and had twin boys, Lias and Ibrahim. Lias died of measles, and Ibrahim, aged seven, was sent by his uncle, Abud, to the monastery of St John. Here, in the hands of a monk from Aleppo called Procopius, he was trained in the healing arts. When he grew up he became a monk himself, but then at the age of thirty-two left the monastery and went to Acre where he worked as a doctor and got married.

By the time Ibrahim became Daher's adviser he had four (possibly five) grown-up sons. Some played a part in Daher's government, others helped Ibrahim in his many commercial activities.

Yusuf became deputy governor of Jaffa, Habib looked after the Sabbagh trading activities in Acre, Niqula became a doctor like his father, and Abud – my direct ancestor – ran the family soap factory.

Daher and Ibrahim were obviously close, although they had very different personalities. Daher had no interest in wealth, whereas Ibrahim was interested in little else. Daher was generous with what he had, while Ibrahim begrudged giving anyone a single piastre of his fortune. Volney wrote: '[Ibrahim's] passion for money was so sordid, that, amid the wealth he was amassing, he lived only on cheese and olives; and so great was his parsimony, that he frequently stopped at the shops of the poorest merchants, and partook of their frugal repast. He never wore any thing but dirty and ragged garments. To behold this meagre, one-eyed wretch, one would have taken him rather for a beggar than the minister of a considerable state.'

It must have hurt Ibrahim considerably when his master ordered him to assign a monthly stipend for the poor. And during droughts, when the farmers in his territory could not afford to pay the Ottoman tax, Daher paid it from his own treasury or borrowed from his minister, a loan Ibrahim really could not refuse.

Daher also had several sons. They divided their time between helping their father and fighting him. Each one controlled a region of Palestine from the citadels and fortresses Daher had built across northern Palestine. Fighting broke out from time to time when one son or another, sometimes two or more, declared war on Daher to gain some advantage over the other brothers or to redress some slight, real or imagined, at the hands of their father. The sons could also be bribed or seduced by Daher's enemies – such as the ruling governor of Damascus – to join in battle against their father.

In 1753 Daher's son Uthman rebelled and fled to Jenin. In 1761 three more sons, led by Ali, barricaded themselves in the fortress at

Tiberias and declared war against Daher. Truce was followed by revolt and revolt by truce, rather like an elaborate war game. Usually either Uthman or Ali was the instigator, but accounts of their battles and the outcomes suggest that these events weren't always as serious as one might think.[11]

Constantine de Volney warned his readers not to imagine that Arab battles were anything like European ones.

> The reader must not here figure to himself a number of complicated and artificial movements, such as those which within the last century, have reduced war with us to a science of system and calculation; the Asiatics are unacquainted with the first elements of this conduct. Their armies are mobs, their marches ravages, their campaigns mere inroads, and their battles, bloody frays; the strongest or the most adventurous party goes in search of the other, which not unfrequently flies without offering resistance; if they stand their ground, they engage pell-mell, discharge their carbines, break their spears, and hack each other with their sabres, for they rarely have any cannon; and when they have they are but of little service. A panic frequently diffuses itself without cause; one party flies, the other pursues, and shouts victory; the vanquished submit to the will of the conqueror, and the campaign often terminates without a battle.[12]

While real wounds were sometimes inflicted, there was a code of honour that prevented too much harm being done by one close relative to another. If Daher was on the losing side and his forces were routed, his son would not pursue him once it was obvious who had won. When on one occasion Daher fell off his horse and shouted 'I am Daher!', a cavalryman from the opposing side came, helped him up, kissed the hem of his coat and led him to safety, before getting back to work attacking his forces.[13]

The French Consul in Sidon explained to his government how these things were done: 'These fights have at first an alarming air because everyone is armed. But they are no less careful not to spill blood, and apart from the furor and the noise these battles cause they are merely family quarrels, which paternal love always brings to an end; and in any case, at the slightest danger they will reunite to oppose the enemies of the family.'[14]

These regular fights between Daher and his sons rather destroyed some of the benefits of the security he had brought to the area. In Volney's words they led to 'general disorder, resulted in an unnecessary power split, retarded development [and] disrupted the economy'. Nevertheless, during the second half of the eighteenth century, Daher's rule, with the help of Ibrahim's advice, made Acre the principal port in the whole stretch of Mediterranean coast from northern Syria down to Gaza. He made it the centre of a region that was developing great economic potential. Acre was transformed from an insignificant village to a great trading post. One sign of its prosperity is a list of the properties owned by Daher al-Omar and Ibrahim Sabbagh, found in the archives of the Ottoman Empire. It gives details of over a hundred shops, a soap factory, probably Abud's, several gardens and a new Turkish bath, as well as two new mosques.

The port in the old town of Acre is now a marina and fishing boat harbour, but many of the stone structures Daher built still stand, including his impressive walls and ramparts and his citadel, dominating the middle of the town. They are the western end of a whole chain of fortresses, mosques and caravanserais that Daher and his sons built at the height of his power. But Daher was growing old, his sons were restless and rivals were eyeing-up his 'kingdom'.

3

DAHER'S DECLINE

• • •

Daher's rule over Palestine was brought to an end by Ottoman politics. While Palestine was relatively calm, Egypt, a neighbouring part of the Ottoman Empire, was more turbulent. It was ruled by a group called the Mamluks, former slaves who in a reversal of status had become an elite force. But because each member was deemed to be the equal of all the others, there was constant jostling for power and control. This is how Volney described the chaotic state of Egyptian politics at the end of the eighteenth century:

> In a society where the passions of individuals are not
> directed to one general end, where each man, attentive
> only to himself, considers the uncertainty of the next day,
> merely as a motive to improve the advantage of the
> moment; where the chiefs, impressing no sentiment of
> respect, are unable to maintain subordination; in such a
> society, a fixed and regular state of affairs is impossible;
> and the incessant jarring of the incoherent parts must give
> a perpetual vibration to the whole machine. This is what
> continually happens among the body of the Mamlouks at
> Cairo.[1]

One of the Mamluks ruling Egypt in the 1760s was Ali Bey al-Kabir, who was noted for his extravagant tastes. Volney described the public murmurings against him after one of his new purchases: 'When Ali Bey expended two hundred and twenty-five thousand livres (above nine thousand pounds) in the useless handle of a kandjar [a poniard carried in the belt] though jewellers might applaud his magnificence, had not the people reason to detest his luxury?' Not surprisingly Ali Bey got on rather well with Ibrahim Sabbagh, who knew him through the network of Christian Arabs in Egypt, some of whom had emigrated to Cairo to avoid persecution in Syria.

Ibrahim forged an alliance between Daher and Ali Bey, which although strategically useful, was to hasten Daher's downfall. In the words of one recent historian: 'In November 1770 Ali Bey al-Kabir sent the first Egyptian troops to Gaza and Jaffa. With that step he set the stage for the last act of Daher al-Omar's rule in Acre, five years which in human greed, hubris and bravery, in dramatic, unforeseen turns of events, and in grandeur and catastrophe lacked nothing of Greek tragedy.'[2] It was natural for Daher and Ali Bey to unite to attack Othman, the pasha of Damascus. After several battles they gained almost total control of the largest city in Syria. If they succeeded in crushing Othman, Ali Bey would have Daher's state as a buffer between Egypt and the Ottoman rulers in Constantinople.

In fact, Daher's relations with the central government were quite good at this time. In 1768, he had demanded to be proclaimed 'Sheikh of Acre, Prince of Princes, Governor of Nazareth, Taberias, and Safad, and Sheikh of all Galilee' and the Porte agreed. For the time being he was too powerful for them to control. In the same year the Ottomans inadvertently created a new ally for Daher by declaring war on Russia. In skirmishes, sieges and battles against the Ottomans and their allies over the next few years Daher could now appeal for back-up to the Russian fleet, which had appeared in the Mediterranean and annihilated the entire Ottoman navy.

Daher was now an old man, eighty years old or so. There is a touching picture of him, still fighting, in a biography of Ali Bey by a Portuguese traveller, Sauveur Lusignan. While the army of Daher and Ali Bey was fighting Othman in Egypt, one of Daher's sons, Salibi, was killed. Lusignan and some of Ali Bey's soldiers and slaves travelled to Gaza to break the news to Daher. 'When the good old Sheik Daher saw us approach,' Lusignan wrote, 'and heard of the death of his eldest son, and the loss of his friends and army, he fell on the ground on his face, crying out, "From this day I am undone." [We] strove to comfort him as much as we could, but, alas, we were ourselves inconsolable for the loss of our prince, and all our property.'[3]

At the root of the problems that beset Daher from now on was Ibrahim Sabbagh and the advice he gave. The Ottoman government was going through a bad phase. It was eventually defeated by the Russians and faced a series of rebellions from minor leaders in different parts of the empire, so the Porte offered a peace settlement to Daher. The old sheikh was willing to accept but Ibrahim would not have it. He felt that Ali Bey would conquer the whole of Syria in the coming year or so and hand over a part of it to Daher, enlarging his territory to the north of Palestine. '[Ibrahim] hoped for the advancement of his own private fortune,' Volney wrote, 'and the means of adding fresh treasures to those he had already amassed by his insatiable advice. Seduced by this brilliant prospect, Daher rejected the propositions of the Porte, and prepared to carry on the war with redoubled activity.'[4]

In addition to amassing yet more wealth, Ibrahim was motivated by a belief that the Ottoman Empire was about to collapse, in which case he and Daher, although they were both old men, might live to see their territories stretch far beyond Palestine. In 1773 Ibrahim said to the French Consul, de Taules, 'The Ottoman Empire is no more, and there is only one nation in the world, Russia, just as there is only one God in the heavens.' De Taules replied: 'Whatever you say, the Ottoman Empire will not fall. There are forces with an interest in keeping it powerful and it is when it's in danger of being entirely overcome that you will see how help will arrive.'[5] In fact, de Taules' assessment was more accurate than Ibrahim's. Another seventy years passed before the Ottoman Empire was recognized as 'the sick man of Europe' and it was sixty years after that before it finally fell apart.

While Ali Bey was fighting battles in Palestine, there were intrigues in Cairo which led to him being ousted by another Mamluk called Abu Dhahab. On the basis that 'my enemy's friend is my enemy', Abu Dhahab, having called Ali Bey back to Egypt and

Acre, a few years after the time of Daher al-Omar. The arches are the remains of the cotton market Daher built for foreign traders to meet Palestinian cotton merchants.

killed him, turned to Daher. Abu Dhahab's name means 'father of gold' and he seems to have rivalled Ibrahim in his avarice. He had heard rumours of Ibrahim's wealth and wanted to get at it. On one occasion, when Acre changed hands for a short period and Abu Dhahab captured the town, he went in search of Ibrahim's treasure. Knowing Ibrahim's friendship with some Catholic friars in Nazareth, he sent for them on a pretext and when they arrived he asked them to show him where Ibrahim kept his treasure, which he believed had been deposited in their monastery. The friars said they did not know about any treasure, and Abu Dhahab beheaded three of them to encourage the others to speak. But they knew nothing and were thrown in prison.

By all accounts, Abu Dhahab's behaviour towards the inhabitants of Acre was brutal, so it was fortunate for them that he was found dead one morning, having gone to bed the night before feeling perfectly well. His army, fearing the return of Daher, fled back to Egypt, and two days after Abu Dhahab's death, Daher was back in control of the town.

Tensions were growing at this time between Daher's surviving sons and Ibrahim Sabbagh, who was seen as getting in the way of their own access to their father. The sons were also growing weary of Daher's longevity, and worried that their inheritance might be slipping away from them, into Ibrahim's hands.

> [Ibrahim] neglected no means, however unjust, by which he could amass money. He monopolized every article of commerce; he alone had the sale of corn, cotton, and other articles of exportation; and he alone purchased cloths, indigo, sugars, and other merchandise. His avarice had frequently invaded the supposed privileges, and even the real rights of the Shaiks [Daher's sons]; they did not

pardon this abuse of power, and every day, furnishing
fresh subjects of complaint, was productive of new
disturbances. Daher, whose understanding began to be
impaired by his extreme old age, did not adopt measures
calculated to appease them. He called his children rebels,
and ungrateful, and imagined he had no faithful and
disinterested servant but Ibrahim: this infatuation served
only to destroy all respect for his person, and to inflame
and justify their discontents.[6]

The crisis came in 1775, when the Porte sent a small fleet of ships
under the control of Hassan Pasha, the admiral of the Ottoman
navy, to collect several years' outstanding taxes which Daher was
meant to have remitted to Constantinople. What happened next
depends on which of Daher's biographers you believe. The
Sabbaghs, uncle and nephew, found no fault with Ibrahim's part in
the drama that was about to unfold. Others hold him entirely
responsible. A close associate of Daher's, Ahmad al-Dinkizli, was a
Moroccan mercenary who had fought well over the years in a
number of Daher's campaigns, and had also developed an antipathy
to Ibrahim Sabbagh. So the Sabbaghs blame him for the final events
in Daher's reign, whereas other biographers blame Ibrahim.

The central issue was whether to pay the back taxes or not.
Ibrahim, as you might imagine, was all for holding on to what must
have been quite a large amount of money. Dinkizli advised Daher
to pay up, in return for a peaceful resolution of the dispute, and
Daher was inclined to follow his advice. 'This is the right thing to
do,' Daher said. 'I am an old man and I don't have the nerve any
more for fighting and endless marches in the mountains. For me
the most important issue is to die with a calm mind as an obedient
[servant] of the Sultan.'

Ibrahim would have none of it, claiming that if the taxes were paid the Ottoman government would just ask for more, and in any case there was not enough money in the coffers to make the payments. Daher changed his mind and supported this, and Dinkizli replied, with more than a hint of sarcasm, 'The Shaik is in the right; his servants have long known that his generosity does not suffer his money to stagnate in his coffers; but does not the money they obtain from him belong to him? And can it be believed that thus entitled to them, we know not where to find two thousand purses?'

Volney described this scene vividly: 'At these words Ibrahim, interrupting him, exclaimed, that as for himself, no man could be poorer. "Say 'baser'," resumed Degnizla, transported with rage. "Who doesn't know that for the last fourteen years you have been heaping up enormous treasures; that you have monopolized all the trade of the country; that you sell all the lands, and keep back the payments that are due; that in the war of Mohammad Bey, you plundered the whole territory of Gaza, carried away all the corn, and left the inhabitants of Yafa without the necessaries of life?"'[7]

But to no avail. Faithful to the last to his minister, Daher sent a message to Hassan Pasha refusing to pay the taxes, whereupon Hassan Pasha launched an attack. Al-Dinkizli, disgusted by Ibrahim's advice and Daher's acceptance, said 'We are Muslim people, obedient to the Sultan. For the Muslim, believing in One God, it is not permitted to fight against the Sultan in any form.' He then gave orders to the Moroccan troops under his charge not to resist the Ottoman admiral, and Hassan Pasha's ships began to bombard Acre. Daher tried to respond but without Dinkizli's forces he had little to respond with.

When it was clear that all was lost, Daher mounted his horse and rode out of the city. Then, the eighty-five-year-old ruler of Palestine, who had recently married a young and beautiful woman, made a fatal decision. He decided to turn back for his bride, and on his way to fetch her was shot by one of Dinkizli's Moroccan soldiers. Daher fell to the ground and was surrounded by the Moroccans, who beheaded him and took his head to Hassan Pasha. He, as was the custom, first showered it with insults and then pickled it and shipped it off to Constantinople to prove that the troublesome sheikh was no more. 'Such was the tragical end of a man, in many respects, worthy of a better fate,' Volney wrote. 'It is long since Syria has beheld among her chiefs so great a character.... [It was not] till he had taken Ibrahim for his minister that his conduct was blemished with a sort of duplicity which that Christian called Prudence.'[8]

But what of Ibrahim? Where was he while his master was being cut down by his own soldiers? He had fled the town and sought refuge with a tribe who had been friendly to Daher in the past, who returned him with a guarantee of safety to Acre. But the guarantee was ignored and he was given up to Hassan Pasha, 'to whom no present could be more acceptable', according to Volney. Reports of Ibrahim's vast riches were known throughout the empire and Hassan Pasha was determined to track them down. But Ibrahim denied that they existed. 'In vain did the Pasha employ caresses, menaces, and the torture; all were ineffectual,' Volney wrote.

With Ibrahim firmly in chains, it wasn't too long before the location of his treasures was revealed to be – as had been suspected by Abu Dhahab – in a Christian monastery. There were several chests, 'so large and so full of gold, that the biggest required eight men to carry it'. There were also jewels and trinkets, including Ali Bey's famous dagger with the £9,000 handle. Ibrahim Sabbagh and his treasure were shipped to Constantinople where he was subjected to new tortures in an attempt to find if he had hidden any more money and valuables. But wily old Ibrahim was at least consistent to the last, and said nothing. He was executed, dying, Volney said, 'with a courage worthy of a better cause'.

The story of Daher al-Omar and Ibrahim Sabbagh might seem to be a sideshow in the history of the Ottoman Empire. But it is significant for several reasons. Historians have described it as the first introduction of European power to the area, through the contacts Daher made with the French and the Russians as well as with other European countries. Daher also brought a unified trading policy to a whole swathe of Palestine and Syria, tying farmers, middlemen, and merchants from abroad into a well-run economic system which brought prosperity to his people for the short period of his rule. But it did more than that. Daher's administration of Palestine was taken over by successor sheikhs and Ottoman governors so that the benefits were felt well into the nineteenth century.

This story is worth telling in some detail because it proves the existence of a complex and multilayered Palestinian society in the second half of the eighteenth century. These people didn't all disappear in the nineteenth century. Palestine was not an empty country fifty years after Daher. My family tree shows that Ibrahim's sons went on to do what most people do: marry and have children, and the Zaydani family, Daher's descendants, did the same. So did all the bit part players in the story of Daher's Palestine – the Jews, Christians and Muslims he attracted to his state, the cotton farmers and traders, the foot-soldiers and horsemen, the Bedouin tribesmen and townspeople of Safad, Acre, Tiberias and Nazareth. They stayed and put down roots and built houses, and their children stayed on, in towns and villages that survived from the time of Daher. Nowadays, the majority of those descendants are in refugee camps or in cities thousands of miles from their ancestral homes in Palestine, having been expelled by the Israelis in 1948.

But a few of the descendants of Ibrahim remained, particularly in northern Palestine, now Israel, as I discovered when I travelled in the autumn of 2003 in search of one of Daher's most formidable strongholds, the fortress of Deir Hanna, a town on the road between Tiberias and Acre. I wanted to photograph the ruins, but they were not easy to find. Instead of the village I had expected, Deir Hanna is now a small Arab town. I could see nothing very fortress-like on the hill, so I asked directions of a man who was walking slowly along carrying some worry-beads. He told me that I had to drive a little further and indicated the direction. He then asked me where I was from and I told him I was from 'Beit Sabbagh', the house of Sabbagh. His face lit up. 'There are many of your relatives here!' he exclaimed. 'I will come with you and show you the ruins.' His name was Hanna.

I parked in a patch of shade and we started walking. 'This house used to be the house of the Sabbagh family,' said Hanna, pointing to a derelict stone building surrounded by some land. 'No one lives there now.'

As we walked along the village street, he noticed an elderly couple sitting on the balcony of a house. 'This man is from Beit Sabbagh,' he shouted to them. 'He has come from outside,' (meaning abroad). There was a shouted reply I didn't hear. Hanna turned to me. 'What was your father's name?' I told him and a further shouted conversation revealed that they knew my father. They insisted I come to their house and lunch with them (it was about ten in the morning). I shouted back that I had some research to carry out and maybe I would come back later. We had barely gone another fifty metres when an old woman leaned over a balcony.

'Here's another of your relatives,' said Hanna, and shouted up to the old woman that I was the son of Isa Khalil Sabbagh. The old woman launched into an account of how her sister was married to a man whose daughter was the wife of another member of the Sabbagh family. She seemed about to fall off the balcony with excitement and insisted I come to her house NOW for lunch. I politely declined, eager to find the ruins. How many more relatives was I going to meet?

We found the old fortress: a well-built series of rooms around a courtyard. Hanna showed me into the bedroom of somebody's house before he realized his mistake. Like hermit crabs, many of the villagers have made their homes in the rooms there. The unoccupied rooms opening off this courtyard were knee-deep in rubble and rubbish, but it was still possible to make out some of the fine decorative masonry and the alternating light and dark bands of stone that characterize Daher's buildings.

When I had seen enough, we walked back to the house of the couple on the balcony and I decided I should really stop for five minutes. I was there for an hour. Like me, Abu Hatem and his wife were descendants of Ibrahim Sabbagh. Cups of strong Arab coffee were produced and the interrogation started. My Arabic was good enough to tell them most of what they wanted to know, though I could not always understand what they told me.

They knew a lot about my immediate family – my uncles and aunts and which parts of the world they had gone to. Abu Hatem claimed to know my father, proving this by showing me three out-of-focus photographs. The blurred man in the middle was definitely my father, standing with younger versions of Abu Hatem and his wife. I was also shown photographs of Georgette, my aunt, and of Abu Hatem's mother, a real beauty called Kurjiyi. I heard that some members of the family had ended up in America, like my father. 'My sister has two children in America,' said one of the women, 'and their Arabic is broken, just like yours.' (I thought I'd been doing rather well.)

Kurjiyi, née Sabbagh, mother of Abu Hatem in Deir Hanna.

'Well, I'd better go,' I said, looking at my watch, but it had no effect.

'You haven't eaten anything yet,' said Abu Hatem's wife.

'I had breakfast not long ago.'

'It's nearly ready,' said Abu Hatem. 'Please, come.'

I entered a large room with windows overlooking the beautiful countryside. Abu Hatem seized my arm and led me on to the balcony.

'All of that mountain used to belong to the Sabbagh family,' he said, pointing to a large hill in the distance. He steered me around the corner and waved his arm at the fields below which stretched into the distance. 'A third of that land also was Beit Sabbagh.'

I sat down to a familiar-looking feast of Palestinian dishes. 'Eat, eat,' they all said in a chorus. 'Try this, and this. It's home made. It comes from our land.'

At last I really had to move on.

'No, no,' they all cried. 'Wait a moment for the olives and the olive oil.'

Out of the kitchen came five large plastic bottles containing many different types of the family's olives. 'These are large green olives in peppers; these are large black ones in oil; these are small green ones in oil; this is olive oil from our olives, and this is a bag of za'ater [dried thyme and sesame].'

I tried to leave three of the bottles behind, hoping to travel light, but they were firmly gathered up by Hatem. I said my farewells, with promises to return for longer next time, with my wife and children, and headed downstairs to the car. As I opened the boot for Hatem to deposit all five bottles, I was seized by the arm, swung around, and kissed on both cheeks by a strange woman. She was wearing traditional Palestinian costume and accompanied by a toothless old man, also traditionally dressed and as short as she was. More relatives. Word had reached their ears that I was in town, and they were both effusive in their greetings, so grateful to me for honouring them and their village with a visit, and insistent that I come to their house for lunch.

As I drove down the hill I rather wished I had taken a photo of the other side of the Sabbagh house, which I had glimpsed from the balcony. But I knew that to stop and get out of the car once more would risk more relatives appearing and I might never get away.

A Sabbagh family group, still living in Deir Hanna, now part of Israel.

4

PALESTINE IN THE NINETEENTH CENTURY

• • •

At the time of the death of Ibrahim in Constantinople, the port of Acre, fortified and expanded by Daher, was assuming an increased importance in the area, at the expense of Safad, which had previously been the administrative centre. But many of the Sabbagh family still lived in the old hilltop town. Ibrahim had four sons who had either helped their father in managing Daher's affairs or had run various parts of Ibrahim's trading empire. For their time, they were clearly among the more cultured families of Palestine. They could read and write, calculate accounts, even bargain with the foreign merchants who came to Acre to trade in cotton and the other Palestinian goods Daher had brought into the market place.

Much of our knowledge of the state of the country during the nineteenth century comes from the writings of Christian travellers from the West. Palestine was a focus of interest for gentiles for two reasons. First, it was 'the Land of Israel' where Old Testament Jewish history unfolded. Second, it was the landscape of Christ, where all the New Testament events that were a staple part of every Christian child's religious upbringing took place. In the tragedy that was to unfold for the Palestinians, this had one important consequence – an innate sympathy for the idea of Palestine becoming a Jewish nation.

Christian travellers to Palestine were fond of trying to associate every site in the Holy Land with some biblical location or event. 'Influential segments of Christian society in Britain had long been receptive to the prospect of a revival of the historic connection between the Children of Israel and the Land of the Bible,' writes the historian Stuart Cohen. 'The literary public of Victorian England was still affected by the residual influence of earlier millenarian visions of a Second Coming. Throughout the period, it was also supplied with more recent ... jogs to its scriptural memories. An entire school of travellers, Orientalists, archaeologists, artists, and writers of fiction gave prominence to both the Holy Land and its ancient inhabitants.'[1]

W.M. Thomson, describing a visit he made to Safad in 1833, says: 'The wall is mostly modern, but built on one more ancient ... By creeping under these broken vaults, you obtain a site of the true antiquities of Safed. Here are bevelled stones, as heavy, and as aged in appearance as those of the most celebrated ruins in the country; and they prove that this has been a place of importance from a remote age.'[2] When Jesus in the Sermon on the Mount said 'a city built on a hill cannot be hidden' he may have been referring to Safad, the highest town visible from the edge of the Sea of Galilee.

For several hundred years the town was a centre of Jewish learning and mysticism and one of the four holy cities of the Jews, although the Jewish population never rose above 50 per cent. In the sixteenth century many synagogues were built and the first printing press in the Middle East was set up. Before the Jews came, the town was inhabited by Arab families, and when the Jewish population expanded in the sixteenth century, with an influx of Jews from Eastern Europe, principally Poland, the two groups lived side by side reasonably harmoniously.

When I visited the town in 2003 it had been entirely Jewish for fifty-five years. I stopped in a bookshop and asked the owner where I could get a good cup of coffee in Safad. 'In my estimation you can't get a good cup of coffee in *Israel*,' he said with feeling. I told him that my family came originally from Safad, and could be traced back several hundred years, and he told me that he was from Phoenix, Arizona, and before that, Skokie, Illinois.

When Lawrence Oliphant, the Victorian English traveller and Zionist, visited the town, he showed the traditional English finickiness about Oriental hygiene:

> However prepossessing Safed may look from a distance, it does not bear a close acquaintance. Down the centre of every street runs an open sewer, which renders it the most odoriferous and pestiferous place that it has ever been my fate to sleep in. The aspect of the population is in keeping with the general smell. One seems transported into the ghetto of some Roumanian or Russian town, with a few Eastern disagreeables added. The population here have not adopted the Oriental costume as they have at Tiberias, but wear the high hats, greasy gabardines, and ear-curls of the Jews of Europe. Instead of Arabic, one hears nothing in the streets but 'jargon,' as the dialect used by the Jews in eastern Europe is called. The total population of Ashkenazim, or German Jews, who are hived in this unenviable locality, is between five and six thousand; besides these there are about twelve hundred *Sephardim*, or Spanish Jews, who wear Oriental costumes, and in the other quarter of the town from six to

seven thousand Muslims, making the total number of inhabitants about fourteen thousand.[3]

For a man who was instrumental in promoting to the English the idea of Palestine as a home for the Jews, he showed a remarkable distaste for those Jews who lived there already. 'As there is nothing approaching to a hotel or boarding-house in the place, I was of course dependent on the native hospitality for board and lodging, and thus able to acquire an insight into the mode of life of rather a curious section of the human family. The majority of the Jews here are supported by a charitable fund called the Haluka, which is sub-scribed to by pious Jews all over the world as a sacred duty ... The practical result of this system is to maintain in idleness and mendicancy a set of useless bigots, who combine superstitious observance with immoral practice ...'

In fact, Oliphant's objection to this group of Jews was that they had no interest in promoting the development of Palestine: '... they

When the British traveller Laurence Oliphant visited Haifa and Acre he met well-off middle-class Palestinians like these.

regard with alarm the establishment of agricultural colonies, or the inauguration of an era of any kind of labour by Jews in Palestine. They are bitterly hostile to schools in which any secular teaching is carried on, and agree with those Western Jews who consider that any scheme for developing the material resources of Palestine by means of Jewish industry is fantastic and visionary.'[4]

Oliphant noted in passing the 'six or seven thousand Muslims' who also lived in Safad, but doesn't mention Christians. Perhaps he thought all Arabs were Muslims or perhaps he just didn't have an estimate for the numbers of Christians in addition to the Muslims. At the time Christians probably formed something less than 5 per cent of the Arab population of Safad, and were members of four families of notables, the Bishoutis, Haddads, Khourys and Sabbaghs.

Among them were my ancestors, the descendants of Ibrahim Sabbagh. After Daher and Ibrahim died, Ibrahim's sons left and went north to the area around Sidon. In the early part of the nineteenth century, several grandsons of Ibrahim moved back to Safad in northern Palestine and settled in what was then the Christian quarter, building fine stone houses with vaulted ceilings and roof terraces with views over the surrounding valleys.

But some time in the 1780s one of Ibrahim's sons, Niqula Sabbagh, moved his family to Egypt. Here, one of his two sons, Mikhail, learned to read and write classical Arabic. He would have spoken colloquial Palestinian Arabic at home but to read and write the classical language fluently required considerable study. In the 1790s, Mikhail toured Upper Egypt, the southern part of the country, and learned more about its towns and villages and the history of the country. When the French under Napoleon occupied Egypt, Mikhail got in touch with them, and worked with them for the rest of their stay in the country.

Perhaps he was with Napoleon's army when it passed by Mikhail's birthplace of Acre in 1799. This visit was memorable for a speech made by Napoleon at his camp outside the city walls in which he offered Palestine to the Jews of the world, under French protection. His proclamation began: 'Israelites, unique nation, France offers you at this very time … Israel's patrimony; take over what has been conquered and with that nation's warranty and support, maintain it against all comers.'[5]

This first disposal of Palestine by a statesman giving a land he didn't own to a people who had little right to it presumably didn't put off Mikhail from continuing to work with Napoleon's army, with his considerable skills in the French language. And when the French withdrew from the Middle East in 1801, Mikhail went with them to France.

It was here that an intriguing series of events took place. In Paris Mikhail came to the attention of a famous orientalist, Baron Antoine Sylvestre de Sacy, a gifted linguist and author of an Arabic grammar, described as 'the greatest Arabic scholar of his age'. Mikhail worked first in the official government printers, organizing the printing of texts in Arabic. Then he worked with de Sacy as a copyist of Arabic manuscripts, developing the Arab and Egyptian archives in the King's Library. Mikhail Sabbagh also produced several poems in Arabic, memorializing contemporary events, including 'In Praise of Pope Pius VII', 'Tribute to the Minister of Justice on the Occasion of his Visit to the National Press', 'Verses on the Occasion of the Marriage of Napoleon', and 'Hymn on the Birth of the King of Rome'.

Clearly his combination of literary and linguistic skills had made him in demand in early nineteenth century Paris, when the cultural results of Napoleon's expeditions had led to an upsurge of interest in the Orient. Napoleon appointed to the School of

Oriental Languages in Paris an Egyptian whom de Sacy disliked and, on his resignation some years later, Mikhail took over his job. His brief, originally laid down by Napoleon, was 'to give public lessons in colloquial Arabic'. De Sacy also paid Mikhail the compliment of translating into French a small work he had written in Arabic about carrier pigeons, called *La Colombe, messagère plus rapide que l'éclair* (The Dove, a messenger faster than lightning).

While working in the library, Mikhail Sabbagh helped to organize the collection of Arabic texts for an edition of the *Arabian Nights*. Versions of these stories had been available in French and English for about a hundred years, but Arabic manuscripts of the stories had been in existence for at least six hundred years, so an Arabic scholar like Mikhail could seek out stories that had not been available to the original translators. His researches were associated with two stories in particular, *Sinbad the Sailor* and *Aladdin, or the Wonderful Lamp*.[6]

Sir Richard Burton, the nineteenth-century explorer, linguist, translator and writer, based an eighteen-volume translation of the *Arabian Nights*, or the *Thousand Nights and a Night*, as its Arabic title has it, on a whole range of manuscripts which he dug up from libraries or purchased from dealers. He also scoured Middle East markets and drank coffee with storytellers in souqs to gather as comprehensive a collection of material for this voluminous work, a work so long that superstition has it that anyone who reads it in its entirety will die. (Literally true, of course.)

When Burton was gathering material for his version, there was already in existence an earlier translation, by a French writer, Antoine Galland, who used a fourteenth- or fifteenth-century manuscript from Syria for most of his translation. But this manuscript did not include *Aladdin, or the Wonderful Lamp*, a story that has become one of the best known. Since the story was included in

Galland's translation, Burton wondered about its source. In the foreword to one of his volumes, Burton described how he discovered it, or thought he did, on a visit to Paris in 1887:

> At the Bibliothèque Nationale I had the pleasure of meeting M. Hermann Zotenberg, keeper of Eastern manuscripts, an Orientalist of high and varied talents, and especially famous for his admirable *Chronique de Tabari*. Happily for me, he had lately purchased for the National Library, from a vendor who was utterly ignorant of its history, a MS. copy of The Nights, containing the Arabic originals of Zayn al-Asnam and Alaeddin.... The highly characteristic writing, which is the same throughout the two folios, is easily recognized as that of Michel (Mikhaíl) Sabbágh, author of the *Colombe Messagère*, published in Paris A.D. 1805...

Burton then quoted from a note on the manuscript:

> And the finishing thereof was during the first decade of Jamádi the Second, of the one thousand and one hundred and fifteenth year of the Hegirah by the transcription of the neediest of His slaves unto Almighty Allah, Ahmad bin Mohammed al-Tarádí, in Baghdad City: he was a Sháfi'í of school, and a Mosuli by birth, and a Baghdadi by residence, and he wrote it for his own use, and upon it he imprinted his signet. So Allah save our lord Mohammed and His Kin and Companions and assain them!

This note was in Mikhail's handwriting, so the manuscript clearly wasn't the original by 'Mohammed al-Taradi'. But Burton was convinced it was an authentic copy by Mikhail. However, even if it was, there was the possibility that it was not the original story in Arabic, but that al-Taradi – or someone else – had translated Galland's *Aladdin* back into Arabic from French. Burton dismissed this possibility:

> … as this date corresponds with A.D. 1703, whereas Galland did not begin publishing until 1705, the original MS. of Ahmad al-Tarádí could not have been translated or adapted from the French; and although the transcription by Mikhail Sabbagh, writing in 1805–10, may have introduced modifications borrowed from Galland, yet the scrupulous fidelity of his copy, shown by sundry marginal and other notes, lays the suspicion that changes of importance have been introduced by him. Remains now only to find the original codex of Al-Tarádí.[7]

In fact, it seems that Burton was wrong. There was such a demand for *Arabian Nights* stories in Europe that several scribes, including Mikhail Sabbagh, turned their hands to satisfying the need. It now seems likely that Mikhail cobbled together most of the 'al-Taradi' manuscript from various odd Syrian and Egyptian manuscripts he found lying around Paris. But he couldn't find an original source for *Aladdin*, so he retranslated the story from Galland's French back into Arabic. 'His "discovery" of this alleged Baghdad manuscript,' writes Robert Irwin, a modern Arabist, 'earned him money as well as some academic fame.'[8]

It seems the villainous genes of Ibrahim Sabbagh had found their way down to his grandson. What a shame his 'Tribute to the Minister of Justice on the Occasion of his Visit to the National Press' or even his pioneering work on carrier pigeons are not more widely known, to compensate for this lapse into plagiarism.

• • •

In 1837 the Sabbagh home town of Safad was all but demolished by an earthquake, as were many other towns in Palestine. The Revd W. M. Thomson, a Christian missionary, was in Beirut at the time and felt the effects of the quake while taking a communion service on New Year's Day. In the following week he received several letters from Palestine describing the dreadful damage and loss of life in Safad, so he arranged a relief expedition.

> On the morning of the 18th, we reached Safed, and I then understood, for the first time, what desolation God can work when he ariseth to shake terribly the earth.... All anticipation, every imagination was utterly confounded when the reality burst upon our sight.... Not a house remained standing.... The town was built upon the side of the mountain, which is so steep that the roofs of the houses below formed the street for those above; when, therefore, the shock dashed all to the ground, the highest fell on the next below, that upon the third, and so on to the bottom, burying each successive row of houses deeper and deeper under accumulated masses of rubbish.... many who were not instantaneously killed perished before they could be rescued, and others were rescued five, six, and even seven days after the earthquake, still alive. A friend of mine told me that he found his wife dead, with one child under her arm, and the babe with the nipple in its mouth: it had died of hunger, trying to draw life from its dead mother.[9]

Muslims, Jews and Christians lived side by side in Safad, and both Arabs and Jews spoke Arabic. From time to time, there was friction between the three religious communities, although it rarely resulted in violence. One Hebrew newspaper of the time reported that Arab merchants had begun to take over some of the important commercial functions of the Jews:

> All the negotiations with the fellahs, the purchase of the crops, the items needed for food and clothing – they all are in the hands of Arab merchants. Formerly, this trading was made by Jewish merchants, but with the cultural development of the Arab residents in the town, the Arab merchants began to push the Jewish traders away and overtook the trading business. The Jews did not oppose this; they withdrew from the negotiations with the gentiles. However, the Arab merchants started to compete also in the market of the Jewish commerce. They did not buy at fixed interest but by cash payment, their needs were less and they were satisfied with small benefits, and Jews began to leap at Arab merchandise.[10]

There was clearly competition between the two communities. In this respect, the economic ups and downs of Safad were no different from any other Palestinian town.

Another key centre of trade, agriculture and administration in nineteenth-century Palestine was Nablus, a large town about seventy-five miles south-west of Safad on the hill plateau of central Palestine. A rival centre to Safad and Tiberias, it was under the jurisdiction of the pasha of Damascus. Daher had made several attempts to add the territory to his own possessions, and ruled over it at certain periods. Like each of the main towns in Palestine, Nablus was at the centre of a web of connections with outlying villages, connections defined by families, trading partnerships, religious affiliations and labour needs.

For English travellers of the time, the main interest of Nablus was that it was the home of a surviving community of Samaritans,

The large Arab town of Nablus had a soap industry based on olive oil, which still thrived in the twentieth century.

believed to be descended from the people of the northern kingdom of Israel. W. M. Thomson devoted several pages of his book on 'the manners and customs, the scenes and the scenery of the Holy Land' to the Samaritans. He outlined the arguments for and against the identification of particular Old Testament sites in the area, including the place where Abraham offered his son Isaac to Jahweh. He described Nablus as 'a queer old place. The streets are narrow, and vaulted over; and in the winter time it is difficult to pass along many of them on account of brooks which rush over the pavement with deafening roar.... [I]t has mulberry, orange, pomegranate, and other trees, mingled in with the houses, whose odoriferous flowers load the air with delicious perfume during the months of April and May. Here the bulbul [nightingale] delights to sit and sing, and thousands of other birds unite to swell the chorus. The inhabitants maintain that theirs is the most *musical* vale in Palestine, and my experience does not enable me to contradict them.'[11]

One modern Palestinian historian, Beshara Doumani, has explained the attitudes underlying this kind of writing: 'Small in size and of unexceptionable economic potential, the dominant image of Palestine was that of the "Holy Land," waiting to be reclaimed both spiritually and physically. Pilgrims, businessmen, government representatives, and tourists all landed on its shores in increasing numbers, but often with a single fervent wish in their hearts: to traverse an unchanged landscape where biblical journeys could be endlessly re-enacted.'[12]

All this concentration on the picturesque failed to convey any sense of the complex society that lived and worked in towns and villages throughout Palestine. Doumani studied Nablus, in partic- ular, using Arabic sources. It is in the centre of a rich, olive-growing area and he paints a very different picture of the town from Thompson's fruit-laden aviary:

> The hustle and bustle of tons of [olive] oil being deposited
> in the underground wells of huge soap factory buildings
> after the olive harvest in the fall, for instance, were
> perhaps only surpassed by the commotion of raw cotton
> arriving in the city to be ginned and spun in the summer.
> Thus there were no sharp dividing lines between city and
> country. Indeed, Nablus was, in some ways, akin to a very
> large village: at sunrise many Nabulsis exited the city
> gates to work on the extensive olive groves, vineyards and
> orchards that covered the terraced slopes, as well as in the
> fields, vegetable gardens, and grain mills that were
> scattered across the valley.
>
> In a reverse flow, peasants poured into the city to sell
> their goods and to search for wedding clothes, work tools,
> cooking utensils rice, coffee, and a host of other items.

For them, as for their urban counterparts, Nablus was (to
use a common metaphor) the beating heart of the
surrounding hinterland....

Hundreds of shops lined each artery and spilled over into
smaller streets and alleys, which connected them with each other
and with the six major quarters of the city.'[13]

Palestine was a small but complex society, with a class structure
of sorts, containing a range of people from the highly educated to
peasants, in a community with roads, towns, villages, fine castles
and palaces, a tax-collecting mechanism, some kind of legal system
and so on. As in any society, the families, like mine, produced
descendants whose fortunes varied, some going up in the world,
others falling on hard times.

Laurence Oliphant, after his dismissive tirade against the Jews
of Safad, described the much more congenial company of a
Palestinian married couple who lived in Haifa. Even here,
however, he can't resist a barb: 'owing to the march of civilization,
the richer classes have of late years taken to travel and the study of
languages, persons occupying this position generally speak either
French or Italian, have visited Paris, Constantinople, or Alexandria,
and have a thin varnish of European civilization overlaying their
native barbarism'.

As a guest in the house of a middle-class Palestinian, Oliphant
seems to have been treated to a close-up view of home life, starting
with his host's wife:

If we are on sufficiently intimate terms with him to stay as
a guest in his house, we find that his pretty wife, with her
Paris dress and dainty chaussure, walks about in the
privacy of the domestic home with bare, or at best

stockinged, feet, thrust into high wooden pattens, with
which she clatters over the handsome marble hall that
forms the central chamber of the house, slipping out her
feet and leaving the pattens at the door of any of the
rooms she may be about to enter. She wears a loose
morning-wrapper, which she is not particular about
buttoning, but in this respect she is outdone by sundry
dishevelled maid-servants, who also clatter about the
house in pattens and in light garments that seem to
require very little fastening in front. As for the husband,
who, when he called upon you, might have come off the
boulevards of Paris, barring always the red cap, he has
now reverted absolutely into the Oriental. He wears a
long white and not unbecoming garment that reaches
from his throat to his heels, and his feet are thrust into red
slippers. As he sips his matutinal cup of coffee and
smokes his first narghileh of the day, there is nothing
about him to remind you that he knows a word of any
other language than Arabic, or has ever worn any other
costume than that of his Eastern ancestors. He is sitting
in his own little den, with his feet tucked under him on
the divan which runs around the room, and with his wife
in close proximity, her feet tucked under her, and also
smoking a narghileh and sipping coffee.[14]

The furniture in the house struck Oliphant as rather showy:

'[It] consists of massive tables with marble tops, and
handsome arm-chairs and couches covered with costly
satins. The walls are resplendent with gilt mirrors and
with heavy hanging curtains. The floors are covered with
rich carpets. There is a three-hundred-dollar piano, on

which the lady never plays; and there are pictures, of
which the frames are more artistic than the subjects.

Oliphant was fed well – 'the huge pillaw of rice, the chicken
stew with rich and greasy gravy, the lamb stuffed with pistachio
nuts, the leben or sour milk, the indescribable sweet dishes, crisp,
sticky, and nutty' – but left a little unsatisfied when it came to his
host's provision of intellectual nourishment. 'His conversational
powers and ideas are limited, which is not to be wondered at, considering that there is not a book in the house. He tells you that the
house cost him $9000, which does not seem likely to be an exag-
geration when we look at the handsome marble floors and
staircase, massive arches, and the extent of ground which is
covered by spacious halls and ample courts.'

But of course, always a problem with these Orientals, Jew or
Arab, is the hygiene: 'The kitchen and offices, if you have the
curiosity to look into them, are filthy in the extreme, and the
process of cooking the dinner, performed by a slovenly female, had
better not be too closely examined.'

Haifa, Safad, Nablus, Tiberias and Acre were all bustling towns
with large populations of Palestinian Arabs from a variety of social
groups. Further south, Jenin, Jerusalem, Ramallah, Jaffa, Gaza and
Beersheba were similarly populated, not to mention the hundreds
of villages and hamlets scattered across the hills and in the valleys.
I know the names of thirty-two Sabbaghs who were alive in the
second half of the nineteenth century, and my knowledge of my
family history is less comprehensive than that of many Palestinians
today. How strange it would be, then, for someone to claim that
Palestine in the nineteenth century was an empty land.

Nevertheless, this is the claim in modern books and articles
which seek to justify the takeover of Palestine on the basis that

before the Jews arrived no one was living there anyway. In fact, there were hundreds of thousands of Arabs in Palestine in the seventeenth, eighteenth and nineteenth centuries increasingly recorded by Ottoman censuses. But as we will see in the next chapter, writers on this topic often ignore these figures and instead turn to the most unlikely material to demonstrate that Palestine was deserted.

5

TRAVELLERS' TALES

• • •

In the nineteenth century improved methods of travel brought an increase in tourism to Palestine from Europe and America. Most of the tourists wanted to visit the land of the Bible. They were interested in seeing (and chipping bits off) the sites mentioned in the Old and New Testaments. Landscapes that might have been seen by Moses or Jesus, the sites of the Nativity and Crucifixion, the Stations of the Cross in Jerusalem, plains and valleys where Old Testament battles might have been fought – these places attracted groups of pale, perspiring tourists with sketchpads, journals and parasols.

Books with titles like *The Land and the Book, Excursions in the Holy Land, Letters from Palestine, Things Seen in Palestine*, and *Palestine Past and Present* were produced in increasing numbers. For many of these visitors, the contemporary inhabitants of Palestine were insignificant figures in the landscape, as Doumani explains: 'They regularly appeared in nineteenth-century photographs and postcards as decorations and icons of ancient times: the shepherd tending his flock, the woman drawing water from a well, the peasant plowing his field. They also filled a variety of roles, often exotic stereotypes of the Orient – the pompous pasha,

Western visitors to Palestine in the nineteenth century
were mainly interested in revisiting biblical sites.

the harem girl, the devious merchant – in traveller books and the popular press.'[1]

The American traveller writer Mark Twain was particularly scathing about a writer he called Grimes – actually William C. Prime, author of *Tent Life in the Holy Land*. Arriving in Jerusalem, Prime wrote: 'I stood in the road, my hand on my horse's neck, and with my dim eyes sought to trace the outlines of the holy places which I had long before fixed in my mind, but the fast-flowing tears forbade my succeeding. There were our Mohammedan servants, a Latin monk, two Armenians and a Jew in our cortege, and all alike gazed with flowing eyes.' After quoting this passage, Twain added disparagingly: 'If Latin monks and Arabs cried, I know to a moral certainty that the horses cried also … [Grimes] never bored but he struck water.'[2]

The travel writings of Twain and other travellers have been used to support the idea that Palestine had been devoid of Arabs for the last three hundred years. Here's a typical example of this usage: 'In the sixteenth, seventeenth, eighteenth and nineteenth centuries, a litany of Christian travelers – Siebald Rieter and Johann Tucker, Arnold Van Harff and Father Michael Nuad, Martin Kabatnik and Felix Fabri, Count Constantine François Volney and Alphonse de Lamartine, Mark Twain and Sir George Gawler, Sir George Adam Smith and Edward Robinson – found Palestine virtually empty, except for Jewish communities in Jerusalem, Safed, Shechem, Hebron, Gaza, Ramleh, Acre, Sidon, Tyre, Haifa, Irsuf, Caesarea, and El Arish, and throughout Galilee towns – Kfar Alma, Ein Zeitim, Biria, Pekiin, Kfar Hanania, Kfar Kana and Kufr Yassif.'

This comes from a pro-Israeli book,[3] and you can't imagine a firmer and more convincing statement of fact. No doubts, no caveats, just a sober list of authorities implying an accumulation of data that point to one conclusion: the population of Palestine from seventeenth to the nineteenth century was sparse and almost entirely Jewish.

The Palestinian claim to Palestine is based on the assertion that the Muslim and Christian Arabs have always formed a majority of the indigenous population of the area and that Jews have always formed a minority, sometimes a very small minority of only a few per cent. Now, in quotes like that above, here comes an impressive array of apparently reputable people – a brace of knights, a count, a priest and some famous writers – all testifying to the contrary.

In his learned study *The Jews in Palestine 1800–1882*, Tudor Parfitt, a lecturer in Hebrew at London University, gives the following set of figures for the number of Jews in six of the sites mentioned above, at the dates given during the nineteenth century. Parfitt's work is based on a wide-ranging and thorough analysis of available population estimates.

Jerusalem	(1800)	–	2,000+
Safad	(1836)	–	1,500

Nablus	(1829)	–	50
Nablus	(1860)	–	300
Hebron	(1847)	–	2,500
Acre	(1843)	–	150
Haifa	(1829)	–	50
Haifa	(1870)	–	900

A 'virtually empty' country indeed if this is any indication of the inhabitants of some of the major towns. But Parfitt also gives the figures for the *total* population of each of these places. We can assume that most of the non-Jews, aside from a few visitors or immigrants, were Muslim or Christian Arabs:

Jerusalem	(1800)	–	12,000
Safad	(1836)	–	6,000
Nablus	(1829)	–	15,000
Nablus	(1860)	–	24,000
Hebron	(1847)	–	28,500
Acre	(1843)	–	8,000
Haifa	(1829)	–	2,500
Haifa	(1870)	–	3,180

This is not a country 'virtually empty' apart from the Jews. Even in the main Jewish centres, Safad and Haifa, the Jews usually formed less than 50 per cent of the population, and in the others the percentage was much lower – a third of 1 per cent in Nablus in 1829. These are verifiable statistics compiled by people who are interested in getting at the facts objectively, whereas the authorities for the statement that Palestine was 'virtually empty' are a group of dilettante travel writers whose demographic data was largely restricted to what they could (or couldn't) see through the flaps of the luxury tent that was put up by their friendly Arab guides, or out of the windows of their stone caravanserais.

Mark Twain, in particular, is always quoted to prove that Palestine was deserted:

> Stirring scenes ... occur in the valley (Jezreel) no more.
> There is not a solitary village throughout its whole extent
> – not for thirty miles in either direction. There are two or
> three small clusters of Bedouin tents, but not a single
> permanent habitation. One may ride ten miles hereabouts
> and not see ten human beings. [To find] the sort of
> solitude to make one dreary ... come to Galilee
> for ... these unpeopled deserts, these rusty mounds of
> barrenness, that never, never, never do shake the glare
> from their harsh outlines, and fade and faint into vague
> perspective, that melancholy ruin of Capernaum: this
> stupid village of Tiberias, slumbering under its six funeral
> palms.... Palestine sits in sackcloth and ashes....
> desolate and unlovely.

This comes from *The Innocents Abroad*, a humorous travel book. Although Mark Twain's observations are refuted by every scholarly analysis of the true figures, that doesn't stop them being used to bolster the Zionist cause. In the US Senate in 2002 Twain's journalistic musings were presented as one of seven reasons why the State of Israel was entitled to the land. A Republican politician from Oklahoma, Senator James M. Inhofe, said: 'There was not a huge Arab population in the land at that time, and there is a reason for that. The land was not able to sustain a large population of people.... Nobody really wanted this land. It was considered to be worthless land.... Mark Twain – Samuel Clemens – took a tour of Palestine in 1867. This is how he described that land. We are talking about Israel now. He said: "A desolate country whose soil is rich enough but is given over wholly to weeds ...'"

One or two of Senator Inhofe's other reasons for the justice of Israel's claims are equally dubious. 'Archaeological evidence', for example: 'Every time there is a dig in Israel, it does nothing but support the fact that Israelis have had a presence there for 3,000 years.' Not quite. Many digs, when allowed by the Israelis, confirm the longer-lasting and more recent presence of the Palestinian Arabs and their ancestors. Inhofe's reason number 7 is 'Because G–d said so. As I said a minute ago, look it up in the book of Genesis. It is right up there on the desk ...' (Inhofe's objectivity in Middle East matters can be gauged by the fact that he also said in the Senate that the 9/11 attacks were G–d's punishment of America for persuading Israel to restrain itself in the face of terrorist attacks.)

Mark Twain, alias Samuel Clemens, was an American humorist and anti-Semite. I use the word in its literal sense, as applied to all

Mark Twain and other Western tourists had little real contact with the country or its people, as they stayed in luxury tents and were waited on by Arab servants.

Semites, Arabs and Jews. In *Innocents Abroad*, Twain was venomously anti-Arab, and in other writings he was anti-Jew. But many supporters of the State of Israel are happy to ignore his anti-Jewish statements and prefer to concentrate on his anti-Arab writings.

Twain's conclusion that Palestine was 'desolate and unlovely' makes it sound like just the sort of place that needs revitalizing and repopulating with a lively thrusting group of people who can make the desert bloom. His quote can be found on the site of a group called *Palestine Facts*,[4] for example, which claims to be 'dedicated to providing comprehensive and accurate information regarding the historical, military, and political background to the on-going struggle between the State of Israel and the Palestinian Arabs'. Here are some other appearances of the Twain quote on the internet, increasingly used as a source of information in preference to reference books:

- '...when the American writer Mark Twain toured Palestine in 1867, he wrote with remorse: "Stirring scenes ... occur in the valley [Jezreel] no more. There is not a solitary village throughout its whole extent – not for thirty miles in either direction..."'[5]
- 'The most famous [traveller] was Mark Twain, who recorded after his visit in 1867: "Stirring scenes occur in the valley [Jezreel] no more. There is not a solitary village throughout its whole extent – not for thirty miles in either direction."'[6]
- 'But *eretz yisrael*, the land of Israel was still sparsely populated. In 1867, Mark Twain wrote, "Stirring scenes.... occur in the valley [Jezreel] no more. There is not a solitary village throughout in whole extent – not for thirty miles in either direction."'[7]

- 'In one location after another, Twain registered gloom at his findings. "Stirring scenes.... occur in the valley [Jezreel] no more. There is not a solitary village throughout in whole extent – not for thirty miles in either direction."'[8]
- 'When Mark Twain visited the Holy Land in 1867, he found to his dismay that the land was barren. "Stirring scenes ... occur in the valley (Jezreel) no more. There is not a solitary village throughout its whole extent – not for 30 miles in either direction."'[9]

However, at least one eyewitness account – a particularly significant one – by a Western traveller to Palestine in the 1860s contradicts Twain's description of a desolate, unpopulated place:

> Here were evidences of cultivation, an acre or two of rich soil studded with last season's dead corn-stalks of the thickness of your thumb and very wide apart.... it was a thrilling spectacle.... The view presented from its highest peak was almost beautiful. Below, was the broad, level plain of Esdraelon, [also known as the Vale of Jezreel] checkered with fields like a chess-board, and full as smooth and level, seemingly; dotted about its borders with white, compact villages, and faintly pencilled, far and near, with the curving lines of roads and trails. When it is robed in the fresh verdure of spring, it must form a charming picture, even by itself. Nazareth is wonderfully interesting ... We found here a grove of lemon trees – cool, shady, hung with fruit.... We jogged along peacefully over the great caravan route from Damascus to Jerusalem and Egypt, past Lubia and other Syrian hamlets, perched, in the unvarying style, upon the

summit of steep mounds and hills ... It was beautiful. I do not overestimate it. I must always remember Shunem gratefully, as a place which gave to us this leafy shelter after our long, hot ride. We lunched, rested, chatted, smoked our pipes an hour, and then mounted and moved on.... The narrow cañon in which Nablous, or Shechem, is situated, is under high cultivation, and the soil is exceedingly black and fertile. It is well watered, and its affluent vegetation gains effect by contrast with the barren hills that tower on either side.... Perched on its eternal hills, white and domed and solid, massed together and hooped with high gray walls, the venerable city gleamed in the sun. Jerusalem numbers fourteen thousand people ... We came finally to the noble grove of orange-trees in which the Oriental city of Jaffa lies buried; we passed through the walls, and rode again down narrow streets ... Sometimes, in the glens, we came upon luxuriant orchards of figs, apricots, pomegranates, and such things ...

So who was this traveller who disagreed so strongly with the accounts of desolation and barrenness given by Mark Twain? Step forward: Mark Twain. From other chapters of *Innocents Abroad* I have selected phrases and sentences as carelessly and with as little attention to conventions of academic citation as the earlier quotes used by supporters of Israel. While they too are presented as if they were continuous text, they are actually taken from many pages apart.

What is going on here? How can the most frequently quoted source of demographic and economic data about mid-nineteenth-century Palestine be a writer whose description of the territory is so subjective and inconsistent? In fact, *Innocents Abroad* is written in such an exaggerated, tongue-in-cheek style that Twain's observations can hardly be taken as factual descriptions. At one point he claims to have taken an old sword. 'I tried it on a Muslim,' he writes, 'and clove him in twain like a doughnut.' And here's some more: 'It was a tiresome ride to us, and perfectly exhausting to the horses. We were compelled to jump over upwards of eighteen hundred donkeys, and only one person in the party was unseated less than sixty times by the camels … After a while we came to a shapeless mass of ruins, which still bears the name of Bethel. It was here that Jacob lay down and had that superb vision of angels … The pilgrims took what was left of the hallowed ruin, and we pressed on toward the goal of our crusade, renowned Jerusalem.'

It should be clear by now that one cannot base the case for the takeover of Palestine on the facetious remarks of an American humorist, especially since everything Mark Twain wrote about the Arab inhabitants of Palestine is loaded with prejudice and hatred. He refers to 'filthy Arabs' who 'smell like a camel' living in 'barbarous ignorance and savagery'. He objects to their 'ugly features' and their 'disagreeable jabbering in unknown tongues'. It's charming stuff. As for factual accuracy, what did it matter to the readers of the San Francisco newspaper for whom Twain wrote? None of them would be likely to pick up on his errors, exaggerations and fabrications.

Why then is he quoted so often, in preference to more objective, academic and reliable sources of information? In particular, the ubiquitous sentence about 'Stirring scenes … occur in the valley [Jezreel] no more. There is not a solitary village …' is easily checkable and, it turns out, nonsense. A short visit to Israel, the West Bank and Gaza will reveal hundreds of Arab towns and villages with histories of continuous population that stretch back at least to the eighteenth century and many for hundreds of years before that. And there are many reliable sources that back this up.

It didn't take me long to realize how this idea had got about, and indeed was being kept alive. Most of the people quoting from Twain have probably never read *Innocents Abroad*. However, they may have read *From Time Immemorial* (1984) by Joan Peters, a wildly inaccurate account of the history of Palestine and one of the most comprehensively demolished non-fiction books of recent years. In spite of numerous detailed and well-referenced condemnations of this pro-Israel book, it has not been withdrawn, and continues to nourish the anti-Palestinian rhetoricians of the internet.

Embedded in the much-repeated Twain quote, like a piece of DNA passed down the generations, is that mysterious word 'Jezreel' in brackets. If those quoting the passage had read the original they would have realized that this is *not* what Twain wrote, it's what Peters added in her book to make it clear Twain was describing the Valley of Jezreel. Only he wasn't, as a glance at a map of Palestine would have shown. Twain's 'not a solitary village' passage was written while camping at Ain Mellahah, a village situated by 'one of the most copious springs in Palestine, yielding between 1,800 and 2,700 cubic meters of water per hour', according to a more reliable historian than Twain.[10] But Ain Mellahah no longer exists: it was one of hundreds of Palestinian villages whose inhabitants were expelled in 1948 and their villages razed to the ground. It was near Lake Huleh (the biblical Waters of Merom), about ten miles north-east of Safad and twenty-five miles north of the larger town of Tiberias. It is nowhere near the Valley of Jezreel – and it is not clear why Peters thought it was.

Twain's statement that there was not a solitary village 'for thirty miles in either direction' is plain wrong. Mid-nineteenth-century maps of Palestine show that within a sixty-mile radius of Ain Mellahah there were more than a hundred towns and villages including Safad and Tiberias. Why did Twain ignore them? Even more astonishing is the credence given to his observations, which are contradicted by a wealth of modern scholarship concerning the demography of Ottoman Palestine in the eighteenth and nineteenth centuries.

'Palestine is a country without a people; the Jews are a people without a country,'[11] said Israel Zangwill in 1901. Despite its inaccuracy, this snappy slogan has had a remarkably long life. It perfectly embodies the desire of Zionists at the turn of the century to establish a Jewish national home in Palestine. However, one can still hear it used today to justify the State of Israel, even though it flies in the face of the established historical facts.

In *The Population of Palestine*, Professor Justin McCarthy provides the statistics for 1860 and 1877, covering the period of Twain's visit. He corrects the raw figures (which underestimate the numbers of women and children) and cites 369,000 and 440,000 respectively.[12] Even if we take a figure of about 400,000, it is hardly insignificant for a country of 27,000 square kilometres. That's about fourteen people per square kilometre, several times the population density of the United States at the time, which no one would have considered 'a country without a people'. It seems that the facts get in the way of the Zionist cause.

The Zionists are named after Zion (or Sion), a hill in Jerusalem that later gave its name to the whole city. The Zionists held their first meeting as an organized group in 1897 in Basle, Switzerland. 'The aim of Zionism,' they agreed at this meeting, 'is to create for the Jewish people a home in Palestine secured by public law.' The official aim was only to have 'a home *in* Palestine', but Theodore Herzl, the first president of the Zionist Organization, made it clear in his diary that much more was at stake: 'If I were to sum up the Congress in a word – which I shall take care not to publish – it would be this: At Basle I founded the Jewish State. If I said this out loud today I would be greeted by universal laughter. In five years perhaps, and certainly in fifty years, everyone will perceive it.'[13]

The Zionists threw all their considerable energies into promoting the idea that Palestine was deserted, although some of them who had actually seen the land for themselves had to admit that the indigenous population of Palestine might well present a problem: 'There are now only five hundred [thousand] Arabs, who are not very strong, and from whom we shall easily take away the country if only we do it through stratagems [and] without drawing upon us their hostility before we become the strong and populous ones.'[14]

Asher Ginsburg, writing under the pseudonym 'Ahad Ha'am', might be described as a spiritual Zionist who wanted to keep alive the philosophical and cultural traditions of Judaism. Yet he fiercely criticized any Zionist who thought Palestine was there for the taking. In 1891 he wrote: 'We abroad are used to believing that Palestine is now almost totally desolate, a desert that is not sowed, and that anyone who wishes to purchase land there may come and do so to his heart's content. But in truth this is not the case. Throughout the country it is difficult to find fields that are not sowed. Only sand dunes and stony mountains that are not fit to grow anything but fruit trees ... are not cultivated.'[15]

Ginsburg sounded a warning note for those Zionists who assumed the takeover would be easy: 'We are used to thinking of the Arabs as primitive men of the desert, as a donkey-like nation that neither sees nor understands what is going on around it. But this is a great error. The Arab, like all sons of Shem, has a sharp and crafty mind ... Should the time come when the life of our people in

Palestine imposes to a smaller or greater extent on the natives, they will not easily step aside.'[16]

Four years after writing that Palestine was 'a country without a people', even Israel Zangwill was forced to admit that 'Palestine proper has already its inhabitants. The pashalik [an Ottoman administrative area] of Jerusalem is already twice as thickly populated as the United States, having fifty-two souls to the square mile, and not 25% of them Jews ... [We] must be prepared either to drive out by the sword the [Arab] tribes in possession as our forefathers did or to grapple with the problem of a large alien population, mostly Mohammedan [Muslim] and accustomed for centuries to despise us.'[17]

The situation was summed up in a pithy telegram from a Zionist delegation who visited Palestine in 1898 to assess the feasibility of making it a Jewish state. 'The bride is beautiful,' said the telegram, 'but she is married to another man.'[18]

In 1904, two months before his death, Theodore Herzl wrote his last letter to a friend, saying 'Don't do anything foolish while I am dead.'[19]

The denial of Palestinian history was just one of many foolish things that were to be done 'while Herzl was dead', as the twentieth century began to deliver a series of blows to the indigenous population. For when the Zionist Organization was determined to commit adultery with the beautiful bride it turned out that the British government was only too happy to help them.

6

BIBLE STORIES

• • •

The Jewish people have always sought to maintain their ties to their 'Promised Land', a promise some of them believe was made by their God to Abraham, Isaac and Jacob.

Between 1897 and 1917 – a mere twenty years – a small group of dedicated Zionists managed to convince some of the West's most powerful politicians and statesmen that Palestine should become a Jewish state – against the wishes of the majority of the land's inhabitants. How did they do this? How did they achieve this anti-democratic goal at a time when early ideas of democracy and self-determination were setting the agenda for twentieth-century attitudes to nationhood? The answer lies partly in religion.

Western culture is founded on the Bible. Paintings, sculptures, works of literature, even common phrases and metaphors in the English language are derived from the Old and New Testaments. Judaism itself was a minority religion in all Western countries, but the ideas, places, people and events of the Jewish religion were familiar to many. The Bible was even presented as being literally true, as a kind of guidebook to Palestine. This is why European travellers went to see the walls of Jericho, the temple of Solomon or the Witch of Endor's cave. In Britain, where so many of the important decisions about the modern history of Palestine were to be made, the sentimental link with Palestine claimed by Jews was looked on benignly by many Christians. As one Zionist has written: 'In British homes the people of the Old Testament and the ancient land they had made famous touched not only the imagination but the very heart-strings of the common folk.'[1]

The Zionist claim to Palestine was based on two assumptions. First, that God had given the land to the Jews three millennia ago. 'This land is ours,' said the Israeli Prime Minister Ariel Sharon in 2002, speaking to a group of Christians. 'God gave us the title deeds.'[2] He was not speaking metaphorically. Many Jews today believe in the literal truth of this divine promise. Second, the Bible describes a long association of the Jews with Palestine which only ended when they were expelled by the Romans in AD 70.

Professor Philip Davies summarizes the biblical story of the Jews as follows:

> It begins with the ancestor Jacob, who is given the name 'Israel' … the 'children of Israel' consist of twelve 'tribes', each traced back to a son (or grandson) of Jacob/Israel. These 'tribes' originate in Palestine (which is called, among other names, 'Canaan'), migrate to Egypt, where they are enslaved, then escape and after wandering between Egypt and their destination for forty years, conquer the 'land of Canaan', though not completely. Thereafter, they are ruled by 'judges' who 'judge' all Israel … They later elect a king, Saul; he is killed, and then succeeded by another, David, who is already king of Judah … but becomes king of a kingdom of the twelve 'tribes' called 'Israel', although within this kingdom the

'house of Israel' and the 'house of Judah' are distinguished.
David rules over an empire from the borders of Egypt to
the Euphrates, as does his successor Solomon. Under
Solomon's successor, the kingdom redivides into 'Judah'
and 'Israel', the latter being regarded as religiously
illegitimate. Israel (i.e. the northern kingdom) falls to the
Assyrians and later Judah falls to the Babylonians. Its
rulers are deported, but after about fifty years are allowed
to return to Judah. Some do so, and rebuild Jerusalem and
its Temple, instituting the law of Moses and preserving
their ethnic purity. Yet, 'Israel' continues to include the
descendants of the former kingdoms still living elsewhere,
whose return is often hoped for.[3]

This account, rich in detail, full of dramatic characters and stirring events, is the basis of Jewish religious belief and also for the
case of their right to 'return' to Palestine.

In Tel Aviv on 14 May 1948 a new State of Israel was proclaimed
using these words: 'The Land of Israel was the birthplace of the
Jewish people. Here their spiritual, religious and national identity
was formed. Here they achieved independence and created a
culture of national and universal significance. Here they wrote and
gave the Bible to the world. Exiled from the Land of Israel the
Jewish people remained faithful to it in all the countries of their
dispersion, never ceasing to pray and hope for their return and the
restoration of their national freedom.'[4]

Zionists may regard these ancient beliefs as a sufficient basis for
taking over Palestine, but do they really justify displacing hundreds
of thousands of indigenous Arabs from the land – Arabs who can
trace their ancestry back hundreds of years and whose distant
ancestors may have coexisted with the Jews?

But there is a much stronger objection to the proclamation of the State of Israel than merely the lapse of time since these biblical events occurred. The fact of the matter is that much of the Old Testament is fictional. At first glance, this statement may seem unlikely. There are people and events mentioned in the Bible whose existence is confirmed by independent evidence. Ahab and Jehu, Sennacherib's siege of Jerusalem, the Babylonian invasion of Judaea: all are mentioned either in Assyrian or Babylonian inscriptions. And the writing style of the Bible, the daring deeds spelt out with much circumstantial detail, the human frailties portrayed, all have the ring of truth about them. But then so does Tolstoy's *War and Peace*. And while Napoleon certainly marched on Moscow, Natasha Rostov never danced her peasant dance in the cottage of her uncle, and Pierre Bezukhov never wandered the battlefield of Borodino.

Like *War and Peace* the Old Testament sometimes draws on historical fact, but it remains a religious and literary construction rather than an accurate description of events that actually happened. The books of the Old Testament were written as much as a thousand or more years after the events they describe and there is no archaeological evidence – in spite of immense efforts in recent years – for the existence of many key figures and events in these ancient stories.

'The empire of David and Solomon believed to have existed in the 10th century BCE is evidently based on a fictional representation of the past,' writes the biblical scholar Niels Peter Lemche. 'Many things speak in favour of this conclusion. One of them has to do with the status of Jerusalem in the 10th century BCE when Jerusalem was at most a village or a small town.'[5]

And according to historian Professor Philip Davies,[6] 'The biblical empire of David and Solomon has not the faintest echo in the archaeological record.' 'There is no archaeological evidence for this important symbol of power [the temple of Solomon].... Despite the biblical description of a forty-year reign for David, ironically enough we have very few archaeological remains from the Davidic period. There are no monuments that can positively be identified as Davidic,'[7] writes Professor Keith Whitelam. 'The chronology of Judges and Samuel is a purely fictitious creation to provide a 1000-year scheme covering Israel's existence in Canaan. As such it cannot be used to provide a chronology for a history of Israel.... The picture of Israel's past as presented in much of the Hebrew Bible is a fiction, a fabrication like most pictures of the past constructed by ancient (and, we might add) modern societies.'[8] The only 'Israel' which has left its traces in the soil of Palestine existed between the ninth and late eighth centuries BCE, whereas the 'Israel' described in the biblical literature, an Israel which has been described as merely a 'literary construct', is presented as a society which lived

Palestinian Arabs were seen largely as peasant figures in a landscape, by Western visitors to Palestine. If they could also be posed to represent biblical scenes this was a bonus.

continuously in Palestine from at least 1250 BCE until some time in the fifth century BCE. It is only in the *literary* Israel that characters such as David and Joshua and Abraham have any existence.

As you might expect, there are plenty of older biblical scholars who disagree with this new body of work, but they tend to start from a belief in the literal truth of the Bible. In contrast, the new biblical historians look objectively at any text as just that – a text – without any preconceptions about its contents or origins that cannot be supported by independent evidence. They also point out the limitations of claimed archaeological evidence, such as a stela which might (or might not) bear the inscription 'House of David', and excavations, funded by groups seeking evidence of the king, that are said to reveal a palace of David's.

The anthropologist Edmund Leach has examined a key area in the supposed history of 'ancient Israel': the reigns of David and Solomon. 'Personally I find this most implausible,' he says in his conclusion. 'There is no archaeological evidence for the existence of these heroes or for the occurrence of any of the events with which they were associated. If it were not for the sacredness of these stories their historicity would certainly be rejected.'[9]

Another episode from the Bible with great importance for Zionists is the story of how most of the population of Judah was exiled to Babylonia, leaving behind an empty land. The crucial point for Zionists is that the people who sought to return to the land in the twentieth century were direct descendants of a group of people who were sent into exile. There is no evidence for this and some modern scholars believe it to be highly unlikely. Philip Davies points out that deportations, which were frequent in the ancient Near East, were designed to break up populations, preventing them from retaining a religious and national identity.

The idea that the authentic 'Israel' was preserved by deportees and replanted in Palestine several decades later by their grandchildren is a fairly suspicious piece of ideology on the part of biblical scholars ... The biblical story itself suggests that these 'exiles' did not return even in moderate numbers, and not without need for persuasion, so that the idea of a compact community nurturing memories of home is not borne out even in biblical scholarship's primary source.... I have raised the question of whether these immigrants were really descended from Judaean deportees. The Persians probably told them that they were, they may have believed it themselves, and it may have been true. But whether or not this were the case, they would have made that claim anyway, and the claim itself is therefore no evidence.[10]

Great efforts have been made to excavate archaeological sites in Palestine, both before and after the establishment of the State of Israel, in the hope of corroborating the Bible stories. Nineteenth-century archaeologists believed that it should be possible to uncover evidence of an Israelite empire under King David, bearing in mind the duration and extent of its power, as described in the Bible. A classic book, Professor John Bright's A History of Israel, describes Israel in the tenth century BC as 'one of the ranking powers of the contemporary world'.[11] He bases this entirely on his reading of the Bible and argues that the 'eyewitness flavour' of several of the books of the Old Testament means they must have been written at the time. Today, most scholars believe they were written five or six hundred years later.

What historical facts we do know about the various nations in the area make it rather unlikely that Palestine – with an estimated population of 250,000 living mainly in small rural villages – might rank with Egypt or Assyria with their populations of two or more million people and a much more developed economic infrastructure.[12] Professor Davies writes: 'Evidence of the process of settlement on the Judaean highlands ... makes it extremely difficult to conceive of the formation of a state until 900–800 BCE and the formation of an empire of any size is out of the question.'[13]

According to Keith Whitelam, 'Any meaningful notion of a Davidic empire, the realization of "Greater Israel"... could reasonably be expected to have found corroboration in the bureaucratic output of surrounding cultures or ought to have left a significant impact on the material remains of the region.... Such a large state, let alone an empire, would require significant changes in social and political organization which ought to have left some trace in the archaeological record.'[14]

Yigael Yadin, perhaps the leading Israeli archaeologist during the first decades of the existence of modern Israel, put very clearly the link between the pursuit of archaeology and the need to find results that prove the truth of the Bible story of 'ancient Israel'. 'Everyone feels and knows that he is discovering and excavating findings and artifacts from the days of his fathers. And every finding bears witness to the connection and covenant between the people and the land,' he wrote ... 'As far as Israel is concerned, it seems to me that the factor I mentioned – the search and building of the connection to the people and the land – must be taken into consideration. [Archaeology] in my view reinforces the Hebraic consciousness, let us say – the identification and the connection with ancient Judaism and Jewish consciousness.'[15]

Under such pressure to prove a point, it is sometimes difficult for archaeologists to be objective about their findings. The anthropologist Nadia Abu El-Haj studied the work of archaeologists in

Palestine and discovered that their pre-existing beliefs often led them to unscientific and unreliable conclusions. One of her examples centres on a type of pottery first identified and named by a distinguished American archaeologist, W. F. Albright, who worked for many years on sites in Palestine. While working on one of these sites, Tell el-Ful, he discovered pottery which had a distinctive design feature, known as a 'collared rim' and which was associated with a culture that, by dating methods, he could tell was new to the site and the area. Because Albright believed – from his reading of the Bible and in particular the book of Joshua – that a group of people called the Israelites had conquered the area during a period now called Iron Age I by archaeologists, he named this type of pottery 'Israelite'. Over the years, other sites were excavated by other archaeologists, and sometimes similar types of pottery were found. Albright's designation was applied to these findings and then, by extension, to the sites themselves, so that every new place where this pottery was found was treated as evidence for another 'Israelite' site, confirming the widening presence of 'Israel' in Palestine, even though the use of the world 'Israel' was a dubious assumption about one particular pot design.

Abu El-Haj summed it up by saying: 'It was not on the basis of any specific material finds (say, an inscription) that Albright first identified such pottery forms as characteristically Israelite, however. Rather, that conclusion was derived from his assumption regarding who this new culture in early-Iron Age Palestine had to be. Nevertheless, once detached from that initial textually based reasoning, which specified the identity of the pottery forms, the presence or absence of Israelite pottery enabled subsequent excavators to ascertain the location of Israelite sites and strata, now on the basis of empirical evidence, or archaeological facts.'[16]

In the nineteenth and early twentieth centuries, the research methods were rudimentary and belief in the literal truth of the Bible was much more widespread, but what Davies, Whitelam, Abu El-Haj and others reveal is that this misuse continues today. The Israeli archaeologist Ze'ev Herzog caused an outcry when he summed up these new discoveries in an Israeli newspaper in 1999:

> This is what archaeologists have learned from their excavations in the Land of Israel. The Israelites were never in Egypt, did not wander in the desert, did not conquer the land in a military campaign and did not pass it on to the twelve tribes of Israel. Perhaps even harder to swallow is the fact that the united monarchy of David and Solomon, which is described by the Bible as a regional power, was at most a small tribal kingdom. And it will come as an unpleasant shock to many that the God of Israel, Jehovah, had a female consort and that the early Israelite religion adopted monotheism only in the waning period of the monarchy and not at Mount Sinai. Most of those who are engaged in scientific work in the interlocking spheres of the Bible, archaeology and the history of the Jewish people – and who once went into the field looking for proof to corroborate the Bible story – now agree that the historic events relating to the stages of the Jewish people's emergence are radically different from what that story tells.[17]

Why am I going into these matters in so much detail? Does it really make much difference to an understanding of the situation in the modern Middle East?

I think it is important for two reasons. First, as we will see ad nauseam, the constant refrain from Zionists right up to the era of modern Israel has been that they had a right to take over Palestine

As archaeology became a science in the twentieth century, it was dedicated to 'proving' that Bible stories about Israel were historically accurate.

because 'they' were once powerful rulers of the area for a long period and, apparently, in the absence of anyone else. This message is reinforced through the identification of sites throughout Israel that authenticate the biblical text, or would if there was any independent evidence, and persuade Israelis and diaspora Jews that they are not alien invaders of a land with which, in reality, most of them have no ethnic or ancestral connection.

Unfortunately, this spurious history of the Jewish people has led to the suppression of the legitimate history of the Palestinians and their connection with the land. This wilful ignorance has a long history. Long before the modern State of Israel was established, archaeologists were far more interested in identifying 'Israelites' than any of the other different groups of people who lived in Palestine between 1500 BCE and the Christian era. Now many academics who have studied biblical texts objectively believe that this 'Israel' was a fictional creation. 'Exporting a literary construct,' says Philip Davies, 'and dumping it into Iron Age Palestine has succeeded in creating a "history of ancient Israel". But it has also interfered with the real history of Palestine, which now has a cuckoo in its nest. For of course ... there *was* a population of Iron Age Palestine, including a kingdom called Israel, and real people lived there, real kings ruled, real wars took place and real transportations, in and out, were practised by conquering armies and sovereigns. *These* are the people and societies whose relics archaeologists discover whenever they dig for "ancient Israel".'[18]

It seems that ancient artefacts left behind by other people are far less interesting. 'If these people were not Israelites,' writes the biblical archaeology expert Hershel Shanks, 'they have as much interest to us as Early Bronze Age IV people. This does not mean we are uninterested, but it does mean considerably less interest than if they were Israelites. In short, we want to know what all this evidence – and there is a great deal of it – can plausibly tell us about early Israel.'[19]

Some archaeologists even seem to resist calling the early inhabitants of Palestine 'Palestinians'. They are referred to merely as 'inhabitants of ancient Palestine', even though the archaeologists happily refer to the 'Palestinian coastline', 'Palestinian agriculture' or the 'Palestinian economy'. Nevertheless there is reliable evidence that the Canaanite culture – effectively the most plausible antecedent of native Arab Palestine – coexisted with the various manifestations of Israel. The Canaanite culture was rich, varied and socially sophisticated, though it was deemed a little too racy for early archaeologists and historians. As one English bishop put it in 1903: 'Nothing, I think, that has been discovered makes us feel any regret at the suppression of Canaanite civilization by Israelite civilization ... [The excavations show how] the Bible has not misrepresented at all the abomination of Canaanite culture which was superseded by the Israelite culture.'[20]

Why was Canaanite civilization regarded as inferior to Israelite civilization? Judging by the discoveries that have been made, the Canaanites had a rich tradition of ceramics, faience, glass and jewellery, and some small sculptures reveal a skilful modelling of the human form. However, they are sculptures of naked women and were used in fertility cults and this would not do.

The archaeologist W. F. Albright found the Canaanite culture distasteful and was such a fan of Israelite culture (or what he believed it to be) that as late as 1957 he was prepared to justify 'ancient' Israel's wholesale elimination of its political rivals. In his view it was necessary to ensure the pre-eminence of the founding culture of Western civilization.

> Strictly speaking, this Semitic custom [the extinction of
> the indigenous Palestinian population] was no worse,
> from the humanitarian point of view, than the reciprocal
> massacres of Protestants and Catholics in the
> seventeenth century, or than the massacre of Armenians
> by Turks and of Kirghiz by Russians during the First
> World War, or than the recent slaughter of non-
> combatants in Spain by both sides ...
>
> And we Americans have perhaps less right than most
> modern nations, in spite of our genuine humanitarianism,
> to sit in judgement on the Israelites of the thirteenth
> century BC, since we have, intentionally or otherwise,
> exterminated scores of thousands of Indians in every
> corner of our great nation and have crowded the rest into
> great concentration camps ...
>
> From the impartial standpoint of a philosopher of
> history, it often seems necessary that a people of markedly
> inferior type should vanish before a people of superior

potentialities, since there is a point beyond which racial mixture cannot go without disaster ... Thus the Canaanites, with their orgiastic nature worship, their cult of fertility in the form of serpent symbols and sensuous nudity, and their gross mythology, were replaced by Israel with its pastoral simplicity and purity of life, its lofty monotheism, and its severe code of ethics.[21]

More recent archaeological research has shown, however, that the distinction made in the Bible between 'Israelite' and 'Canaanite' culture is largely fantasy – but it performed the useful function of denigrating the indigenous Palestinian population, as modern Zionist archaeology tries to do.

It's difficult to see how much further blind adherence to Israel past or present could go. But people with a strong religious point of view, Jewish or Christian, do not find it easy to set aside their personal beliefs to take a more objective stance. And when those people were powerful politicians in early twentieth-century Britain, the stage was set for Zionism's great victory.

7

BALFOUR AND FRIENDS

• • •

Palestinian Arabs might have ended up governing their own country if a Russian Jew living in Manchester had not developed a chemical process for extracting nail-varnish remover from horse-chestnuts.

In 1910 an English company wanted to produce two chemicals used in industrial processes: butanol and acetone (nail-varnish remover). It recruited Chaim Weizmann, a Jewish chemist from Manchester University, who began work on a new process he had devised. When the First World War broke out in 1914 there was a big demand for acetone because it was used to produce cordite, necessary for making explosives. Weizmann developed a strain of microbes that could produce acetone from the starch found in potatoes, maize and even horse-chestnuts, which schoolchildren were mobilized to gather for the war effort.

Lloyd George, the Minister of Munitions, faced a crisis of supplies. 'As I marched from gun to gun, from shell to shell,' he later explained. 'I suddenly found that we had not got one of the great motive powers to make cordite.' Fortunately he discovered Weizmann, who had 'trained little animals' (as Lloyd George put it) to produce the necessary acetone.

'You have rendered great service to the State,' said
Lloyd George to Weizmann 'and I should like to ask the
Prime Minister to recommend you to His Majesty for
some honour.'

'All I care for is an opportunity to do something for my
people,' said Weizmann.[1]

Lloyd George later quipped to a meeting of the Jewish Historical
Society: 'Acetone converted me to Zionism.'

When Lloyd George became Prime Minister later in the war, his
support was to prove decisive.

The First World War marked the beginning of the end of the
history of Palestine. Decisions made in a succession of smoke-
filled rooms in Manchester, Kensington and Whitehall sealed the
fate of 700,000 Palestinian Arabs, including members of my family
in Safad, Deir Hanna, Haifa and Tulkarm.

Palestine was still part of the Ottoman Empire, governed from
Constantinople with the light hand that the Turks had used for the
previous three hundred years. But Palestine came to have strategic
significance for the two major blocs fighting in the First World War.
When Turkey sided with Germany, Palestine became a target for
the Allies. If they could wrest control of Palestine (as well as Syria,
Egypt and Arabia) from the Ottomans, they would have control of
major routes to the east, including the Suez Canal. Furthermore, if
the Turks were on the losing side and their empire was up for
grabs, the Allies could divide up the spoils. It occurred to the Allies
that conquest of the area would be easier with Arab support, so
they exploited a general hostility to the Turks. This led to the so-
called Arab Revolt when, in return for certain promises, tribesmen
in Arabia attacked Turkish positions to make it easier for the
British to invade.

Historians have argued about exactly what commitments were made to the Arabs if the Allies won the war. A vast amount of paperwork in the Public Records Office in London shows that a dozen or more British officials of various ranks from ministers down to a second lieutenant (T. E. Lawrence) were eager to persuade the Arabs it would be in their own interest to support the British in the Middle East by rebelling against the Turks. Sherif Hussein, of the Holy City of Mecca, the Arab to whom British promises were made, came from a powerful aristocratic family with its power base in the Hejaz, the area around the port of Jiddah, as well the Muslim holy cities of Mecca and Medina. But Hussein wanted to be king of a much larger territory stretching from the Mediterranean to Persia and from Turkey to Aden. Britain would have to support such a kingdom after the war if it wanted his help.

It is difficult to know precisely what Britain promised Hussein. The documents involved – letters, memos, translations, telegrams – are contradictory and confusing. This was sometimes accidental, the result of poor translation, for example. One of the key figures, Ronald Storrs, believed his Arabic was pretty good but by all accounts it wasn't. In his own memoirs, he makes a mistake in Arabic which would seem to the Arabs as basic as writing about 'jovernment' rather than 'government' seems to us.*[2] What is established is that Sir Harold McMahon, the British High Commissioner for Egypt, a man described by his friends as 'frightfully slow on the uptake' and 'the laziest man I have ever met', wrote a letter to Hussein on behalf of the British government. He promised that after the war Britain would recognize and support the independence of the Arabs within a great swathe of territories

---

* He writes a word that requires a strong letter 'h' and uses a weak one.

which, according to Hussein, included Palestine. In this letter Sir Harold excluded some territories to the west of certain districts of Syria and subsequent arguments have centred on whether this exclusion extended as far south as Palestine. However, as a later writer O. S. Edwardes has pointed out, 'To say that Palestine lies to the west of these [districts] is like saying that Wales is part of the country west of Manchester, Skipton, Appleby and Carlisle, or that the Carolinas and Georgia lie to the east of Richmond (Va.), Washington and Pittsburgh.'³

In fact, Britain's promises to the Arabs were deliberately vague as to which territories would be included in Hussein's 'kingdom', especially where Palestine was involved. Britain had no intention of Palestine becoming independent under an Arab ruler, and had secretly agreed with France to carve up Syria and Palestine between themselves after the war. So some kind of promise was made to Hussein if he agreed to help Britain fight the Turks, but it was sufficiently vague for the British to say after the war that Palestine was excluded.

The reality was that the British were negotiating with a man who had no special relationship with Palestine and whose constituency they overestimated. He was just one of several tribal chiefs in Arabia, though his claim to special status derived from the fact that he was guardian of the Muslim holy cities of Mecca and Medina. He did mount some kind of rebellion, using copious amounts of British gold supplied by T. E. Lawrence. The capture of the port of Aqaba from the land, surprising the Turks whose guns were trained towards the sea, seems to have been an important contribution to the Allied landings in Palestine, although other attacks on the Turks proved less successful. These events were just a sideshow in the war, however, and the negotiations and discussions between the British and Hussein seem to have been carried out by local officials, with occasional and often garbled communication with Whitehall about what was going on.

When Turkey sided with Germany, Herbert Samuel (the only Zionist Jew in the British Cabinet, as minister for local government) confided to Weizmann that he had been considering the possibility of establishing a Jewish community in Palestine. This was music to Weizmann's ears, since behind the scenes he and his fellow Zionists had been pushing for this to happen. Weizmann wrote at the time: 'He [Samuel] told me that, in his own words, at the moment the military situation is cleared up, and he is convinced it will be cleared up favourably, he will act and will expect the Jews all over the world to act ... He mentioned at the end of the interview that those ideas are in the mind of the other Cabinet Ministers ... He advised me to work quietly, continue the investigation, step by step, and prepare for the hour to come.'[4]

Weizmann's 'quiet work' over the next few years was to embroil the British government in endless discussions with a small group of British and European Jews who felt they should have a role in running Palestine after the war. This group of men could be described as 'political Zionists', to distinguish them from those Jews who were in favour of the admission to Palestine of Jews who wished to live there but did not foresee or intend that they should take over the country from its majority inhabitants.

The political Zionists formed a society called the Zionist Organization, led by Dr Chaim Weizmann, the Manchester chemist. They wanted to take possession of Palestine and make it an exclusively Jewish state. However, they had to tread carefully and conceal their true aims. 'It always was and remains a cardinal principle of Zionism as a democratic movement that all races and sects in Palestine should enjoy full justice and liberty,'[5] Weizmann announced in a letter to *The Times* in May 1916. But in secret correspondence with the British government the previous October, the Zionist Organization had made their position rather clearer – and it was far less democratic: 'The Jewish Chartered Company [there was no such company at the time] is to have power to exercise the right of pre-emption of Crown and other lands [there were, of course, no Crown lands in Palestine then, and Britain had, at the time, no rights in the territory other than military occupation] and to acquire for its own use all or any concessions which may at any time be granted by the suzerain government or governments. The present population, being too small, too poor and too little trained to make rapid progress, requires the introduction of a new and progressive element in the population.'[6]

And so began a sustained campaign of deception over the next thirty years, crucial years for the history of Palestine. If the Zionists had made their real aims obvious from the beginning, those members of the British government who saw no reason why 90 per cent of Palestine's inhabitants should be subsumed under Jewish rule might have been alerted sooner and perhaps the whole ill-fated enterprise would have been aborted.

There were anti-Zionist Jews who criticized the political Zionists. Each group had its own Jewish organization and they attacked one another at meetings and in books and pamphlets, newspaper articles and letters. 'The Zionists sharpened their caricatures of [the anti-Zionists] as Establishment toadies,' says the historian Stuart A. Cohen, while the anti-Zionists 'responded that the Zionists were a pack of uncouth louts, whose lack of manners could probably be attributed to the fact that "they are all foreign Jews, bearing no quality to speak for the native Jews of the United Kingdom".'[7]

Harry Sacher, a staunch political Zionist, wrote to one leading anti-Zionist in the following threatening terms: 'We are determined to go forward even without them [the anti-Zionist Jews] and against them. If they stand aside it will be for the future historian of the Jewish people to pass judgement on them. If they oppose us we shall, however reluctantly, do what within us lies to destroy any authority they may claim in Jewry or beyond Jewry to speak for the Jewish people. We know we have the power to do it.'[8]

The hostility of one group of British Jews to the other had all the characteristics of anti-Semitism. Weizmann himself, a Russian Jew who had adopted Great Britain as his country, made an extraordinary statement about German Jews when he was visiting Arthur Balfour. It is ironic that some people consider Balfour himself a bit of an anti-Semite. When he was Prime Minister in 1905 his government passed an Aliens Bill, restricting immigration to the United Kingdom. In the House of Commons Balfour spoke of 'the undoubted evils that had fallen upon the country from an immigration which was largely Jewish'.[9]

Weizmann described a conversation with Balfour: '[Balfour] expounded to me his view of the Jewish question and said that, in his opinion the question would remain insoluble until either the Jews here [in Britain] became entirely assimilated, or there was a normal Jewish community in Palestine – and he had in mind Western Jews rather than Eastern. He told me that he had once had a long talk with Cosima Wagner [the wife of the German composer Richard Wagner, who believed in the superiority of the Germans and the inferiority of the Jews] in Bayreuth and that he shared many of her anti-Semitic ideas. I pointed out to him that we too are in agreement with the cultural anti-Semites, in so far as we believe that Germans of the Mosaic faith are an undesirable, demoralizing phenomenon.'[10]

Balfour was converted to Weizmann's Zionist views after a series of long conversations about Palestine which brought tears to

Balfour's eyes. Nevertheless, he continued to be suspicious of Jews in general. After the Russian Revolution in 1917, Balfour told Colonel House (US President Woodrow Wilson's aide) that 'nearly all Bolshevism and disorder of that sort is directly traceable to Jews'. House wrote: 'I suggested putting them, or the best of them, in Palestine, and holding them responsible for the orderly behaviour of Jews throughout the world. Balfour thought the plan had possibilities.'[11] Some British supporters of a Jewish state in Palestine were certainly motivated by a dislike of the Jews. If Jews had their own state, they reasoned, further immigration to Britain or America could be restricted.

The Zionist Organization wanted to convey the impression that they represented British Jewry as a whole, but they didn't. When they promoted the idea of turning Palestine into a Jewish state a number of leading British Jews protested. They were led by the presidents of two major British-Jewish organizations: the Board of Deputies and the Anglo-Jewish Association. They objected that 'the establishment of a Jewish nationality in Palestine founded on the theory of Jewish homelessness, must have the effect throughout the world of stamping the Jews as strangers in their native lands and of undermining their hard-won positions as citizens and nationals of those lands.'[12] They also forecast the dire consequences of pursuing this plan: 'The proposal is all the more inadmissible because the Jews are and probably long will remain a minority of the population of Palestine, and it might involve them in the bitterest feuds with their neighbours of other races and religions, which would severely retard their progress and find deplorable echoes through the Orient.'[13] Several prominent British Jews agreed with them.

The political Zionists were outraged at these attempts to pour cold water on their scheme, which was gathering momentum thanks to their friends in high places in Britain and the United States. 'It was absolutely essential,' wrote Samuel Landman, the secretary of the World Zionist Organization, 'to convince the Cabinet that Anglo-Jewry was Zionist in sympathy and outlook, in view of the constant denial of this which they heard from the leading Jews.'

Weizmann took on his detractors in *The Times*: 'I should like to express my regret,' he wrote, 'that there should be even two Jews who think it their duty to exert such influence as they may command against the realization of a hope which has sustained the Jewish nation through 2,000 years of exile, persecution and temptation.'[14]

Samuel Landman described how a rapid campaign was mounted against the president of the Board of Deputies, and his officers, by organizing a pro-Zionist resolution against him. 'The President ... resigned,' wrote Landman, 'thus leaving the field clear for the Zionists.'

The political Zionists sought official support for their plan at the highest government level. With the help of sympathizers in the civil service and by meeting individual ministers in private, a drip-feed of memoranda, letters and proposals was directed at the British government. This was at the height of the First World War when the Cabinet had other things on its mind. But the political Zionists suggested that a Jewish Palestine would aid the war effort. The support of millions of Jews in Russia might be useful to the Allies, they said, and American Jews would view favourably the entry of the United States into the war on Britain's side.

'It is a little difficult to see why the sympathies of the Jewish community should have been considered as particularly vital to the British interests at that moment,' says the writer Nevill Barbour. 'The United States of America had entered the War some months

before; and the Russian Revolution had removed any unwilling-
ness of the Russian Jews to fight on the side of the Allies. Dr
Weizmann himself stated before the Royal Commission in 1936
that most of the rich Jews were not Zionists, and that, therefore, no
question of seeking Jewish financial assistance was involved. At
the Zionist Congress of 1921 he was even more explicit. "During
the War," he said, "we Zionists had neither the force of arms, nor
gold, nor influence".'[15]

Nevertheless, the British Cabinet allowed itself to be persuaded
that a Jewish Palestine might help to win the war. They were
unaware that another group of Zionists was approaching Britain's
enemies just in case Britain lost the war and Germany won, along
with Turkey who were still the rulers of the country. Richard
Lichtheim, the Zionist representative in Istanbul, urged the advan-
tages of a pro-Zionist policy upon the Turkish and German
governments: 'We wish to establish, on the eastern shore of the
Mediterranean, a modern cultural and commercial centre which
will be both directly and indirectly a prop of Germanism.' He told a
colleague in Berlin about the arguments he had used to show how
useful the Jews could be to Britain's enemies: 'I brought every argument to bear, the German language and business connections of
the Jews; their pro-Turkish sentiment; their possibilities as a counterweight to the Arabs; their international influence in the Press
and finance; the gratitude of all Jews – for example in America –
towards Germany if she supports us; the political significance of a
cultural base for Germany as the future leading power in the Near
East. I write all this to you in order that we may say the same thing
here and in Berlin.'[16]

The Zionist promise to Germany and Turkey was summed up in
one sentence: 'Palestine by Jewish immigration ... could become a
politico-commercial base, a Turkish-German Gibraltar, on the

A Turkish delegation visiting Jerusalem.
Ottoman control of Palestine lasted 400 years.

frontiers of the Anglo-Arab ocean.'[17] The unique status of Jews in global politics made this sort of double-dealing possible. The British political Zionists had dual loyalties, to Britain and Jewry; the German political Zionists were loyal to Germany and Jewry. Lichtheim even offered to arrange a legion of Jews to fight the British in the Middle East, alongside Germany's Turkish allies.[18]

But it was the British government that became the recipient of the poisoned chalice of a Jewish Palestine, when they were persuaded by the Zionists to publish the most notorious document in the history of the Middle East: the Balfour Declaration.

8

A LETTER TO LORD ROTHSCHILD

· · ·

The letter known as the Balfour Declaration has caused nearly ninety years of death and disruption in the Middle East, yet it was issued as calmly as if it were granting planning permission for a new bus shelter in Solihull. Except that a new bus shelter in Solihull would have been of some use to someone.

The Balfour Declaration was presented as a major statement of British policy in the Middle East. It was a factor in the peace talks after the First World War and was enshrined in the League of Nations mandate by which Britain effectively governed Palestine (ineffectually). As Palestine descended into chaos in the 1930s and 1940s, it was often described as a treaty which Britain could not breach, despite what a later British government described as its 'vagueness'.[1]

According to Arthur Koestler, the Balfour Declaration meant that 'one nation solemnly promised to a second nation the country of a third',[2] but that is not quite true. In fact, one nation promised the country of another nation to a small group of men who claimed to represent an ethnic group, although they had the support of only half of them.

The Balfour Declaration was quite a coup for the political

Zionists. Although they had generated proposals and memoranda in 1915 and 1916, their deputations had never reached Cabinet level. The Prime Minister Herbert Asquith was not particularly sympathetic. But when the leadership changed in 1916 and Lloyd George became Prime Minister, the Zionists had a strong supporter in a position of real power, as well as support from senior MPs such as the new Foreign Minister, Arthur Balfour.

Weizmann was not on friendly terms with other leading Zionists in Britain, so he gathered around him what he called 'a small band of workers, not official, not recognized, out of contact with Jewry at large'.[3] They were a youthful group of eager British Zionists, and it might be wondered why, at a time when, in the words of Lloyd George, 'the fortunes of the Allies [were] at their lowest ebb', they were not fighting at the Front. But as one of them, Samuel Landman, explained: 'Dr. Weizmann was able, about this time, to secure from the Government the services of half a dozen younger Zionists for active work on behalf of Zionism. At the time, conscription was in force, and only those who were engaged on work of national importance could be released from active service at the Front.'[4] Thus a letter from Weizmann to the Director of Military Operations soon led to his young men being excused conscription for their 'work of national importance', even if the nation concerned was not Great Britain.

'From that time onwards for several years,' Landman wrote, 'Zionism was considered an ally of the British government, and every help and assistance was forthcoming from each government department. Passport or travel difficulties did not exist when a man was recommended by our office. For instance, a certificate signed by me was accepted by the Home Office at that time as evidence that an Ottoman Jew was to be treated as a friendly alien and not as an enemy, which was the case with the Turkish subjects.'[5]

Communication between British Jews and Jews on the continent where the war was raging was achieved through the Foreign Office, using the official government cipher.

Weizmann had now acquired important friends and sympathizers in high places. They included the editors of *The Times* and the *Manchester Guardian*, as well as Arthur Balfour, Lloyd George, Sir Edward Grey, Winston Churchill and Herbert Samuel. Their support would prove vital when it came to government decision-making. Samuel was a key player. He was even more Zionist than Weizmann and he attended and spoke at Cabinet meetings as Minister for Local Government. In June 1917, Weizmann and Lord Rothschild went to see Balfour at the Foreign Office to suggest that the British government issue 'a definite declaration of support and encouragement' to the Zionists, a declaration they were then asked to draft. 'The walls of the Foreign Office without doubt have enclosed many a singular scene,' wrote J. M. N. Jeffries, a *Daily Mail* editor, but here was 'the spectacle of a Secretary of State asking a visitor from Russia to give him a draft of his own Cabinet's measures'.[6]

Weizmann's 'small band of workers' set to work among themselves to draft a statement of aims, spelling out the powers they would like Great Britain to hand over to the Zionist Organization after the war. Some Zionists wanted to ask for everything – a speedy takeover of Palestine and the establishment of a Jewish government as soon as possible. Others advised caution, realizing that to demand a swift transition to a Jewish minority government over a vast Arab majority might not have an easy passage through the British Cabinet.

The task of drafting the statement was approached with astonishing casualness. Harry Sacher, a young disciple of Weizmann's, wrote to him: 'It is good news that B[alfour] wants us to frame a declaration and I shall be happy to try my hand at a draft.'[7] At the time, Sacher was a journalist on the staff of the *Manchester Guardian*, and a passionate Zionist. He was also very close to Weizmann, who wrote to him as 'Darling Harry' and signed his letters 'Love, Chaim'.

The prospect of this young journalist on the staff of the *Manchester Guardian* 'trying his hand' at a draft of a declaration of British government policy on the Middle East – at the request of the British Foreign Minister – is an indication of the complete victory of Zionism over Whitehall. The political Zionists were simply dictating to the British government what they wanted to do about Palestine. Sacher was Machiavellian: 'I should like it to be at once precise and vague, precise in what it excludes, vague in the means by which what we want is to be realized.'[8] Within a month he and other members of the group had produced several different drafts which were gathered together and sent to Leon Simon, a sympathetic member of the civil service.

There were six drafts of varying lengths, all promising that Palestine should be recognized as the national home of the Jewish people and a Jewish state. 'Jewish in the same sense as the dominant national character of England is English, of Canada Canadian and of Australia Australian,' said the draft written by another *Guardian* journalist, Herbert Sidebotham.

None of these drafts made any reference to the existing population of Palestine. In fact, the Palestinian Arabs had not figured widely in the discussions so far. Even the Jews who objected to political Zionism did so on the grounds of its effects on the status of British Jews in the United Kingdom rather than because there was already an indigenous population which might want some say in the future of their country after the war. However, some Zionists did refer privately to the inhabitants of Palestine. Sacher, for instance, wrote: 'At the back of my mind there is firmly fixed the recognition that even if all our political schemings turn out in the way we desire, the Arabs will remain our most tremendous problem.'[9] To use the word 'remain' rather implies that the Arabs were already a problem although in fact at that time Jewish-Arab relations in Palestine were no problem at all.

Sacher began his draft with the words, 'The British Government declares ...' and went on to describe an essential post-war aim as 'the reconstitution of Palestine as a Jewish state and as the national home of the Jewish people'.[10] The Zionists wanted total control of Palestine with no political participation by the indigenous population in their own government. 'We look forward to Palestine becoming ultimately an autonomous Jewish polity,' wrote Sacher in a note on his memorandum. 'Jewish because the predominance in population, talent and wealth will rest with the Jewish inhabitants, although of course such predominance will not conflict with the individual and nationality rights of the non-Jewish citizens ... We have ... deliberately omitted any reference to the political organization of Palestine as a whole. We shall endeavour, however, from the first to secure as the administrative head of all Palestine a Jew sympathetic to the national cause, and to staff the Palestine Civil Service as largely as possible with competent Jews, principally from England.'[11]

Every draft was carefully worded. 'I beg you to note the phrase "the reconstitution of Palestine"; "of" not "in",' wrote Sacher to Nahum Sokolow, a leading Polish-Russian Jew. 'The "of" is fundamental. It is our charter against Arab domination and the poisonous tomfoolery which Gaster preached some time ago and apparently is still preaching.* We must control the <u>state</u> machinery

---

* Moses Gaster was the spiritual head of the Sephardi Community.

in Palestine: if we don't the Arabs will. Give the Arabs all the guar-antees they like for cultural autonomy; but the state must be Jewish.'[12]

The hostility of British Jews to the Arabs seems to have had two main causes. First, the Palestinian Arabs were the predominant population in a territory the Jews wanted for themselves. This was not, of course, the Arabs' fault. Second, they were seen as an infer-ior people who could not be trusted to govern themselves. 'We must not forget that we are dealing here with a semi-savage people, which has extremely primitive concepts,' wrote Moshe Smilansky, a Zionist activist in Palestine in 1914. 'And this is his [the Arab's] nature,' he went on. 'If he senses in you power he will submit and will hide his hatred for you. And if he senses weakness he will dom-inate you ... Moreover ... owing to the many tourists and urban Christians, there developed among the Arabs base values which are not common among other primitive people ... to lie, to cheat, to harbor grave [unfounded] suspicions and to tell tales.... and a hidden hatred for the Jews. These Semites – they are anti-Semites.'[13]

Although Sacher mentioned the Arabs in private correspon-dence, none of the Zionist draft declarations give any indication of the existence of an indigenous population. In fact, when a refer-ence to the rights of the 'non-Jewish' population was finally inserted by the Cabinet, it irritated many Zionists. They did not like to be reminded that they were claiming an inhabited land.

When the United States entered the war in April 1917, President Wilson set out fourteen points that should apply in any peace set-tlement. Point number 12 was that all nationalities under Turkish rule 'should be assured an absolutely unmolested opportunity of autonomous development'. Wilson's goal was 'a world ... made safe for democracy'. However, these moves towards democracy for the formerly colonial peoples posed a problem for the Zionists unless some way could be found to redefine the word 'democracy'. So Harry Sacher duly did this in a publication he wrote for the Zionist Organization, by defining American ideas of democracy as somehow weird and inapplicable to peoples in other parts of the world:

> Democracy in America too commonly means majority rule without regard to diversities of types or stages of civilization or differences of quality ... This doubtless is natural in America, and works on the whole very well. But if the American idea were applied as an American administration might apply it to Palestine, what would happen? The numerical majority in Palestine today is [Palestinian] Arab, not Jewish. *Qualitatively* [my italics], it is a simple fact that the Jews are now predominant in Palestine, and given proper conditions they will be predominant quantitatively also in a generation or two. But if the crude arithmetical conception of democracy were to be applied now, or at some early stage in the future to Palestinian conditions, the majority that would rule would be the Arab majority, and the task of establishing and developing a great Jewish Palestine would be infinitely more difficult.[14]

Fortunately – for the rest of the world at least – the 'crude arithmetical conception of democracy' is the one that has caught on in global politics. Without it, Catholics and Protestants in Northern Ireland, Sunnis in Iraq, even perhaps university graduates in the United Kingdom, would each be trying to make a case for ruling over their qualitatively less-predominant fellow citizens.

With this insight into Zionist thinking, it must be clear that any 'declaration' that the Zionists presented to the British government to sign would seek the maximum control over the territory and people of Palestine after the war. But surely the British Cabinet would not, to a man, swallow this unfair policy? In fact, reading the correspondence of the parties involved, and the Cabinet minutes, it is clear that some kind of infatuation had taken hold of the Cabinet, whenever issues came up to do with the Jews or Zionism.

In France, the British and French armies were in the middle of one of the worst battles of the First World War. The fight for Passchendaele resulted in 325,000 Allied and 260,000 German casualties. Nevertheless, in Whitehall on 2 September 1917, the War Cabinet found time to discuss the unfolding saga of the various draft 'declarations' that were arriving on the desks of ministers and civil servants, some of them forwarded by Lord Rothschild, others prepared by interested members of the government. At the meeting was Edwin Montagu, Secretary of State for India and the leading British Jew in the government.

Montagu was a constant source of irritation and frustration to the political Zionists. Weizmann and his team had persuaded the British government that their views were shared by most British Jews, but Montagu was passionately against the movement to make Palestine a Jewish state, and laid out his case forcefully in a series of letters, pamphlets and speeches. At the Cabinet meeting he picked out the phrase 'the home of the Jewish people' and objected that it would 'vitally prejudice the position of every Jew elsewhere'.

In a memorandum to the Cabinet, Montagu wrote: 'I wish to place on record my view that the policy (toward Palestine) of His Majesty's Government is anti-Semitic in result and will prove a rallying ground for anti-Semites in every corner of the world … Zionism has always seemed to me to be a mischievous political creed, untenable by any patriotic citizen of the United Kingdom. If a Jewish Englishman sets his eyes on the Mount of Olives and longs for the day when he will shake British soil from his shoes and go back to agricultural pursuits in Palestine, he has always seemed to me to have acknowledged aims inconsistent with British citizenship and to have admitted that he is unfit for a share in public life in Great Britain or to be treated as an Englishman.'[15]

'Our Jewish opponents have not been idle,' wrote Weizmann to an American supporter of Zionism. 'They have found an excellent champion of their cause in the person of Mr Edwin Montagu, who is a member of the government and has certainly made use of his position to injure the Zionist cause as much as possible.'

For public consumption, Blanche Dugdale, Arthur Balfour's niece and a leading British Zionist, wrote that the Balfour Declaration was 'the result of a decision come to after very careful consideration by the whole British Cabinet, and for which the whole British Cabinet shared responsibility ... It was not Balfour who gave the pledge, it was the whole British Government... statesmen of outstanding quality, with great experience, who devoted deep and unhurried consideration to the policy which they eventually endorsed.'[16] However, the *Daily Mail* journalist Joseph Jeffries gave a very different account based on an interview with Edwin Montagu revealing how ill-informed most of the Cabinet had been about the momentous topic they were discussing.

> [Montagu] said that not the slightest consideration was given to our previous pledges to the Arabs. The whole question was treated as a close preserve between Great Britain and the Zionists. Nothing was thrashed out properly. As the autumn came on, members of the Cabinet were overwhelmed with their several duties and with the general crisis of the time, when the Allies'

fortunes were at a very low ebb indeed. There was a marked disposition for each Minister to stick to his particular province and to accept the word of the others upon theirs. The Premier and Balfour tried to push the Zionist project briskly through, both of them possessed with an *idée fixe*. Up to the time of his departure for India, said Mr Montagu, the terms of the Declaration and its consequences had never been properly analysed by all members of the Cabinet, and certainly had not been grasped by the non-partisan members after a fashion which would enable them to hold out against their pro-Zionist colleagues.[17]

The minutes of that all-important Cabinet meeting on 31 October 1917 show how little the British government understood the central issue: 'The Secretary of State for Foreign Affairs [Balfour] stated that he gathered that every one was now agreed that, from a purely diplomatic and political point of view it was desirable that some declaration favourable to the aspirations of the Jewish nationalists should now be made. The vast majority of Jews in Russia and America, as, indeed, all over the world, now appeared to be favourable to Zionism. If we could make a declaration favourable to such an ideal, we should be able to carry on extremely useful propaganda both in Russia and America.'[18]

The minutes noted only two possible objections: '(a) That Palestine was inadequate to form a home for either the Jewish or any other people. (b) The difficulty felt with regard to the future position of Jews in western countries.' There is no mention of the fact that making Palestine a national home for the Jews would necessitate the permanent denial of self-determination to 670,000 Palestinians who formed nine-tenths of the population.

After a few more i's were dotted and t's crossed, the Cabinet agreed the final draft of the letter that Mr Balfour would send on behalf of the British government to Lord Rothschild and his friends, who had drafted the letter in the first place.

Foreign Office,
2 November 1917

Dear Lord Rothschild:

I have much pleasure in conveying to you, on behalf of His Majesty's Government, the following declaration of sympathy with Jewish Zionist aspirations which has been submitted to, and approved by, the Cabinet.

His Majesty's Government view with favour the establishment in Palestine of a National Home for the Jewish people, and will use their best endeavours to facilitate the achievement of this object, it being clearly understood that nothing shall be done which may prejudice the civil and religious rights of existing non-Jewish communities in Palestine, or the rights and political status enjoyed by Jews in any other country.

I should be grateful if you would bring this declaration to the knowledge of the Zionist Federation.

Yours sincerely

Arthur James Balfour.

The Balfour Declaration appeared in British newspapers on 9 November 1917 and generated a range of reactions. One MP,

William Ormsby-Gore, said at a public meeting that 'he supported the Jewish claim as a member of the Church of England. He felt that behind it all was the finger of Almighty God.'[19] Some years later, Weizmann revealed his own surprise at how the deal had come about: 'We Jews got the Balfour Declaration quite unexpectedly; or, in other words, we are the greatest war profiteers. We never dreamt of the Balfour Declaration; to be quite frank, it came to us overnight ... The Balfour Declaration of 1917 was built on air.'[20]

To all appearances it was a letter that emerged spontaneously from the pen of the British Foreign Minister and his advisers. J. M. N. Jeffries later wrote: 'It was given forth ... under the guise of an entirely British communication embodying an entirely British conception. Everyone concerned was made the victim of this false pretence. The British people were given to believe that it was an unadulterated product of their own Government. To the mass of Jews it was presented as a guarantee sprung of nothing but the conscience of the Cabinet – and thereby it served to allure them towards political Zionism. As for the Arabs, when it was proclaimed eventually upon their soil (which was not till much later), to them too a text in which Zionists of all nationalities had collaborated was announced as the voice of Britain. They were told that it was a pledge made to the Zionists: they were not told that the Zionists had written most of it. They were asked to respect it on the ground that it was given to the world by the British government out of its native magnanimity, after the said government had extended its profound, solitary and single-minded consideration to the "problem of Palestine".'[21]

According to Jeffries the drafters of the Balfour Declaration 'set out to conceal the fact that the Arabs to all intents constituted the population of the country. It called them the "non-Jewish communities in Palestine"! It called the multitude the non-few; it called

In 1917, the British army captured Jerusalem from
the Turks and General Allenby took over the city.

the 670,000 the non-60,000. You might just as well call the British
people "the non-Continental communities of Great Britain". It
would be as suitable to define the mass of working men as "the
non-idling communities in the world," ... or the sane as "the non-
lunatic section of thinkers" – or the grass of the countryside as the
"non-dandelion portion of the pastures".'[22]

The role of British Zionists in drafting the Balfour Declaration
was not publicized and the letter from Balfour to Rothschild
acquired an undeserved aura of respectability, as if it had emerged
as a result of a massive national and international movement.
Indeed, many Jews believed, and still believe, that the Balfour
Declaration was 'the recorded wish of the British nation and of all
the other civilized nations of the world',[23] as one Jewish immigrant
to Palestine wrote ten years after it was written. We can now see

how untrue that was. Balfour's letter acquired the status of an international treaty or a binding agreement, to such an extent that successive British governments were to turn down any request for self-determination by the Palestinians on the grounds that their hands were tied.

In February 1918 Richard Meinertzhagen, a British civil servant who was strongly Zionist, was having lunch with Balfour and asked him: 'At the back of your mind do you regard this declaration as a charter for ultimate Jewish sovereignty in Palestine or are you trying to graft a Jewish population on to an Arab Palestine?' 'My personal hope,' said Balfour, 'is that the Jews will make good in Palestine and eventually found a Jewish State. It is up to them now; we have given them their great opportunity.'[24]

• • •

With Turkey and Germany defeated, a victorious Allied army marched into Jerusalem on 9 December 1917 and a military administration was established under General Allenby.

At about the time that Allenby was preparing to march into Jerusalem, and the Zionists were drafting the Balfour Declaration,

Khalil Sabbagh, great-great-grandson of Ibrahim Sabbagh, and the author's grandfather.

a ship from Brazil was easing its way into the harbour at Haifa, Palestine's major port. A pregnant woman was on board, maiden name Josefina de Fereira, with her husband, a Palestinian lawyer. Their two daughters, called Constanza and Tekla, were with them. The man's name was Khalil Sabbagh and he was my grandfather. Having gone to South America as many Arabs did at the time to build up savings and start a career, he had also acquired a Brazilian wife. With the beginnings of a family that would eventually expand to seven children, he had decided to return to his homeland and settle down. The war was all but over, he had relatives in Safad, Deir Hanna and Haifa, and could look forward to a successful career as a lawyer in what he and other Palestinians assumed would be an independent Palestine after the war.

9

PICKING UP THE PEACE

• • •

As the victorious Allied armies occupied more and more of Palestine, the Palestinians looked forward to a more stable future. The rule of Ottoman Turkey had been replaced by the less benign government of the 'Young Turks' who wanted the citizens of the empire to be Turks rather than express their own nationalities. Palestinians hoped for a fairer future under the British as a prelude to their promised independence.

But what was that future to be? Life was lived in towns and villages which many people hardly strayed from during their lifetimes, although middle- and upper-class Palestinian Arabs travelled to Cairo, Damascus, Constantinople or even Europe. Most Palestinians (Jews as well as Arabs) brought up their families in traditional ways. They paid taxes to the government in charge and were happy to continue like that.

However, some leaders in the area took a less parochial view. Even in the absence of national boundaries under the Ottomans, the Middle East could be divided into cultural and national regions, 'divisible at the joints'. Greater Syria, including Lebanon and Palestine, had characteristics which set it apart from Iraq and Jordan, which in turn had a different character from the Arabian

Peninsula. And there were aspects of greater Syria itself – from religion to history and geography – that suggested that further sub-divisions might be desirable. Palestine was one obvious area that was thought of by its inhabitants, as well as by visitors from all over the world, as having a separate cultural and social identity.

To some Arab leaders the twentieth-century ideal of independence from colonial rule and the formation of distinct states with their own governments seemed perfectly applicable to the Arab world. Indeed, in order to gain the support of Arab tribes against Turkey, the Allies had agreed to grant independence in some form to some peoples, after the war. This promise was confirmed in a document sent to seven Arab notables in Cairo who, hearing of the Balfour Declaration, wrote to the British government for immediate clarification. At the time, the Balfour Declaration had not been promulgated in the Middle East, and so was not known to the general public. But once it had been published in Britain, educated Arabs knew of it.

The British government replied on 16 June 1918, seven months after the Declaration was published, at a time when they occupied part of Palestine while the rest was still under Turkish control:

> In regard to the areas occupied by Allied forces it is the wish and desire of His Majesty's Government that the future government of these regions should be based on the principle of the consent of the governed, and this policy has and will continue to have the support of His Majesty's Government.
>
> In regard to [the areas still under Turkish control] it is the wish and desire of HMG that the oppressed peoples of these areas should obtain their freedom and independence, and towards the achievement of this object HMG continue to labour.[1]

US President Wilson also realized that some major shift would be needed after the war in those countries formerly ruled by Turkey. As we have seen, one of the points that he considered important for the world to adhere to for the sake of justice and peace was that 'nationalities under Turkish rule' would have 'an absolutely unmolested opportunity of autonomous development'. Palestine had been 'a nationality under Turkish rule', so the Palestinians naturally assumed they could look forward to being given their independence. In 1918 Wilson returned to this point: 'The settlement of every question, whether of territory, of sovereignty, of economic arrangement, or of political relationship [should be] upon the basis of the free acceptance of that settlement by the people immediately concerned, and not upon the basis of the material interest or advantage of any other nation or people which may desire a different settlement for the sake of its own exterior influence or mastery.'

A mere two months later, however, President Wilson wrote of 'the satisfaction I have felt in the progress made by the Zionist movement in the United States and in the Allied countries since the declaration by Mr Balfour on behalf of the British Government'. Wilson appears to have been won over by Balfour's letter to Lord Rothschild.

Meanwhile, it was the British rather than the Americans who had to deal with the immediate situation in Palestine, a country of which they were largely ignorant. 'What in 1917 did the war-torn British public ... know about the composition of the population of Palestine?' asked J. M. N. Jeffries. 'Nothing. It was upon this, then, that the drafters of the [Balfour] Declaration played. They concealed the Arabs' very name and called them "existing non-Jewish communities in Palestine", as though they were packets of monks who had strayed into the country and here and there got a foothold in it. The qualification "existing" provides the finishing touch. The impression given is that these Arabs have just managed to survive, that an explorer has returned and reported to Lord Balfour that he has discovered non-Jews existing in the hills.'[2]

When the Allies took control, Palestine became part of the Occupied Enemy Territory Administration (OETA) and a British military government was established. It was clear that the power of Turkey as an empire-builder was over, while Allies, with the beginnings of some kind of global awareness, faced the problem of what to do with the dismembered empire. Colonialism was not dead in the Middle East: France had its eyes on Lebanon and Syria and the British wanted to maintain their influence in Mesopotamia and Arabia. Palestine had been pondered by both powers and various ideas were bandied around Whitehall and the Quai d'Orsay about how to carve up the area.

In 1918 plans were laid for a springtime offensive to advance into areas of Palestine still occupied by the Turks with the help of the Germans. The Allied army, including soldiers from Australia and

Field Marshal Lord Plumer, like all High Commissioners for Palestine, preserved in daily life the manners and customs of English society.

British soldiers became familiar with the streets of Palestine as they tried to deal with growing Arab–Jew hostility in the 1920s.

New Zealand, made a swift advance north. In October 1918 the Allies – accompanied by a small Arab army and Colonel T. E. Lawrence – marched into Damascus and Turkish control was eliminated from the Arab world.

• • •

My father, Isa Khalil Sabbagh, was about ten months old at this time. He was named after his grandfather, and his second name, as custom dictated, was his father's. This tradition leads to a rather monotonous alternation of names in Arab families, at least for the eldest son. My name should really be Khalil Isa, but because of my mother's shaky ability to pronounce either of those names, the 'Isa' was dropped and I was called 'Karl'.

My grandfather Khalil Sabbagh was born in Safad about 1880. Eventually the family moved from Safad to the village of Deir Hanna in search of a better life. Khalil trained as a lawyer and some time early in the twentieth century he visited Brazil. He met Josefina in Belem (coincidentally the Portuguese name for the

Palestinian village of Bethlehem), a city at the mouth of the Amazon. Palestinian families often pooled their resources to send ambitious family members overseas to earn their fortune, and perhaps that's why my grandfather arrived in Belem, an important commercial centre for the export of rubber, timber, jute, nuts and other products of the Amazon basin.

Josefina's family were not happy with the match. Her brothers tried to prevent it and when the couple married, the brothers' resentment did not diminish. When Josefina's daughters Constanza and Tekla were about five and three and she was pregnant again, some kind of confrontation took place between her brothers and Khalil. There was a shoot-out and one of Josefina's brothers was killed. Khalil knew that if he stayed in Brazil he would be killed in retaliation. He gave Josefina the opportunity of staying with her family or travelling to Palestine with him. She chose him.

The war was nearing its end and it was clear that Ottoman rule over Palestine was over. Khalil had three brothers and two sisters, and many cousins, so there was an extensive network of relatives he could turn to all over northern Palestine, in Haifa, Safad and Deir Hanna. He moved to a large house in Tulkarm and his prospects were good. He looked forward to a successful career as a lawyer in post-war Palestine. His brothers in Deir Hanna started small businesses and were soon owners of property and land in the area. The majority of families in Deir Hanna were Muslim and the Sabbaghs were one of a handful of Christian families. Nevertheless, Khalil's brother Hanna was made Mukhtar of the village, the official representative of the government.

Khalil was descended from Ibrahim's son, Abud, the soap-maker, but there was a group of Sabbaghs descended from another of Ibrahim's sons, Niqula, who virtually formed a community of their own in Safad, living in several large stone houses in the Christian quarter. One of them, Tuma, was the French consul in Safad and Tiberias, and had a brother, Jeris, who fathered three daughters and two sons, one of whom, a boy called Hasib, was born in 1920 in Tiberias. Hasib's subsequent life in and out of Palestine was to form a counterpoint to my father's, and as the two boys grew up, Hasib, a few years younger, sometimes followed in my father's footsteps.

Isa grew up in a land under British military occupation. According to the *Manual of Military Law*, the OETA was not allowed to 'alter the existing form of Government [or] ignore the rights of the inhabitants'. This presented the temporary government of Palestine with a considerable dilemma over the next few years.

The OETA was generally a good administration as far as the Arabs were concerned and it tried to be fair to all the inhabitants of Palestine. Military engineers installed a water supply in Jerusalem; British officials reorganized the post office, public health and education, and British soldiers controlled the traffic. Their knowledge of the country was often shaky, but the average Tommy did his best. One British official asked a soldier in the Old City of Jerusalem the way to the Mount of Olives. The soldier didn't know, though he'd been in Palestine for three weeks. 'Three weeks and you don't know the way to the Mount of Olives?' the officer said. 'No, sir,' said the soldier, 'but might it be a pub, sir?'[3]

For much of Palestine, the First World War ended with the surrender of Jerusalem in 1917, though fighting did not end in all sectors until November 1918. By this time, Zionists had stepped up their activities in London, Washington and Palestine, impressing on politicians, diplomats, civil servants and, indeed, the ordinary people of Palestine that the British government now had an obligation to put into operation the terms of the Balfour Declaration. In fact, at that stage, the British government had no such obligation. The military administration was actually committed under international law to preserve the status quo until after a peace agreement had been signed with Turkey.

Nevertheless, Palestinians became increasingly worried about the aims of the Zionists during 1918. The British government did its best to allay their fears. A group of Zionists led by Weizmann formed themselves into the Zionist Commission and planned a trip to Palestine to make sure the British administration was favouring Zionist aims in the way it ran the country. A few days before leaving for Palestine, Weizmann had lunch with the eccentric English Zionist Richard Meinertzhagen, who had been a British spy during the war and was soon to assume a political role in running Palestine.

Meinertzhagen described in his diary his impressions of Weizmann. 'Weizmann is an enthusiast about Palestine and the Zionists, and a fanatic if such a clever man can be so termed ... He is very naturally a violent enemy of the Arabs.'[4] Meinertzhagen himself idolized the Jews and detested the Arabs. 'The Jew means progress,' he wrote in his diary, 'the Arab is stagnation and stands for immorality, rotten government, corrupt and dishonest society.' That a man with such views should be entrusted with the sensitive task of helping to run Palestine over the next few years is extraordinary and suggests how little consideration the British government gave to the rights of the Palestinian Arabs.

In Palestine Weizmann met senior Syrian and Palestinian Arabs and lied to them about the Zionists' intentions. He told them 'that a Jewish government would be fatal to his plans and that it was simply his wish to provide a home for the Jews in the Holy Land where they could live their own national life, sharing equal rights with the other inhabitants.'[5] Three months after his visit, Palestinian Zionist Jews paraded in the streets of Jerusalem on the first anniversary of the Balfour Declaration (2 November 1918). It was their way of showing how much they appreciated what they knew the Declaration meant: that Palestine would be turned into a national home for the Jews.

'Several Jewish friends of mine,' wrote Sir Ronald Storrs, the Military Governor in Palestine, 'ardent Zionists, but with a knowledge of the country, expressed their surprise that so much public parade, which could not fail to arouse strong resentment in non-Jewish [sic] circles had been found necessary, when the gratitude of the Jewish people could have been equally well expressed by meetings within four walls and loyal telegrams to the British Government.'[6]

This demonstration outraged many Arabs in Jerusalem and a hurriedly assembled group of representatives of some of the main Muslim and Christian organizations wrote a letter of protest which they presented to Sir Ronald the following day. It appealed to Britain not to allow Palestine to be changed from an Arab to a Jewish state, revealing a rather touching faith in the British government. Originally written in Arabic, the inelegant way the letter has been translated (presumably by a British government translator) creates the unjustified impression that it came from a rather unsophisticated group of people:

> We have noticed yesterday a large crowd of Jews carrying
> banners and overrunning the streets shouting words
> which hurt the feelings and wound the soul. They pretend
> with open voice that Palestine, which is the Holy Land of
> our Fathers and the graveyard of our ancestors, which has
> been inhabited by the Arabs for long ages who loved it and
> died in defending it, it is now a national home for them.
> These are words which displease the heavens. How do
> the Jews expect Palestine to be a national home when the
> Muslims and the Christians never asked that it should be

a national home for those of them who are not inhabitants of Palestine? … We Arabs, Muslim and Christian, have always sympathized profoundly with the persecuted Jews and their misfortunes in other countries as much as we sympathized with the persecuted Armenians and other weaker nations. We hoped for their deliverance and prosperity.

But there is a wide difference between this sympathy and the acceptance of such a nation in our country (to be made by them a national home), ruling over us and disposing of our affairs…. The Arabs occupied Spain over seven centuries, and having established themselves there they were scattered all over the globe. Is it now permitted to them to claim the country ruled by them in the past and their old native home, where they left traces of their civilization which still stir their imagination. This is the law of God – a country flourishes and faints, and one dynasty is built on another. Is it now permissible therefore to raise in the twentieth century the feeling of fanaticism and to excite the evil ambition which brought on the present War, destroyed the world, and loaded men with misfortunes which could not be supported even by mountains?…

The history of Great Britain which never attained their greatness except by administering justice attests the standard of righteousness and the character of her men. It is therefore impossible that it should be blackened by this injustice. We are perfectly sure that nothing will be realized of what the Zionists and their Agents pretend throughout the country and we expect that a Power like

Great Britain well known for justice and progress will put
a stop to the Zionists cry ...

In conclusion, we Muslims and Christians desire to
live with our brothers, the Jews of Palestine in peace and
happiness and with equal rights. Our privileges are theirs,
and their duties ours.[7]

The letter was stamped with the seals of more than a hundred
religious, political and educational societies in Palestine. A few
days later Sir Ronald received another letter from a group of Arab
notables in Jaffa. They drily observed that the Zionist claim to
Palestine on the basis that Jews had lived there 3,000 years ago suggested 'the impracticable necessity of drawing up quite a new map
of the world in which the immediate state of affairs that obtained
after the Deluge should be taken into consideration'.[8] The Jewish
parade, the Arab reaction, and attempts by British soldiers and
later British civil administrators to keep the peace were to become
a pattern over the next twenty years.

Meanwhile, the Zionist Commission had set up offices in
Palestine and was laying the groundwork for a 'state within a state'.
They demanded that Jews should participate in the British military
administration; that there should be a Jewish Land Commission
and a Jewish agricultural bank; that the Zionists should be allowed
to nominate Jews for the Palestine police force who would be paid
more than Arabs; and that the Jews should have their own army in
Palestine – all at a time when Palestinian Jews formed less than 10
per cent of the population.

General Clayton, the Military Governor of Palestine, was bombarded with letters, memos and telegrams from the Zionists, hoping
to persuade him to support them. 'The Jewish people as a whole
expected rather more,' wrote Weizmann in one such letter, more in

The town of Safad, original home of the Sabbagh family.

sorrow than anger, 'and from what one gathers it seems that a considerable disappointment is felt in the masses [He meant the Jewish masses.] ... Unless we get something which will secure a normal and rapid development of a Jewish Commonwealth under British auspices, it is no use speaking of [a] National Home.'[9]

Nevertheless, Clayton knew that there were significant groups of Jews even in Palestine, who disagreed with the Zionists. In a telegram to the Foreign Office in November 1918 he wrote: 'The Zionists have not yet succeeded in bringing over the whole Palestine Jewry to their side: the ultra religious community of Jerusalem still stands aloof and elements in it are actually hostile. There are indications that local Zionists contemplate a much more extended programme than is justified by the terms of Mr Balfour's declaration and open expression of their views has done much to stimulate Arab hostility.'[10] Palestinian Arabs were further perturbed by newspaper reports in October and November 1918 describing the borders of the state the Zionists eventually wanted to control. One scheme extended Palestine northwards to Beirut; another took in much of present-day Jordan.[11]

Other British officials, even at this early stage, predicted long-term disastrous consequences from pursuing the idea of a Jewish Palestine. Major General Money, the Chief Administrator, wrote to Whitehall: 'I am convinced that any such policy as giving the Jews a preferential share of the government of Palestine in the near future would be disastrous [and] would react powerfully and most unfavourably on the Arabs all over the British Empire.'[12] Major General Money was attacked by the Zionists for his reluctance to decree that official paperwork, from stamps and railway tickets to government notices, should be printed in Hebrew, even though some of the minority Jewish population had lived quite happily in Palestine for generations, speaking Arabic rather than Hebrew. Major General Money was eventually relieved of his duties as Chief Administrator at the insistence of the Zionists who claimed he was anti-Semitic. Shortly afterwards, Hebrew became an official language.

Similarly, Vladimir Jabotinsky, an outspoken Zionist, told Weizmann that a new 'postage stamp has been sanctioned by the Berne Bureau and is now the official stamp of liberated Palestine: it is English and Arabic, without Hebrew, within a year after Balfour's Declaration and a few months after the laying of the foundation stone of a University which proclaimed Hebrew as the vehicle of civilization in Palestine'.[13] Jabotinsky had a theory as to why the British officials were anti-Zionist. 'When they come here they find, on the one side, Arabs whose position is simple and clear, who are just the same old "natives" whom the Englishman has ruled and led for centuries, nothing new, no problems; on the other side, the Zionist who is a problem from top to toe, a problem bristling with difficulties in every way – small in numbers yet somehow strong and influential, ignorant of English yet imbued with European culture, claiming complicated claims, etc. The kindest of Englishmen hates problems and riddles. This is the natural difficulty of our position here.'[14]

The very public activities of the Zionist Commission in Palestine were alarming the Palestinian Arabs, who frequently asked the British administration what was happening. As Jabotinsky noted: 'Everywhere Arabs are making the same inquiry – is it true you are going to "hand over" the country? – and everywhere, so far as we know, the answer is "no", which, I quite agree is a natural and necessary answer to give without due reservations without pointing out that … the Arabs had better come to terms with Jews because the National Home policy is a resolve immutable.'[15]

The Palestinian Arabs were further angered when secret correspondence between the British and Sherif Hussein was made public. It had promised independence for large areas of the former Ottoman Empire, including Palestine. Although the British government tried to deny that Palestine was included, one secret Foreign Office document prepared in 1919 leaves no doubt. 'With regard to Palestine, His Majesty's Government are committed by Sir H. McMahon's letter to the Sherif on the 24th October 1915, to its inclusion in the boundaries of Arab independence.' However, it then added that 'the Jewish opinion of the world is in favour of a return of Jews to Palestine, and inasmuch as this opinion must remain a constant factor, and further, as His Majesty's Government view with favour the realization of this aspiration, His Majesty's Government are determined that in so far as is compatible with the freedom of the existing population, both economic and political, no obstacle should be put in the way of the realization of this ideal.'[16] In other words, the Palestinian Arabs had been promised independence, but they were not going to get it.

Back in Europe a system was being devised to ensure that the former Ottoman territories made a transition to some form of stable government. It was decided they should not be returned to Turkish rule but should come under the tutelage or supervision of more experienced states. Thus was born the system of 'mandates', whereby Allied victors were 'mandated', or charged with, shepherding various countries to independence over an unspecified period. Britain had already promised Palestine to two separate groups of its inhabitants and the League of Nations would now have to decide the country's fate.

MANDATE

• • •

A Peace Conference to conclude the First World War began in Paris in January 1919. Thirty-two nations attended and the sessions were held in secret. The talks were attended by the British Prime Minister Lloyd George and his Foreign Secretary Arthur Balfour. In Paris during the peace talks Balfour described himself to Richard Meinertzhagen as 'an ardent Zionist', adding that the British government 'was committed to Zionism as our policy in Palestine'.

As Meinertzhagen noted, Balfour 'defined the policy of HMG as follows: All development, industrial schemes of all kinds, and financial assistance must be based on the principle that Zionists are the Most-favoured Nation in Palestine.... He thought President Wilson a sincere and capable man, but ... considered the famous fourteen points were badly conceived and positively harmful, more especially the one encouraging small nations to self-determine.... He agreed ... in principle to the creed of self determination, but it could not be indiscriminately applied to the whole world, and Palestine was a case in point, and a most exceptional one.'[1]

Balfour had no intention of consulting the Palestinians on how they would like to be governed in the future, thereby handing 'the

Arabs ... an overwhelming majority' (as he told Meinertzhagen). He had a better idea. 'In any Palestine Plebiscite, the Jews of the world must be consulted; in which case he sincerely believed that an overwhelming majority would declare for Zionism under a British Mandate.'[2]

Meinertzhagen's diaries are full of such titbits and they have been criticized for mixing fact with fiction. It is pretty certain, for example, that he made up some – possibly all – of the entries relating to his friendship with T. E. Lawrence. He claimed that he and Lawrence released a huge roll of toilet paper down the central stairwell of the Hotel Astoria, the British delegation headquarters in Paris, while Lloyd George, Balfour and Lord Hardinge were talking at the bottom. According to Meinertzhagen, Hardinge said later 'There is nothing funny about toilet paper.' Meinertzhagen also claimed to have spanked Lawrence of Arabia on the bottom 'when he ran off with my knobkerry'. This knobkerry, or one similar to it, had been used to kill Germans, whom Meinertzhagen actually claimed to admire, even after the First World War. 'I see no reason,' he wrote, 'why [Germany] should not for the future be one of the leading moral lights in the family of Nations.' However, although clearly a loose cannon, Meinertzhagen had real political power, the ear of the Foreign Office and a bullying way with memos and telegrams, sometimes countermanding the orders of the British officials who were meant to be administering Palestine.

The Zionists also addressed the Peace Conference. Weizmann dismissed the idea that Zionism would prove a problem for the Palestinians, echoing something he had written in *The Times*: 'It is not likely that there will ever be an "Arab question" in Palestine: non-Jews [sic] need not fear that they will suffer at our hands. For two thousand years we have known what it means to be strangers.

We Jews know the heart of the stranger: are we likely to deal out oppression?'[3]

But while Weizmann was reassuring the Peace Conference that the 'non-Jews' of Palestine need not worry, an informal meeting of Zionists and British officials in London was discussing how the Zionists' aims might be achieved. The minutes of this meeting read: 'Major Rothschild ... suggested that it would be well if his Majesty's government would also consider whether some comprehensive emigration scheme to the south (Egypt) as well as to the north (Damascus) could not be arranged for the Arab Palestinian peasantry in conjunction with schemes for the immigration of the Jews. Miss [Gertrude] Bell and Colonel Lawrence agreed and Miss Bell added that there was scope in Mesopotamia for such immigrants. It was pointed out that it was not impossible to move Arab peasantry from their lands as had been shown when the original Zionist colonies were established.'[4] This is not the earliest mention of the 'transfer' of large numbers of Palestinian inhabitants. The idea was raised by Zionists as early as 1882. It gathered momentum in the 1930s, in parallel with Nazi plans to 'transfer' Jews out of Germany.

Palestinian Arabs were represented at the Paris Peace Conference by the Emir Feisal from the Hejaz. He was not Palestinian, but he was the nearest thing they had to a statesman (he had been groomed by T. E. Lawrence at the time of the Arab revolt). He was also the son of Sherif Hussein, who had been promised Palestine by the British. Feisal came to Europe with a delegation of Palestinians and Syrians. Some of them, wearing dark suits, visited an MP, Colonel Clifton Brown, at the House of Commons. They were shown into the central lobby to wait for him, but after fifteen minutes he had not appeared. They sent a message but were told that the MP was not in the House. They waited another half-hour and then, in the words of one member of the delegation, Izzat Tannous, 'a gentleman walked up to us and asked gently who we were. "The Arab delegation from Palestine," was our answer. "I am extremely sorry for keeping you waiting," he said very apologetically, "I have been standing over there for forty-five minutes anxiously waiting for the Arab delegation in their beautiful colourful Arab robes to enter the hall as I wanted to welcome them at the entrance. Please come in."' [5]

In Paris, Feisal gave a speech to a group of Allied leaders known as the 'Council of Six'. 'It was an unsatisfactory affair,' said J. M. N. Jeffries, 'for no one has ever known exactly what he said. His speech was unfinished at the close of the hearing and does not appear ever to have been completed. On the morrow of it the Council of Six was transformed into the smaller Supreme Inter-allied Council, the "Big Four", and the rest of Feisal's speech was put off to an unfixed ulterior date at the convenience of the new body. But no date ever was found for it. Feisal spoke in Arabic, from

As the main representative of the Arab nations at the Peace Conference, Emir Feisal was no match for the Zionists, even with the help of Lawrence of Arabia (*third from right*).

manuscript notes. There was no official interpreter. [T. E.] Lawrence translated at intervals, and questions were put to Feisal. But Lawrence, as we know, was not at all a sworn interpreter. Neither the Emir nor his secretaries (at the time) understood what Lawrence said in English, and of course none of the Europeans there but Lawrence had any Arabic.'[6]

Lawrence once admitted that his 'fluency [in Arabic] had a lack of grammar, which made my talk a perpetual adventure for my hearers'.[7] This suggests that Feisal and other senior Arabs were not well served by his interpretation of their speeches. Feisal was not an uncultured man and is likely to have made a spirited and learned case for Palestinian independence, but Lawrence's inadequate linguistic skills may well have destroyed any impact.

In Paris, Feisal was courted by Weizmann, who felt he needed some Arab support for the Zionist cause, or at least for a diluted version of it that concealed the intention to make Palestine a National Home for the Jews. But Feisal complained bitterly to his secretaries about Weizmann's importuning. 'What does this man want?' he is alleged to have said. 'I would do anything to get rid of him. He tires me out by his long speeches.'[8]

Feisel was not persuaded. Weizmann's attempts to allay Feisal's fears were not helped by a speech made at that time by Israel Zangwill at a public meeting, in which he said: 'Many [of the Arabs of Palestine] are semi-nomad, they have given nothing to Palestine and are not entitled to the rules of democracy.' In an interview with the *Jewish Chronicle*, Feisal hit back at Zangwill, saying that Palestine had a deeply rooted Arab population and could not be transformed into a Jewish state.

Most decisions about the fate of the Middle East seem to have been made behind closed doors. Balfour and Lloyd George had made up their minds. In the proceedings of the Peace Conference the Zionists tried to put a moderate face on their demands, although there were occasional lapses into the truth. On one occasion, the US Secretary of State asked Weizmann what in fact was meant by the 'National Home'. Weizmann had been warned by 'a leading British official' not to use a phrase like 'Jewish Palestine' because it would embarrass the British government. In the words of J. M. N. Jeffries, 'He threw the protocol to the winds and answered that the "National Home" meant that there should be established such conditions ultimately in Palestine that "Palestine shall be just as Jewish as America is American and England is English." ... The cat had bounded out of the bag, had torn its way out of it, rending the material with its claws and miaowing on its highest note.'[9]

Ordinary Palestinians, meanwhile, knew almost nothing about the Paris Peace Conference. Aside from Emir Feisal's inconsequential intervention in Paris, the views of the Palestinians played no part in discussions of their future. However, an attempt was made to consult them a few months after the war when the first of at least six commissions arrived in Palestine to examine the situation created by the Balfour Declaration.

The King-Crane Commission was the least welcome to the British and the Zionists, and potentially the most useful to the Palestinians. It took place at a time when the French and the British were squabbling over who would control which bits of territory between Turkey and Egypt. France wanted Syria and Palestine but might settle for Syria; Britain wanted Palestine for the Jews and for strategic reasons. It was suspected that the Syrians didn't want France as a Mandatory power and that the Palestinian Arabs preferred the British, though they did not want any more Jews than were there already. President Woodrow Wilson sent out a commission to the Middle East to discover the truth. It was supposed to be an international commission, but the British, French and Italians dropped out, leaving only two Americans, Henry King and Charles Crane. As it happened, the fate of Palestine was settled without anyone looking at the King-Crane Commission's findings. Travelling, taking evidence and writing a report took a long time, and King and Crane were overtaken by events in Paris. By the time the Commission returned to the United States to deliver their report, President Wilson was too ill to consider it and the King-Crane report disappeared into the American archives, only to surface some years later after Palestine's fate had been sealed.

Who knows what would have happened if the King-Crane Commission had set off promptly, done its research quickly and published its report while the discussions in Paris were still going on? Its recommendations were unambiguous. The final report quoted Wilson's speech in which he called for "'the settlement of every question, whether of territory, of sovereignty, of economic arrangement, or of political relationship upon the basis of the free acceptance of that settlement by the people immediately concerned,'" and then it said: 'If that principle is to rule, and so the wishes of Palestine's population are to be decisive as to what is to be done with Palestine, then it is to be remembered that the non-Jewish population of Palestine – nearly nine tenths of the whole – are emphatically against the entire Zionist program. The tables [in the Report] show that there was no one thing upon which the population of Palestine were more agreed than upon this. To subject a people so minded to unlimited Jewish immigration, and to steady financial and social pressure to surrender the land, would be a gross violation of the principle just quoted, and of the people's rights, though it kept within the forms of law.'[10] President Wilson's biographer later found no record that Wilson had even seen the report and discovered that the President's copy had been removed from his archives.[11]

Meanwhile, the authorities in Palestine were trying to reassure the Palestinians about their future as rumours circulated about the French, the British and the Zionists. Fully aware of the promises that had been made to the Arabs if they helped to defeat the Turks, and also that they had fulfilled their side of the bargain, General Allenby felt duty-bound to make public the fact that the British would keep their promise. In November 1919 he issued a proclamation throughout Palestine. It began:

> The French Government, in agreement with the British Government, has decided to issue the following joint declaration in order to give to the non-Turkish [sic] populations between the Taurus and the Persian Gulf the assurance that the two countries, each in its own sphere, intend to secure for them the amplest autonomy, with the aim of guaranteeing their liberation and the development of their civilization.
>
> The end that France and Britain have in pursuing in the East the war unloosed by German ambition is the complete and definite freeing of the peoples so long oppressed by the Turks, and the establishment of National Governments and Administrations deriving their authority from the initiative and the free choice of the native populations.[12]

General Allenby's original text, drawn up in Paris and agreed by Britain and France, was in French. When it was published in an English translation in *The Times* the first paragraph was mysteriously omitted. This was the only part of the proclamation that applied unambiguously to the people of Palestine, who were clearly included in 'the non-Turkish populations between the Taurus and the Persian Gulf'. There were of course other territories than Palestine previously under the Turks which clearly were to have 'National Governments ... deriving their authority from ... the native populations' and perhaps it was hoped that the proclamation would be taken as referring to Iraq, Syria, Arabia and so on.

It was at this point that the Zionists achieved what was probably their greatest coup. Until that point, whatever gloss was put on it, the Balfour Declaration was still just a letter. However, Britain was likely to acquire the Mandate for Palestine and a team was assembled to draft the terms of that Mandate, laying out how the country was to be governed and what steps were to be taken towards eventual independence. A Commission was appointed under Lord Milner (a strong supporter of Zionism) and the drafting process soon became an exchange of views between the Commission and representatives of the Zionist Organization, including Sir Herbert Samuel, who was to play an important part in the first few years of the Mandate. As a result, the final draft incorporated the Balfour Declaration as a principle to which the Mandatory power had to adhere, including the dubious phrase about the 'historical connection of the Jewish people with Palestine'. The Mandate was also to include clauses which were virtually direct quotes from various Zionist documents put before the Peace Conference. Article 6, for instance, said 'The administration of Palestine ... shall facilitate Jewish immigration ... and shall encourage close settlement by Jews on the land.'[13]

In Whitehall, there was a sense of urgency about establishing the Mandate for Palestine. Once in place, it would allow the British government much more freedom in running the country than existed under the rules governing the administration of an occupied enemy territory, which is what Palestine still was. These rules were getting in the way of what Weizmann and his colleagues wanted to achieve in Palestine, and members of the military administration were increasingly irritated by the Zionist Commission telling them what to do, often backed by the Foreign Office in London, where Lloyd George and Balfour firmly supported the Zionist cause.

To his own surprise, Richard Meinertzhagen (who associated the Arabs with 'immorality, rotten government, corrupt and dishonest society') was appointed Chief Political Officer for Palestine and Syria on General Allenby's staff. Once inside Palestine's military administration, Meinertzhagen manipulated the flow of information from Whitehall to the Palestinian people to the advantage of the Zionists. He sent a telegram to Lord Curzon, saying, 'The people of Palestine are not at present in a fit state to be told openly that the establishment of Zionism in Palestine is the policy to which HMG, America and France are committed. They certainly do not realize this fact. It has therefore been found advisable to withhold for the present your telegram No. 245 of 4 August 1919 from general publication. So soon as Dr Weizmann arrives, I intend to draw up with him and the Chief Administrator a statement giving in the most moderate language what Zionism means, the gradual manner of its introduction, its freedom from religious or industrial intolerance, its eventual benefits to Palestine, and the denial that immigration spells the flooding of Palestine with the dregs of Eastern Europe.'[14] In his diaries, he continues, 'My conviction that anti-Zionist feeling is largely artificial and has been exaggerated both locally and at home is more than ever confirmed on further investigation. I do not anticipate any serious trouble in the initial stages of Zionism with the present moderation displayed by Zionist leaders.'[15]

However, this view was not shared by the rest of the administration. In 1920 Sir Louis Bols, the Chief Administrator of Palestine, complained to his bosses in Whitehall: 'My own authority and that of every department of my Administration is claimed or impinged upon by the Zionist Commission, and I am definitely of opinion that this state of affairs cannot continue without grave danger to the public peace and to the prejudice of my Administration ... It is no use saying to the Muslim and Christian elements of the population that our declaration as to the maintenance of the status quo on our entry into Jerusalem has been observed. Facts witness otherwise: the introduction of the Hebrew tongue as an official language; the setting up of a Jewish judicature, the whole fabric of Government of the Zionist Commission, of which they are well aware; the special travelling privileges to members of the Zionist Commission; these have firmly and absolutely convinced the non-Jewish elements of our partiality. On the other hand, the Zionist Commission accuses me and my officers of anti-Zionism. The situation is intolerable, and in justice to my officers and myself must be fairly faced.'[16]

Sir Louis wanted the Zionist Commission abolished and two consultative bodies set up, one for the Arabs and one for the Jews, with no special privileges given to either group. What his outburst achieved was the complete opposite: the Zionist Commission lobbied for Sir Louis to be abolished along with his administration. They demanded that a civil government be established in Palestine with much more freedom; one that would toe the line when it came to setting up the Jewish state. As Sir Louis said in his report: 'It is manifestly impossible to please partisans who politically claim nothing more than a "National Home", but in reality will be satisfied with nothing less than a Jewish State and all that it politically implies.'[17]

The Zionists accused Sir Louis and his staff of deliberately trying to thwart their aims and of favouring the Arab population of

Palestine. They attributed this to a pro-Arab, anti-Zionist attitude in the British Foreign Office. It is true that the military administration were supporting the interests of the Arabs, but not for the reasons the Zionists gave. As occupiers of a conquered territory, Sir Louis and his staff had to obey international laws. They were required to preserve the status quo and make no significant changes in the way the territory was run until a final peace agreement had been signed. Palestine's population was 91 per cent Arab and 9 per cent Jew. If the OETA had agreed to the immigration of thousands of Jews, as the Zionists wanted, it would have been in breach of international law.

The pro-Zionist British government saw that the easiest way to gain the freedom of manoeuvre that they needed in Palestine was to put the Mandate (incorporating the Balfour Declaration) into operation as soon as possible, benefiting from the fact that a civilian administration was not bound by the laws applying to military rule of an occupied territory. So Balfour, Lloyd George and their colleagues set about dismantling the OETA and appointing a High Commissioner to Palestine (Herbert Samuel was waiting in the wings) who would set up a civilian government, operating under the terms of the Mandate, which had at its heart the *requirement* to create the conditions by which Palestine would become the National Home of the Jews. The Zionists would get what they wanted.

But the Mandate could only apply after the conclusion of a peace treaty with Turkey. Until then Palestine was occupied by the British army under the terms of the Armistice. In spring 1920 it was believed that Turkey would soon sign a peace treaty, and the British hurriedly got rid of Sir Louis Bols and his men and began setting up a Mandatory government. The first Sir Louis knew of this was when he received a cable from Herbert Samuel asking if he could retain the services of Sir Louis's cook.[18]

Then the Americans threw a spanner in the works. The French and British had agreed to divide between them the proceeds from the sale of Iraqi oil and this would be enshrined in the peace treaty presented to the Turks. But the US government reminded the two European governments that their oil-sharing clauses were in breach of the aim of the peace treaty to ensure equal treatment to the commerce of all countries.

This was a side issue as far as Palestine was concerned, but it had the effect of bringing to a halt the smooth progress of the peace treaty, which in turn meant – or should have meant – that the Mandate over Palestine could not come into effect. It was fortunate for the Zionists (but unfortunate for the Palestinian Arabs) that the British government ignored this problem and went ahead *as if* the peace treaty had been signed. With much greater freedom of operation, then, the new civil government's Zionist High Commissioner could put the Mandate into operation and start to create the conditions for a Jewish National Home. This odd situation, which meant that Britain started governing Palestine with no legal basis, was to continue for three years until a peace treaty between the Allies and Turkey was finally signed in 1923.

None of this was discussed publicly. References to the Mandate in Parliament and in official publications were presented in terms which implied that everything was legal. When the government was accused in the House of Lords in June 1920 of governing Palestine illegally, it failed to answer. It also failed to defend its civil administration in Palestine when J. M. N. Jeffries pointed out in the *Daily Mail* that it was in breach of international law and would continue to be so until a peace treaty was signed with Turkey. 'There is no getting away from the real character of the action of the 1920–3 Government,' Jeffries wrote later. 'It broke international law repeatedly, broke it as a matter of habit, and broke it in affairs of the utmost gravity.'[19]

As the Mandate came (illegally) into operation, the British government was boxed in by a document of its own choosing, and one which bound successive governments, however much they disliked it. Once the Mandate for Palestine had the Balfour Declaration enshrined as one of its clauses it was like a card on which was printed on one side *'The statement on the other side of this card is true'* and when you turn it over it says *'The statement on the other side of this card is false'*. Whichever way you looked at it, it was self-contradictory. In the case of Palestine the card said on one side *'Palestine shall be turned into a National Home for the Jewish people'* and on the other *'The rights of the existing inhabitants of Palestine shall be preserved'*.

Over the next thirty years the British government was to be reminded of this paradox by several Commissions sent out to Palestine. But if any administration for a moment considered abandoning or adjusting the terms of the Balfour Declaration, it was warned off in no uncertain terms by the Zionist Organization.

The significance of retelling these events today is to make clear two facts. First, the hostility of Zionist Jews to the rights of the Palestinian Arabs began a hundred years or more ago. It is not something that has arisen in recent years as a result of actions by the Arabs against the Israelis. In the light of today's events, then, the attitude of the Israeli government to the Palestinian Arabs is not different from that of the early Zionists. The Palestinians are still seen as presenting an obstacle to an exclusively Jewish state by living in their own homes. Second, by accepting the claim for a Jewish state in Palestine, the British government ignored evidence and advice from the earliest days of their rule there that the course they were pursuing would lead to disaster. Further, as other foreign governments have had a part to play in the Middle East, they too have ignored the fact that making or maintaining Palestine – later Israel – as an exclusively Jewish state was an act of gross injustice to millions of Palestinian Arabs around the world.

It was also more than a hundred years ago that the likely outcome of massive Jewish immigration into Palestine was predicted: 'An infiltration is bound to end in disaster. It continues till the inevitable moment when the native population feels itself threatened and forces the Government to stop the further influx of Jews.'[20] These words were written by Theodore Herzl, the founder of the Zionist movement. And he was right.

11

INTO THE 1920s

• • •

Once the Mandate was established, the pattern of events in Palestine was set for the next two decades. The word 'Arab' is nowhere to be found in the document; 'Muslim' appears once, with reference to buildings; 'Jew' or 'Jewish' appears fifteen times. Anyone ruling Palestine according to the Mandate would have to work hard to preserve the rights of its 'non-Jewish' population.

The Jews of Europe, acting on the 'National Home' clause, set about organizing its realization. They hoped to step up the rate of immigration into Palestine so that hundreds of thousands of Jews could augment the tiny Jewish population already there. These Palestinian Jews had been there for generations, inhabiting well-established communities in ancient towns and villages. There were also more recent Jewish immigrants, some arriving in the last few decades of Turkish rule, who had established new 'colonies' (as they were called), sometimes on unproductive land which they then reclaimed. Immigration to Palestine was now under the control of the British government and in the early years of the Mandate the number of Jews arriving was modest compared with the total population of the country, which was about 700,000.

From 1920 to 1923 just under 10,000 Jews a year came to Palestine officially, though it was a significant figure as a proportion of the Jewish population (which was about 80,000). Authorized immigration rose in 1924 to 12,000 and in 1925 it was 33,000. By 1926 the Jewish population had increased to 150,000, almost 20 per cent of the total population of Palestine.

The British intention to increase Palestine's Jewish population was well known and led to hostility between Arabs and Jews in the early years of the Mandate. Often it was the Arabs who were hostile to the new immigrants, rather than the other way round. The Arabs had barely figured at all in the minds of the Zionists. They were either ignored or seen as so ignorant and uncivilized that the Zionists did not regard the plan to take over their country as an aggressive act. Weizmann tried to conceal the fact that the Arabs were virtually unanimous in their resistance to an eventual Jewish state, and he blamed an unspecified minority. 'There is,' he wrote, 'among the Arabs an implacable minority which simply denies the rights of the Jewish people to Palestine. With this minority, which has consistently opposed the improvement of the lot of Arab masses, it is impossible to argue.'[1] When Jews began arriving in Palestine in greater and greater numbers, they saw only what they expected to see. They also lived apart from Arabs in their own communities. The Palestinian Arabs were still very much figures in a landscape.

'The Jews made no effort to adapt themselves to those aspects of oriental life which would have enriched their own cultural pattern, and at the same time made them appear less provocatively alien to the country,' wrote Arthur Koestler, himself a Jew. 'They did not learn from the Arabs to build cool and spacious houses which would fit the climate and landscape; they brought with them their architecture of the Polish small town and of German functionalism of the 'twenties. Their dress, food, manners and general way of life were transplanted like a prefabricated pattern from their lands of origin. Some of these were improvements in the country's way of life; others unfitting and in bad taste. There was no cultural symbiosis between the two races. The Jews came as conquerors.'[2]

These new arrivals were not necessarily ill-intentioned. Patronizing, certainly, but any ill will largely came from the Arabs who felt patronized. Their ancient culture and society were deemed worthless compared with the European civilization from which most of the Jewish immigrants came. Maurice Samuel was one of the Jewish immigrants from Europe who came to live in Tel Aviv in the 1920s. Tel Aviv was a Jewish city that had sprung up in a very few years, next to the Arab town of Jaffa. In *What Happened in Palestine* he compared Jaffa with its new Jewish neighbour:

Jaffa [is] a very ancient city, a city typical of the decayed
East, with a few rich and many poor – and a poverty of
that awful and indescribable type which can be found
only in the East. There are men in Jaffa who live on ten, or
fifteen cents a day: they eat the flat tasteless cakes – dried
dough, really – which are sold off pushcarts; they sleep in
the open; they gather the clothes off filth heaps.... On
the one side Tel Aviv with its poets and painters and
thinkers. On the other, backward Jaffa, in which
education is a fantastic luxury and modern intellectuality
– in a levantinized form, at that – the possession of a
handful. Only yesterday, too, we had got along so well [he
is referring to the time before a recent wave of Arab–
Jewish violence]. The young bloods of Jaffa used to come
on Fridays (the Muslim Sabbath) to Tel Aviv. This was
their taste of 'Europe', of 'the civilized world'. They sat in

the little cafés we have set up on the beach, opposite the
Casino, and in the Casino. They came to our dances.[3]

For Samuel and most of the immigrants, the natural superiority
and intelligence of the Jews were enough to justify their increasing
presence in Palestine and their ultimate right to take over the land.
Samuel's book suffers from what Edward Said has called
'Orientalism': a blithe assumption of the superiority of the West
and the picturesque deficiencies of the East. Samuel's Orientalism
extends from complaining of the 'tastelessness' of (delicious) Arab
bread to maintaining that only Arabs were poor in 1920s Palestine
(in fact there were plenty of poor, deprived Jews). He also says that
educated Palestinians were hard to find. He obviously never met
my grandfather.

Some Jews tried harder to get inside the Arab mind. Vladimir
Jabotinsky, for instance, understood that Palestinian Arabs 'look
upon Palestine with the same instinctive love and true favour that
any Aztec looked upon Mexico or any Sioux looked upon his
prairie. Palestine will remain for the Palestinians not a borderland,
but their birthplace, the centre and basis of their own national existence.'[4] Although he remained an enthusiastic Zionist, Jabotinsky
was at least aware of the fact that there was passion on both sides.

Many of his fellow Zionists blamed the conflict that was to
escalate in the 1920s and 1930s on Arab agitators. There were agitators, of course, in response to a growing realization among Arabs
that the promised independence for former Ottoman peoples
might not be extended to them. The possibility that they had been
lied to and treated like second-class citizens made them under-
standably angry.

• • •

The first clash occurred in 1920 at the Muslim spring festival of Nebi Musa, around the time Christians celebrate Easter. Nebi Musa usually consists of a boisterous but peaceful procession of thousands of Muslims through the streets of Jerusalem. It passed off without trouble in 1919, but since then a lot more had become known of the plans of the Great Powers for the Middle East, and senior Arab figures condemned Zionism in their speeches to the crowds. They called for independence and waved pictures of Feisal.

There were tens of thousands of Arabs milling around in the Old City, bands of youths on the rampage, and gangs roaming through the Jewish Quarter. As was to happen time and again, the perceived threat of eventual Jewish control of Palestine and the feeling that the British government supported this aim created an anger that was vented on the nearest Jews. In the Nebi Musa riots, five Jews were killed and more than 200 wounded, and there was much looting and destruction of Jewish homes. There were also casualties among the Arabs, four killed and twenty-three wounded, partly at the hands of a Jewish defence force that had been organized by Jabotinsky. More than 200 people were put on trial after the riots, including thirty-nine Jews, as well as the two dignitaries who had made the most inflammatory speeches. Even Jabotinsky was arrested, convicted and imprisoned as a result of his actions and for being found in possession of arms.

Whatever the attitude of the British government in Whitehall, there remained a feeling among the Jews that the administration in Palestine favoured the Arabs. The police and army were criticized for not dealing effectively with the disorder. Richard Meinertzhagen, the Chief Political Officer, thought that the British administration had known the riots would take place but had done nothing to prevent them, just to show Whitehall the likely consequences of fulfilling the Balfour Declaration. However, it has also been suggested that Meinertzhagen said this to cover himself. Just four days before the Nebi Musa riots he had told Whitehall he didn't anticipate any trouble.[5]

There is no need for conspiracy theories. Some 50,000 or more people facing an uncertain future were crammed into the Old City of Jerusalem. Of course there would be outbreaks of verbal and physical abuse, slogans and jostling, fighting and looting. If you add to the mix a sprinkling of rumour and a robust defence by armed Jews who had been parading in the streets in the days and weeks beforehand, this was all that was needed for riots to occur.

A government Court of Inquiry, the Palin Commission, was set up to investigate the causes of the violence. It was subsequently asked to widen its remit to the broader issues of racial feelings in Palestine. The Commission heard evidence from 152 witnesses, 'speaking no less than eight different languages, i.e. English, French, Arabic, Hebrew, Yiddish, Jargon and Hindustani'. Their

The first High Commissioner of Palestine, Herbert Samuel (*right*), although a Zionist, claimed that he was even-handed in the dispute between the Arabs and the Jews.

report was marked 'Secret' and never officially published, but the typescript still lies in the National Archives in London. The Palin Commission found that the immediate cause of the violence was Arab attacks on Jews. However, they went on to give a wide-ranging analysis of the broader causes of the unrest. They concluded 'that the Zionist Commission and the official Zionists by their impatience, indiscretion and attempts to force the hands of the Administration are largely responsible for the present crisis'.[6]

The dramatic use of 'largely responsible' in this context reflected the fact that the Court of Inquiry had been antagonized rather than enlightened by the intolerant and extreme statements they heard from Zionists who gave evidence, and their views were backed up by evidence from British officials of persistent attempts to obtain favourable treatment at the expense of the Arabs. The Commission also had little time for the justifications the Zionists gave for their claims on Palestine:

> Such refinements of argument as Captain Samuel's theory that the 'majority of the potential population of Palestine is outside the country' or Dr. Eder's theory of reconstituting a nation, never crossed [the Palestinian Arabs'] minds, nor if such theories had been propounded to them would they have seemed even intelligible. The Jewish title based on the tenacious historical memory of the race and a profound religious sentiment which appeals so strongly to those European and American peoples who have absorbed the Old Testament narrative and prophecies with their earliest essays in their native tongue, means less than nothing to a people who see themselves menaced with deprivation by a race they have hitherto held in dislike and contempt. So far as the claim

is historic, they can only see in the Jews a people who, after an independent history of less than three hundred years, were twice expelled from their territory, by Great Empires as a standing menace to Imperial peace and order. From the religious point of view they regard them as a race guilty of the greatest religious crime in history and still unrepentant. Such views may be uncritical and unjust but they obtain and make it difficult for the native population to contemplate with equanimity even the most moderate aims of Zionism.[7]

The causes of friction identified by the Commission did not go away. Over the next few years there were more Arab-Jewish attacks in Mandatory Palestine. Often innocent Jews who had lived for generations in Palestine and who were not trying to dominate the Arabs bore the brunt of the violence. Before the rise of Zionism, most Arabs and Jews in Palestine had got on perfectly well, as the Palin Commission had observed: 'Whatever may be alleged against Turkish rule, one fact stands out quite clearly from the evidence. Up to a very recent date the three sects, Muslims, Christians and Jews, lived together in a state of complete amity. The Orthodox Jew of Palestine was a humble, inoffensive creature, largely dependent upon charity for his livelihood in the city of Jerusalem, elsewhere hardly distinguishable from the rest of the peasant population. No serious attack on the Jewish population is recorded since the time of Ibrahim Pasha in 1840.'[8] The more aggressive immigrant Zionists had changed all this and now the Palestinian Arabs feared for their future.

Three months after the Nebi Musa riots, the government of Palestine went from being a military to a civil administration, in anticipation of the League of Nations Mandate coming into operation.

Sir Herbert Samuel was appointed first High Commissioner of Palestine by the British government, although Chaim Weizmann has claimed the credit for it. 'I was mainly responsible for the appointment of Sir Herbert Samuel to Palestine. Sir Herbert Samuel is our friend. At our request he accepted that dif-ficult position,' Weizmann told an American audience in 1921.[9]

Samuel had been somewhat in the wilderness after Lloyd George succeeded Asquith as Prime Minister. He still spoke in the House of Commons, but didn't get the Home Secretary job he thought he deserved. He then lost his seat in the 1918 election. After a brief visit to Palestine, he had doubts about becoming its first High Commissioner when he realized the strength of Arab feeling. 'The more I see of conditions here the more I am con-firmed in my original opinion that it would be inadvisable for any Jew to be the first Governor. It would render more difficult ... and not more easy, the fulfilment of the Zionist programme.'[10] Why an unbiased Governor of Palestine should wish for the easy 'fulfilment of the Zionist programme' is another matter. When he finally accepted the position, many Palestinian Arabs assumed he had been appointed not because of his talents, ability and experience but because he was Jewish. In fact, Samuel made efforts to allay Arab fears about the future of Palestine. This in turn, made him unpopular with the Zionists. They had been so pleased when he was appointed and now felt he wasn't dealing with their com-plaints.

In any normal situation, the first five years of the Mandate was a time when the British could be expected to bring their administra-tive skills to bear on the problem of teaching Palestinians how to develop representative government. Syria, Iraq and Transjordan, for instance, were busy building institutions such as a legislative council, a judicial system, some form of Cabinet of Ministers and so on, leading these countries to a point where the Mandatory power could leave behind a country run by its own people. But British attempts to do the same in Palestine were bedevilled by the Zionists' attempts to ensure that as many as possible of the jobs in the new government were given to Jews.

The other states under the Mandatory system faced no such pressures. There was no clause in the Mandate for Syria insisting that its Armenian minority should eventually be in control of the country and rule over the Syrian Arab majority. There was nothing in the Iraq arrangements that required the country to be handed over eventually to its Kurdish minority. In Iraq and Syria the eventual government was the government of all the people, each community represented through its votes in the electorate. Only Palestine had this extra – and crippling – requirement imposed upon it by the Balfour Declaration.

Three of Khalil Sabbagh's children (*left to right*),
Georgette, Constanza (now Soeur Françoise) and Isa.

Whatever the final form of government for Palestine, Samuel knew that he had to enlist the help of the leaders of the different Arab communities in the country. Palestine was a very patriarchal society, with the different religious groups looking for guidance to their leaders. There were also sub-divisions along political lines: left-wing/right-wing, moderate/hardline.

The largest group by far was the Muslims. Two families were rivals for the allegiance of the Palestinian Muslims: the Husseinis and the Nashashibis. As the Arab–Jewish conflict grew in the 1920s and 1930s, the Husseinis were led by Haj Amin al-Husseini. He had been given the title of Grand Mufti of Jerusalem by the British and was also President of the Supreme Muslim Council of Palestine. He and his followers adamantly opposed the Zionist threat to Palestinian democracy. The Nashashibis, led by Ragheb Nashashibi (the Mayor of Jerusalem from 1920 to 1934), pursued a more diplomatic route. The rivalry between these two groups was to bedevil Arab politics over the next twenty years. However, the only thing on which they agreed was also the sticking point in any relationship with the Jews. Both the Husseinis and the Nashashibis were Palestinian nationalists, and, as such, felt that Palestine should be run by Palestinians.

Successive High Commissioners devised endless schemes to draw the Arab notables into the political community of Palestine, but all of them proved inadequate to the task of reconciling the Arabs of Palestine to Zionism.[11] In Samuel's case this failure led him to try to satisfy each community by devolving power separately to the Arabs and the Jews. This meant the communities were driven further and further apart instead of finding ways to live together. At the same time, British civil servants had different attitudes to the various religious groups they dealt with in trying this complex country. Isaiah Berlin summed up the situation by comparing the Mandate to a minor English public school: 'There was the headmaster, the high commissioner, trying to be firm and impartial: but the assistant masters favoured the sporting stupid boarders (Arabs) against the clever swot dayboys (Jews) who had the deplorable habit of writing home to their parents on the slightest provocation to complain about the quality of the teaching, the food, and so on.'[12]

In fact, the new Jewish immigrants did not suffer from a poor quality of life. Their income levels were usually higher than those of the Arabs, largely because of financial support from Jews abroad, and in all sorts of ways they were given special treatment by the government of Palestine. Nevertheless they still complained. They felt that they had been promised – and certainly felt they deserved – the power to determine the future of Palestine and its inhabitants. Some Jews saw a place for the Arabs in the new Palestine, though very much as a subordinate minority group in a Jewish state. According to Arthur Koestler: '"The Arabs" represented for [the Jews] a political headache, not a human and moral problem .... Palestine was [the Jews'] promised land, doubly promised from Mount Sinai and Downing Street, and they came to take possession of it as its masters. The presence of the Arabs was a mere accident like the presence of some forgotten pieces of furniture in a house which has been temporarily let to strangers... all they expected of them was to sit still and watch them taking the country over and running it.'[13]

Afraid of this outcome, the Palestinian Arabs took a leaf out of the Zionists' book and established a presence in London, where they hoped they would have better access to the British government. They wanted to counter the overwhelming Zionist support that existed in the Cabinet in the persons of Balfour, the Foreign Secretary, and Winston Churchill, who had become Colonial

Secretary. A delegation of leading Palestinians from Jerusalem, Nablus and Haifa (including two members of the Christian Arab community) stayed in London for nine months and took part in a series of largely fruitless discussions with Churchill and his civil servants. On a trip to the League of Nations in Geneva they tried to see Arthur Balfour, the Foreign Secretary, but he initially refused to meet them and – astonishingly – told them to go and see Chaim Weizmann. They insisted on an interview and were seen briefly by Balfour, who refused to discuss any dilution of the aims of the Balfour Declaration.

This was also the tone of a White Paper that was being prepared, which was shown, in draft form, to the Palestinian delegation. A long and detailed correspondence took place between the Palestinians and the Colonial Office, in which they questioned a number of statements, some of which were changed in the final version. The draft said that the Zionist Commission 'has not desired to possess, and does not possess, any share in the general administration of the country'. The Palestinian delegation replied by quoting Charles Crane (of the King-Crane Commission), who had just been reported in *The Times* as saying, 'The Zionist Commission which has so much control over the political machinery of Palestine seems to have more power than the authorized government.' The British maintained that the Zionist Organization was merely looking after the interests of Jews in Palestine, to which the Arab delegation asked: 'Cannot the Administration be trusted with the interests of 7 per cent of the population when the welfare of the 93 per cent are entrusted into its hands?'

Once again, Whitehall was rather patronizing towards the Palestinian Arabs, but the Arabs would not be bamboozled. One small example relates to a point raised in the first letter from the Palestinian delegation to Churchill, which quotes the powers given

The beach at Tel Aviv in the 1930s. Most of the Jewish immigrants to
Palestine brought European values and customs into an Oriental country.

to the High Commissioner 'who we will suppose is impartial'. 'But
when,' the letter continues, 'as is the case with the present High
Commissioner, he is a Zionist ...' Churchill's reply said, 'It is not
correct to state that the High Commissioner is a member of the
Zionist Organization.' This is not, of course, what the delegation
had said, and they justified their actual statement in their next
letter. 'In describing the High Commissioner as Zionist, to which
the Secretary of State takes objection ... the Delegation were
simply repeating the words of the Colonial Secretary which
appeared in his speech of June 11th, 1921, in the House of
Commons, when he referred to Sir Herbert Samuel as "an ardent
Zionist."'[14] It must have been irritating to the British government to
discover that some Arabs were capable of refuting the Zionist arguments that formed the basis of British policy for Palestine, but it
was too late to influence government policy.

The Zionist Organization was worried enough about some of
the Palestinian delegation's arguments to rush into print a reply
entitled *The Truth about Palestine*. In its author's justification of

the Balfour Declaration it made no concessions to the possibility that the Jews of the world were ordinary people like everyone else. 'For two thousand years Palestine has remained the lodestar of Jewish idealism,' it said. 'If the Jews now ask for an opportunity of rebuilding their National Home, they base their claim not merely on the existence of a Jewish state in remote antiquity, but on the unwavering concentration upon Palestine of Jewish hopes and prayers from the moment of the Dispersion to the present day. It is in the interests of the new world order that the discord in the Jewish soul should be resolved and that the Hebrew genius, restored to Hebrew soil, should have an assured opportunity of once more making its characteristic contribution to the common stock.'[15]

When it was published in 1922, the final version of the White Paper reaffirmed Britain's commitment to the Balfour Declaration, however, as well as its intention to continue immigration so that Jews from all over the world could come 'of right and not on sufferance'. It also said that no promise of independence for Palestine had ever been made during the First World War, although this statement was later to be shown to be erroneous. However, the White Paper also denied the Zionist claim that Palestine should become 'as Jewish as England is English': 'His Majesty's Government regard any such expectation as impracticable and have no such aim in view,' it said. 'Nor have they at any time contemplated ... the disappearance or the subordination of the Arabic population, language or culture in Palestine.... His Majesty's Government therefore now declare unequivocally that it is not part of their policy that Palestine should become a Jewish State.'

That was not how the Zionists saw it. While the White Paper was being drafted, Montagu Eder, a senior member of the Zionist Commission, told the Court of Inquiry into the Nebi Musa riots:

'There can be only one National Home in Palestine, and that a Jewish one, and no equality in the partnership between Jews and Arabs, but a Jewish preponderance as soon as the numbers of the race are sufficiently increased.'[16]

12

HOSTILE ACTS

. . .

During the Mandate years my grandfather Khalil became openly anti-British. The story goes that one day in the early 1920s the mayor of the town where Khalil lived told him that because of his critical public statements about the British administration he was on a list of wanted men. He had better leave town or he'd be arrested. So Khalil and Josefina moved, with their four children, to another part of Palestine.

Another story describes a protest march he organized from Tulkarm, where he was living, to the house of the High Commissioner, Herbert Samuel, on the Mount of Olives in Jerusalem. Khalil gave a stirring speech in a mosque in Tulkarm, then the people set off, the crowd swelling as it passed through villages and towns. Most people were walking, though his daughter Tekla, then about nine or ten, rode a camel. When the protest march reached Samuel's residence, Khalil made a speech against the British, telling the High Commissioner that he was not welcome. One of my uncles says that when the angry Palestinian mob attacked his house Samuel hid in the bathroom, in a shower, where he was assaulted and his hand was broken. But I can find no evidence for these colourful details.

Samuel's term of office ended after five years in 1925. There had been more riots, some in Jaffa in which forty-seven Jews and forty-eight Arabs had died, the latter mostly at the hands of the police. The next High Commissioner, Lord Plumer, had a calmer period of rule. Palestine in the mid-1920s had recovered from the effects of the Great War and, thanks to British investment, had much improved roads and railways, better health and sanitation, expanding towns and villages and an increasing population.

My grandfather was a lawyer in Tulkarm, one of twenty or so towns in Palestine large enough to have a Municipal Council. According to the *Handbook of Palestine* (1930), Tulkarm had a railway station on the Lydda–Haifa line but, apparently, 'no history'. Khalil's three brothers Mikhail, Hanna and Jamil lived in the village of Deir Hanna, but because there was no secondary school there, they sent their children to Tulkarm where they became part of the expanding Sabbagh household.

During Ottoman rule only four out of ten children (mostly boys) attended school and the lessons were in Turkish. The British changed the language of instruction to Arabic and Herbert Samuel set a target of one school in every village. After he left, there was a general reluctance to educate the Arabs too much, in case it encouraged them to indulge in political activities. The education budget was only about 5 per cent of total expenditure and the Jewish schools received a third of this, at a time when Jews represented about 20 per cent of the population. Jews also funded many of their own schools. Nevertheless, it was possible for children like my father and his siblings and cousins to get a good education. Some schools, especially the private or church-run ones, were very good indeed. Hilda Wilson, an Englishwoman who taught at a school in Bir Zeit, reported that during a lesson in which the class read *Areopagitica*, John Milton's *Speech for the Liberty of*

Unlicensed Printing, a boy named Khalid asked why Britain had freedom of the press but not Palestine.[1]

My father's cousins, who shared the house in Tulkarm during term time, were called Riz'allah, Fadl'allah, Abdallah, Atallah and Shukrullah. Abdallah was to marry my father's sister, Georgette, and they were among the few Sabbaghs from my part of the family who stayed in Palestine after 1948, where their son eventually married a Jewish girl.

My grandfather was clearly a person of influence. People called at his house all the time, seeking his help with various legal and administrative matters. One day a villager asked him to write a letter. The man was a farmer and like many older Palestinians in those days was unable to read or write. He had recently returned from the pilgrimage to Mecca and while in Arabia he had lost his money belt and his boots. He wanted my grandfather to write a letter to King Abdul Aziz in the hope that he or his servants would find time to look for the missing property. Khalil did as he was asked, but he warned the farmer not to get his hopes up. Two months later the man returned in excitement saying, 'Abu Isa! Abu Isa! What a truly great king they have down in Arabia! Why, he found my boots and my red money belt, and the money was still in it!'*

Khalil was also a high-ranking Freemason. On a visit to a judge one day with his second wife, she was about to knock on the door for him and he stopped her. 'Let me do it,' he said. He knocked in a special Masonic way, whereupon they were let in and he was welcomed as a brother.

---

* 'Abu' means 'father of' and Khalil Sabbagh was known as 'Abu Isa' because of the convention by which an Arab man is known colloquially as the father of his eldest son. So Mahmoud Abbas, elected president of Palestine after the death of Yasser Arafat, is known widely as Abu Mazen. Women are named in a similar way, so Khalil's wife was known as Umm Isa, where 'Umm' means 'mother of'.

According to guidebooks of the period, there was a wide range of companies and services in Palestine's larger towns. It suggests that the middle classes were prosperous, educated and well supplied with consumer goods. For instance, the Palestine Educational Company in Jerusalem and Jaffa supplied 'Novels, Fictions and Periodicals of Every Description, Post Cards, Photos and Albums of Palestine. Illustrated Bibles and Testaments and Prayer Books with Olive Wood Sides', as well as 'Waterman and Wahl Fountain Pens and Eversharp Pencils'. The proprietors were B. Y. and W. A. Said, and W. A.'s son would go on to study in America and become better known as Edward Said, the American-Palestinian intellectual.

The Assicurazioni Generali-Trieste, an Italian insurance company, offered to insure 'Journeys Even by Air'. The Grand Hotel in Jerusalem advertised 'Private Suites of Rooms, with Bathroom, Dressing and Servants Room', and D. N. Tadros specialized in 'sending Cases of Jaffa Oranges direct from my Gardens to

The Balfour Declaration's commitment to make Palestine a national home for the Jews led to riots and demonstrations by the majority Arab population.

Consumers'. Meanwhile, the Allenby Hotel in Jerusalem advertised 'Music before and after Dinner Time; Small dance every Saturday night,' and included the gnomic phrase 'Dragomans meet trains.' ('Dragomans' were guide-translators, a corruption of the Arabic *tarjeman*, interpreter.)

The smaller towns (where tourists rarely ventured) were not so well supplied with commercial establishments. Visitors usually relied on the hospitality of relatives. In Safad, the Sabbagh houses were always open to friends, family and guests who came to lunch or dinner or spent the night. Two Greek Catholic bishops, Monsignors Halim and Hajjar, often stayed with the Sabbaghs when they came to visit their communities in Safad.[2]

• • •

Between 1925 and 1927 the Arabs and the British administration were less concerned about Jewish immigration as the figures fell off due to tighter regulations, deteriorating economic conditions and a drop in revenue to Zionist groups abroad. In 1927 more Jews left than arrived. But in 1928, after a few years of relative calm, Palestine entered a period of increased conflict, due to rivalry between the two religious groups, Jews and Muslims, over the few hundred square metres in the heart of Jerusalem that contained two rival sacred sites.

The hostilities began in September 1928 with an apparently trivial incident at the Wailing Wall in Jerusalem. Above this stretch of wall, sacred to the Jews, is the platform on which two mosques are built, the Dome of the Rock and Al-Aqsa mosque. Jews called this area Temple Mount or Mount Moriah, and believed it was the place where Abraham had offered up his son Isaac and where subsequently the Temple of Jerusalem had stood. A few months earlier, at a post-Passover celebration, a Zionist leader in Palestine,

Menachem Ussishkin, declared rousingly, 'The Jewish people wants a Jewish state without compromises and without concessions, from Dan to Be'ersheva, from the great sea to the desert, including Transjordan ... Let us swear that the Jewish people will not rest and will not remain silent until its national home is built on our Mt. Moriah.'[3]

Palestine's Turkish rulers had allowed the Jews to pray by the Wall, but they forbade any construction that might encroach upon the structures above, which belonged to the Muslims. In 1912, for example, they passed an order that screens and furniture could not be brought to the foot of the Wailing Wall. Under the British administration this situation was preserved, but the Muslims were always on the lookout for any possible infringement of this rule. The events of September 1928 began when a screen was erected at the foot of the Wailing Wall to separate men from women during Jewish prayers. A British policeman asked for it to be removed, but when his men returned to the site, it had been fixed with brackets to the flagstones. A group of Jewish women and old men attacked the police when they tried to remove it. Reinforcements were sent for, who were also attacked. 'The angry ladies hammered us with umbrellas and sticks,' the policeman in charge wrote later. 'One beldame belaboured my back until her parasol broke. The women tore at our clothing, spat in our faces and shrieked obscenities.'[4] Muslims who had assembled from all over the city at the news of this violation tried to join in, but were held back by the police.

This apparently minor incident reveals just how uneasy was the relationship between the two religious groups by this time. For several months afterwards Jews and Muslims tried to work out some kind of modus operandi at the Wall that would leave neither group feeling threatened. A new British High Commissioner, Sir John Chancellor, arrived late in 1928 and soon concluded that the

Balfour Declaration had been '"a colossal blunder", unfair to the Arabs and detrimental to the interests of the British Empire'.[5] Nevertheless, in the following year the British reduced their garrison and were emboldened to report to the Mandates Commission at the League of Nations in July 1929 that 'the relations between the two communities continue to improve. There has been little open friction between them.'

The following month then saw the most horrifying outbreak yet of communal violence. It began when the authorities allowed some building work to take place on the Haram al-Sherif above the Wall. There were 'intemperate articles ... of an exciting character'[6] in the Hebrew press and scuffles at the Wall in which two Jews were injured by Arabs. On 14 August a large group of Jewish youths met in Tel-Aviv to protest at the Muslim building activities and to

The riots of 1929 were sparked by a seemingly trivial dispute over religious practices at the Wailing Wall, beneath the site of the Dome of the Rock.

demand the dismissal of government officials, 'whose clear aim is to defeat the building of the Jewish state'. The following day several hundred of the youths travelled from Tel Aviv to Jerusalem and demonstrated near the Wall against the Arabs. This led to a counter-demonstration by Muslims. The atmosphere remained tense and then a Jew kicked a football into an Arab's garden. There was a quarrel, which led to a fight and the Jew was stabbed and later died from his wounds. His funeral resulted in yet more demonstrations and counter-demonstrations, which the police tried to control, but the hostilities got worse over the next few days and there were injuries and deaths on both sides.

For people outside Jerusalem, it was difficult to get an accurate idea of what was happening. Few people had radios or telephones and relied on word of mouth. The Arabs were alert to any threat from the Jews and by the time word of what was happening got to Hebron, a city about twenty miles south of Jerusalem, the scuffles and injuries at the Wailing Wall had been magnified into a con-certed attack by Jews on Arabs. In an orgy of violence on 24 August 1929, groups of Arabs in the mainly Arab city of Hebron murdered more than sixty Jews. A similar number of Arabs died, mainly at the hands of the British police. The police had only limited resources to prevent such attacks. The British police chief did what he could, but the situation only calmed down when reinforcements arrived from Gaza and Egypt.

The Zionists saw the Hebron massacre as just another sign that the British were in collusion with the Arabs to kill Jews. Some later called it a pogrom, though it was not, since it was not initiated by the British government, nor did the police stand aside and allow the murders to happen. However, they were seriously undermanned and unprepared for such events. A few days later, Jews in Safad suffered from similar attacks by rampaging Arabs. Ten Jews were murdered in the town and forty or so were injured. The local British commander tried to protect Jews by evacuating 4,000 of them from their homes to the courtyard of Government House, but he was criticized for this because it meant their houses were left unprotected and many were looted.[7] Hasib Sabbagh's mother, Faduk, with her two older sons, provided daily meals to the Jewish families among her friends, when houses were burned in the Jewish Quarter.[8]

Many Jews blamed all Arabs for the attacks in Jerusalem, Hebron, Safad and other places, making any Arab a target for the illegal Jewish militias organized by Jabotinsky and others. 'All the Arabs of Hebron did this,' wrote Rehevam Ze'evi, 'with the exception of individuals who provided shelter for their Jewish neighbours.'[9] Another Zionist history of the Hebron massacre says: 'In 1929, [in Hebron] Arab rioters with the passive consent of the British – killed or drove out virtually the entire Jewish community.'[10] In fact, Arab families saved two thirds of the Hebron Jews by sheltering them and protecting them from the rioters. 'Had it not been for a few Arab families, not a Jewish soul would have remained in Hebron,' the local Jewish community reported later.[11] Some Arab families took in dozens of Jews.

More assaults by Arabs on Jews occurred in the following days. Four Jewish quarry workers near Bethlehem were threatened by Arab crowds on the same day as the Hebron massacre. They tried to seek sanctuary in a convent, but the nuns were afraid to shelter them. 'We returned to the quarry,' said one of the Jewish workers later. 'There we took counsel with the foreman of the Arab workers. He told us that the situation was difficult, but that they would defend us to the last drop of their blood. Before our talk was over, fifteen Arabs armed with rifles, revolvers, clubs and knives had surrounded the store. We stood at the door and listened to the discussion between the rioters and the workers. Some of the workers were for giving us up … The Muslim workers from Kfar Zurbahir, Ein Kerem and Kfar Artes stood at the door and prevented the raiders from entering.'

The Arab workers helped to disguise the Jews in Arab clothes and took them to a nearby village. But their hiding place was discovered and surrounded by angry villagers. Two days later, early in the morning, their landlord and three other Arabs smuggled the Jews out of the village and took them to Jerusalem where they were reunited with their families. Maurice Samuel, who tells this story in *What Happened in Palestine*, added that, 'From Kiriath Anavim, from Tul Kerem [Tulkarm], and from other points, similar reports were sent in. By Kiriath Anavim, one Arab notable of Abu Gush came to offer his children as hostages for the safety of the Jews. The Mukhtar of Beth Akiba, near Kiriath Anavim, came with assurances of safety and friendship.'[12]

Such stories show that the hostility between Jews and Arabs in Palestine was neither universal nor inevitable. Many Arabs in senior positions in Palestinian society often protested that they were not anti-Jewish, but that they resented the increasing numbers of German, Polish and Russian Jews who were becoming citizens of Palestine and they feared this influx of uncontrolled immigration.

Today, many elderly Palestinian refugees will testify to the good relations that existed between Jews and Arabs in some of the communities where the two groups lived side by side. One man I visited in 2003 in a refugee camp south of Beirut spoke about the Jews who had always lived in Palestine as 'Arab Jews', an expression I had not heard before. He had lived in Acre and described it as 'the area in the whole Middle East where there was harmony between Christian, Muslim and Jew … We lived upstairs, a Jewish family lived downstairs.' He said, 'We knew each other very well. When I was born, my mother asked the Jewish woman downstairs if she would look after my sister. "Of course," she said. "She is our daughter too."'

Jews and Arabs also lived side by side in Tiberias. While violence erupted further south, senior figures did their utmost to prevent it spreading to their town. The Jews and the Arabs signed proclamations of peace and friendship in Arabic and Hebrew. The Arabic version read in part:

> In the name of Allah the Merciful ... We have assembled with the notables of the Jewish community in the house of his Eminence the Great Mufti, Sheikh Abd al-Selim Effendi Tabri, and have taken council [sic] on the preservation of peace and order. We have resolved that both sides shall urge and warn their respective communities to maintain peace and quiet. We therefore proclaim that we vehemently oppose every action which disturbs the peace of the population, and we pray to God the Omnipotent to inspire us with His will. We warn our brothers that they must maintain the peace and go about their work, for that alone is useful. Let them keep far from ways which are illegal and are not desired by the community. Let them keep far from quarrels, for Allah detests the quarrelsome.[13]

There were other moderate voices, such as Judah Magnes, Chancellor of the Hebrew University in Jerusalem. 'If we cannot find ways of peace and understanding,' he said, 'if the only way of establishing the Jewish National Home is upon the bayonets of some Empire, our whole enterprise is not worthwhile, and it is better that the Eternal People that has outlived many a mighty empire should possess its soul in patience ... It is one of the great civilizing tasks before the Jewish people to enter the promised

Isa's older sister, Tekla, in her early twenties.

land, not in the Joshua way, but bringing peace and culture, hard work and sacrifice and love, and a determination to do nothing that cannot be justified before the conscience of the world.'[14]

In the Zionist archives there is a typewritten document which attempts to build on the traditional good relations that had existed in Palestine in the past between Jews and Arabs. It was written by Haim Kalvaryski, an elderly Palestinian Jew who had lived in the country for thirty-five years and knew Arabs well. He had reason to, since his job involved buying land for Jewish settlements in Galilee from their Arab owners. Even before the Balfour Declaration he realized there was something unjust about what he was required to do. 'I realized how close the Bedouin is to his land,' he said. 'During my twenty-five years of colonial work I have dispossessed many Arabs from their lands, and you understand that this – dispossessing people from the land in which they and maybe their father were born – is not at all an easy thing, especially when one looks at these people as human beings ... I had to do this, because this is what the Yishuv [the Palestine Jewish community] asked for, but I always tried to do it in the best way possible ... I got familiar with the Arabs and the Arab question very early on.'[15]

One Jewish writer has dismissed such sentiments with a Hebrew expression which means 'shooting and crying',[16] but Kalvaryski seems to have been sincere in his respect and affection for the Arabs, so much so that in 1930 he sent a proposal to the Zionist Organization for a covenant to be agreed between the Arabs and Jews of Palestine that would result in mutual benefit and a just sharing of the land of Palestine. 'The danger to which the Arabs are allegedly exposed as a result of Jewish work is imaginary, not real. The penetration into Semitic countries in general and into Palestine in particular of a Semitic race will result in no danger to the Arabs. On the contrary, it will contribute to its vigour and to its inherent strength. We Jews shall not thrust ourselves an alien growth upon the body politic of the Arabs, as many extreme nationalists believe, but we shall form a beautiful ring in the chain of the United Arab Confederation. The Arab Confederation does not alarm us.'[17]

Kalvaryski's covenant may sound naive today, but it represents a voice of moderation, one that was not calling for an eventual Jewish state but for a genuine sharing of the land. But Kalvaryski's message of peace was not welcome. 'This worm,' wrote Asaf Halevi about Kalvaryski in a letter to his parents, 'this detestable provocateur walks through the streets of Jerusalem and no one goes up to him in Jaffa Street to give him a slap on the face that will make his ears ring. No one! So what can we say? Are we a nation, a living nation? No! We are not! We are a dead carcass, decomposing, rotting, stinking, a carcass with which everyone does as they wish.'[18]

More publicly, in a Hebrew newspaper in Palestine, Moshe Beilinson wrote on 4 December 1929 – with a breathtaking lack of logic – that 'There is no answer to this question [of competing claims to Palestine] nor can there be, and we are not obliged to provide it because we are not responsible for the fact that a particular individual man was born in a certain place, and not several kilometres away from there.'[19]

Events in London over the next year or so were to show that the Zionists were able to manipulate the entire British government and produce an astonishing volte-face, just at the point where by resisting Zionist pressure the government might have transformed the situation in Palestine. In the space of a year, a government commission set up to consider the causes of the violence in 1929 was to produce a report that showed a realistic understanding of the situation and some recommendations that could have led to a peaceful sharing of Palestine. But sharing was not what the Zionists wanted, and using the kind of tactics that achieved the Balfour Declaration in the first place they were to get the Commission's report replaced by a document they themselves had drafted, which was then used for the next nine years as a basis for the administration of Palestine.

13

COMMISSIONS GALORE

• • •

On 29 August 1929, six days after the Hebron massacre, Lord Passfield – formerly Sidney Webb, the Fabian socialist and now the Secretary of State for the Colonies – received a letter at his office in Whitehall. It contained some firm orders about how to rule Palestine. The British administration had announced the previous day that it would be disarming the whole population, Arabs and Jews, and the letter to Passfield insisted that this order, as it applied to Jewish special constables and members of the Jewish self-defence force, 'will be immediately countermanded'. It ordered that compensation should be paid to the Jewish victims of the violence and that a 'substantial sum' of money should be placed at the disposal of the Jewish Agency, an organization created by the Palestine Mandate to represent the interests of the Jews in Palestine. Passfield was even told to issue a large number of immigration certificates for the Jewish Agency to allocate so that immigration, which had been stopped by the government, could be resumed.

If the style of this letter has a certain familiarity, it is because it was from the Zionist Organization – from Chaim Weizmann himself – and formed the opening salvo in the Zionists' campaign to step up control over the administration of Palestine. Weizmann's letter also sought to remove two senior members of the British administration who were deemed to be pro-Arab. 'For reasons which are self-evident,' Weizmann wrote, 'I feel regretfully obliged to request that His Majesty's Government may consider the propriety of relieving Mr Luke and Mr Cust of their duties.'[1]

Two weeks after the violence in Palestine a government commission was set up under the chairmanship of Sir Walter Shaw 'to inquire into the immediate causes which led to the recent outbreak in Palestine and to make recommendations as to the steps necessary to avoid a recurrence'. The seven-member team stayed from 24 October to 29 December and interviewed more than a hundred witnesses. They concluded that there had been a combination of causes for the violence, but the incident that had most contributed to it was the Jewish demonstration at the Wailing Wall on 15 August 1929. Next in importance were the activities of the Arab and Jewish groups, which jealously guarded the respective rights over the Wailing Wall and the Haram al-Sherif. The commission also blamed inflammatory articles in the Jewish and Arab press.

The major recommendations of the commission were for a clarification of the passages in the Mandate that safeguarded the rights of the Arabs in Palestine; a re-examination of immigration policy; and a scientific inquiry into land use, to establish whether new methods of cultivation could allow for an increased population, both Arab and Jew, to work on the land.

A concept called the 'economic absorptive capacity' of Palestine had been devised, and it was felt that if such a quantity could be calculated it would give some yardstick for assessing appropriate levels of immigration – to counter Zionist demands for unlimited numbers of Jews to be allowed into the country. Yet another commission, effectively a one-man inquiry by Sir John Hope-Simpson, was sent off to Palestine to answer the land question. He came back with the finding that Jewish land purchases for Jewish immigrants were excluding Arabs from their traditional farming activities. 'As an example,' wrote Edward Said, 'Simpson cited a one-time fertile plain in northern Palestine now become "a sea of thorns" ravaged by field mice, because the Zionists had acquired more land than they needed or were able to cultivate. The Zionist movement not only deprived the Palestinian Arab of his land, it deprived Jewish farms as well as commercial and industrial establishments of Arab produce and labour. Contracts given by Zionist agencies that owned most of the Jewish-acquired land stipulated that only Jews could be employed.'[2] Hope-Simpson's report recommended that immigration and the purchase of land by Jews be restricted. 'It has emerged quite definitely,' he reported, 'that there is at the present time and with the present methods of Arab cultivation no margin of land available for agricultural settlement by new immigrants.'[3]

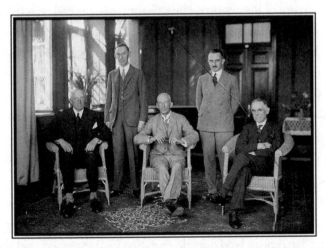

The Shaw Commission of 1929–30 was just one of many well-meaning committees of inquiry to descend on Palestine during the British Mandate.

A decade of government commissions all came to the same conclusion: Britain's National Home policy in Palestine was
'misguided, unjust, and impossible to carry out',[4] as the Israeli
writer Tom Segev has put it. The British Cabinet announced that
immigration should be linked more closely to what Palestine could
support economically. This meant reducing numbers below what
the Zionists wanted. It also made a statement reminding Jews and
Arabs that the government took seriously the obligations of the
Mandate to ensure that the rights of Arabs were not jeopardized by
the requirement to create a Jewish National Home.

The White Paper setting out government policy was issued by
the Colonial Secretary, Lord Passfield, on 21 October 1930, and it
gladdened the hearts of the Palestinian Arabs, since it reiterated
what they had been saying ever since the Balfour Declaration was
issued, although it still affirmed the intention to create a National
Home in Palestine for the Jews. ('*In* Palestine,' not 'to make
Palestine the Jewish National Home.') Passfield also raised the
possibility of a legislative council of Arabs and Jews to share self-
government of the country. The Palestinian Arabs had rejected this
idea in 1922, concerned at the disproportionate representation the
tiny Jewish population would have on such a council. But Passfield
hoped a more equitable mechanism could be devised. This time
the Jews also objected on the grounds that the majority of Arab
peasants were illiterate and would therefore be persuaded by the
effendis, the Palestinian landowning class, to oppose British policy
and the Jewish National Home – although, in truth, they needed
little persuasion.

In a private meeting with Passfield, Weizmann put forward
Zionist plans to encourage an Arab exodus. Jewish money would
be used to buy up land outside Palestine in Transjordan and there
to 'establish a reserve' for the Palestinian Arabs, presumably along

the lines of Indian reservations in America.[5] Another leading Zionist, Menahem Ussishkin, also called for a total handover of Palestine to the Jews. 'If there are other inhabitants there,' he told a group of journalists, 'they must be transferred to some other place.' (By now there could be little doubt that there *were* other inhabitants.) He went on to say: 'We must take over the land. We have a greater and nobler ideal than preserving several hundred thousands of Arab *fellahin* [peasants].'[6] Zionist writings during the Mandate period – when they recognize the majority population of Palestine at all – are rife with such disparaging references to Arabs. Weizmann wrote of 'A vast stretch of territory bordering on the Mediterranean ... sparsely populated by a semi-backward people with a low standard of living ...' Felix Frankfurter, an American Jew, wrote 'The elevation of lowly Arabs and a home for the Wandering Jew are at stake ...'

Fortunately, Passfield realized very well the true nature of Palestinian society and of its right to self-determination. His White Paper was a measured and considered estimate of the situation in Palestine and made explicit the government's obligation to protect the Arabs although, as Lord Passfield admitted, this would probably upset 'the more uncompromising sections of Zionist opinion'.[7] He was right. The outraged political Zionists leapt into action with the intention of cancelling the White Paper and its policies. Weizmann resigned as President of the Zionist Organization in protest, as did other senior Zionist figures in Britain and the United States. In America a campaign was orchestrated that brought tens of thousands of Zionists on to the streets and into mass meetings where Britain was denounced to wild cheers and Lord Passfield was mocked. The pro-Zionist Winston Churchill suggested that the elderly Lord Passfield 'has not given that intense personal attention and original effort to the White Paper that controversial delicacy and importance of subject required'.[8] The only place where the White Paper was welcomed was Palestine itself. The anniversary of the Balfour Declaration – traditionally celebrated by Jews and mourned by Arabs – passed without any demonstrations at all.

Three weeks after its publication, the government announced that in view of the possibility of a misunderstanding over the meaning of some clauses in the White Paper they had invited representatives of the Jewish Agency to confer with them. In a revealing phrase, this announcement referred to the Jewish Agency as one of the 'parties to the Mandate', although in fact they had no such legal status. The Palestinian Arabs were not invited to the party.

In a replay of the Balfour Declaration, the Zionists drafted a statement of British policy diluting the restrictions on immigration and land purchase set out in the White Paper, and toned down any recognition of the rights of the Palestinian Arabs. They expected the government to publish it as a replacement for the White Paper. The document went through several drafts, with the Cabinet and the Zionists haggling over changes. The fifth draft was approved and written up as a letter from Prime Minister Ramsay MacDonald to Chaim Weizmann.

However, when MacDonald announced in the House of Commons, in reply to a question, that he was unwilling to give the letter the status of a White Paper, it caused uproar among the Zionists. On the evening of this announcement, MacDonald rang Weizmann to placate him. The notes of the phone conversation in the Zionist archives show an exchange for which the Yiddish word *chutzpah* might have been invented: 'We want it made clear,' said Weizmann to the Prime Minister, 'that the letter to me containing the authoritative interpretation of the White Paper shall be the basis of the law in Palestine. Unfortunately Lord Passfield still imagines that nothing has happened or changed since the publication of the White Paper. He is causing trouble all the time. If a question is put to you in the House tomorrow, then you can still put matters right. If you will consult the Lord Advocate he will advise you as to the formula to be used. We have to deal with excited and anxious people and it is undesirable that there should be any misunderstanding … We are dealing with an administration in which we have no confidence, and in which I think you should not have any yourself.'[9]

It worked. On 13 February MacDonald laid before the House of Commons the 'letter' that effectively replaced the Passfield White Paper. It was a statement of policy for Palestine drafted by the Zionists. Palestinian Arabs call it the 'Black Letter'. 'In justice to its co-authors,' wrote J. M. N. Jeffries in his account of this period, 'it should not be forgotten that however they veered about, or recanted later, they were the only Prime Minister and Colonial Secretary of Great Britain during two decades who ever showed any passing sign of having listened to the Arabs' fundamental grievances, or having felt a moment's compunction for the Arabs' treatment or a moment's desire to amend it.' The Palestinian Arabs were angered by the letter, although they knew nothing of the goings on in Whitehall or the pressure brought to bear on British politicians and civil servants by the Zionists. How much angrier they would have been had they known the details of MacDonald's volte-face.

Immigration was resumed at ever higher numbers. Between 1931 and 1936 the Jewish population more than doubled, from 174,000 to 384,000. They now formed nearly 30 per cent of the population. No consideration was made of the country's 'economic absorptive capacity'. Fortunately Palestine was experiencing an economic boom as a result of a series of bumper citrus harvests. Middle-class families like the Sabbaghs benefited from the boom. Even when the heads of the family had professional jobs, the traditional family lands where olives or oranges grew generated extra income. And the children of the family pursued the best education they could get in the government educational system and the denominational schools. While my father went to secondary school in Tulkarm, his cousin Hasib attended a co-educational Catholic school in Safad, while his sisters went to a Presbyterian school nearby. But as inhabitants of a multi-faith country, Palestinian Christians were happy to mix with Jews and Muslims when the opportunity arose. Hasib once refused to leave the classroom when Muslim students had their religious instruction because he wanted to learn about Islam.

In 1933 the Palestinian Arabs turned on the British government for the first time in a serious way. Their patience had run out. There were demonstrations outside government buildings in Jerusalem, Jaffa, Haifa and Nablus. These turned nasty and the police response left twenty-six Palestinians dead and nearly 200 injured. From then on, the view spread that British support for Palestinian self-government would never amount to much in the face of Zionist demands for a Jewish National Home. The British in Palestine were subject to increasing violence, first from the Arabs and then increasingly (for different reasons) from the Jews.

There were several reasons for the government's approval of increased immigration, other than Zionist pressure. One High Commissioner in the 1930s, Sir Arthur Wauchope, actually thought that a better balance between the communities would 'cause the lion to lie down with the lamb'. The Colonial Secretary in London thought he could save British taxpayers' money by letting in free of quota any Jew who had more than £1,000 in capital. More than 40,000 Jews arrived legally in Palestine in 1934, most of them from Poland. Their numbers were rising partly because of the increasing menace of anti-Semitism in Europe.

The British government stepped up efforts to establish some form of representative government for Palestine. They proposed a legislative council similar to the one rejected by the Arabs in 1922. This time, however, the Arabs did not reject it outright, the Zionists did. With hindsight, Weizmann admitted that the Zionists' refusal to consider any sort of democratically elected legislative council harmed their cause: 'The position in which we placed ourselves by our refusal to consider the legislative council was ... an unfortunate one. The public heard the words "legislative council for Palestine"; it heard of Zionist opposition; the obvious conclusion was that the Zionists were undemocratic or anti-democratic.'[10] In fact, of course, the Zionists had consistently ignored the wishes of the majority in Palestine ever since the Balfour Declaration, and there was nothing more undemocratic than that.

The Arab middle classes, led by the Mufti of Jerusalem (*centre*), did their best to organize formal protests against the British government's adherence to the Balfour Declaration.

Nevertheless, it began to look as if the idea of a legislative council was making some headway, in spite of the Zionists' refusal to countenance it. So the Jewish Agency leaned on its friends in Parliament to try to quash a new Palestinian Constitution. Their fall guy was the current Colonial Secretary, J. H. Thomas, a British trades unionist whom the Zionists despised. 'Jimmy Thomas will be a very bad colonial secretary from our point of view,' wrote Blanche ('Baffy') Dugdale, the British Zionist and niece of Arthur Balfour. 'Weak, ignorant, blustering and indiscreet. All these qualities have shown themselves ... over Legislative Council controversy.'[11]

As usual, when Parliament discussed Palestine, it was the Zionist view that dominated the speeches. As a later government report observed, 'The debate was a striking illustration of the disadvantage which the Arabs suffer whenever the field of controversy shifts from Palestine to the United Kingdom. The Jews are perfectly entitled to make use of all the opportunities at their command for ensuring that their claims are fully understood; but we believe that their own ultimate interests would have been better served if British public opinion could have been confronted from the outset with a no less clear and cogent statement of the Arab case.'[12] One of the MPs who usually did the Zionists' bidding in the House of Commons was Colonel Josiah Wedgwood. He wrote in a letter to his daughter: 'I have had a successful week ... actually slain the Palestine constitution. I got Churchill and Chamberlain and Amery and Sinclair all to speak, and they did, leaving the Rt. Hon. J. T. Dress-shirt [Thomas] in tears.'[13]

'Baffy' Dugdale returned to her attack on Thomas and planned a one-woman government reshuffle: 'J. Thomas has been acting most annoyingly in affairs of Palestine. I have made up my mind he ought to leave the C.O. .... I shall not rest until Billy Gore reigns in J. H. Thomas' stead. It is not fit that the future of Zion should be in the hands of a drunken ex-engine driver.'[14] She didn't have long to wait. In an almost miraculous turn of events, her enemy disappeared from the political scene shortly afterwards. Thomas was forced to resign as a result of a leak of Budget secrets to some businessmen with whom he played golf. His cry of 'Tee up!' was taken by his golfing partners to mean that the duties on tea were to rise, and this was exactly what Thomas had intended.

The Jewish press in Palestine hailed the demolition in the British Parliament of a legislative council for Palestine as 'a great Jewish victory'. The Arabs saw it as yet another rejection of their right to self-government. Their gloom was reinforced by ever-increasing Jewish immigration – more than 60,000 legal immigrants in 1935. As a proportion of the population, this was equivalent to the United Kingdom accepting three million foreign immigrants in 2005. Much of the immigration pressure on Palestine came from the increasingly harsh measures taken against Jews in Europe. The racist Nuremberg Laws in Germany were an attempt to preserve the 'purity' of the Aryan race by restricting intermarriage and stripping Jews of their German citizenship.

Immigration also increased the smuggling of arms into the country. They were used to arm the militiamen that the Jews in Palestine were organizing illegally. Their stated aim was to protect Jewish communities from Arab attacks, but later they would be turned on the British as well. When some cement cases consigned to Tel Aviv were discovered to contain 254 Mauser pistols, 90 revolvers, 500 bayonets and 500,000 rounds of ammunition, the Arab Labourers Federation of Jaffa sent a telegram to the British administration: 'What is the purpose of the contraband ammunition? Is it to kill the Arabs or expel the English? We demand emphatically equality in armament or the confiscation of Jewish arms, both legal and illegal.'[15] News of illegal Jewish immigrants and caches of illegal arms frightened the Arabs and led to even more suspicion of the Jews.

The influence of the Jewish Agency over the British government continued in the mid-1930s. Early in 1936 the government awarded a construction contract for three Arab schools in the heart of the Arab town of Jaffa to a Jewish company that employed only Jewish labour – at a time when there was a shortage of jobs for Arabs. The Arab Labourers Federation protested to the District Commissioner:

> I beg to draw your kind attention to the fact that giving the construction of the three school premises to a Jewish contractor who engaged only Jewish labourers was a subject of great sensation and protests among the Arab labourers who considered this act to be completely against their legal rights, for the following reasons:
>
> 1. The buildings are situated in an Arab area.
> 2. The government has never given a contract to an Arab in a Jewish area.
> 3. Arab labourers engaged in Jewish areas were dismissed by force in many cases.
> 4. Unemployment among the Arabs is very serious.
>
> I believe that you will agree with me that the government should have studied the present psychological situation of the Arab labourers before signing such a contract which is forcing out their feelings since they are suffering terribly from the present economic crisis and are looking for any kind of work just to keep their families and themselves.
>
> Lately, the labourers held several meetings, and I could

feel that they are determined to have their full rights in these buildings, and I have been urged to request you to deal with this serious question and to give your final decision as soon as possible. I am also requested to inform you that my society is prepared to supply you with any number of labourers of any craft and at any time for this work and for any other work.[16]

The protest had no effect.

• • •

Meanwhile, ordinary Palestinians tried to get on with their lives. My father Isa (now in his teens) applied to the Government Arab College in Jerusalem to study for the higher certificate. It was the top state school in the country and there was fierce competition from all over Palestine for each of the hundred places. The students studied night and day for six days a week, with one day off for sports. The curriculum was a balanced synthesis of the humanities and the sciences as well as Arab Islamic culture and the Western classical heritage, including Greek and Latin.[17] Isa won a place there and a few years later so did his cousin Hasib. Had Palestine gained independence, the Arab College would have been its national university.

By the time my father had finished his education in 1936 the country was in one of its periodic bouts of turmoil and he was unable to take his exams. He decided to teach for a few months, hoping the situation would get back to normal and he could return to Jerusalem. A teacher was needed in Kufr Yassif where my grandfather Khalil had friends, so the whole family moved into a large house in the village. Khalil was now married to Afifa, a Lebanese woman from Tyre who had nursed him after my grandmother died.

My uncle Ghassan (then about five) remembers my grandfather as a very strict person. 'I never remembered sitting on his lap or that he ever even kissed me,' he told me. 'We kids had to be serious all the time in his presence.' Ghassan was taught reading and writing at home by his big sister Tekla. Although he was under school age he was allowed to attend the school where my father Isa was teaching, although he rarely saw him. 'Once only,' Ghassan told me, 'we were taking a religious class and our teacher was away and Isa offered to be a substitute, and he said to the class "Who knows the 'Our Father'?" and we had the habit of raising our fingers and I raised mine and said "Isa! Isa! Isa!" On the way home, he said to me "Don't call me 'Isa' in class. I am 'Mr Sabbagh'. Only at home am I Isa."'

As a student at Jerusalem's Government College,
Isa Khalil Sabbagh won a scholarship to study in England.

'Mr Sabbagh' was about seventeen or eighteen, but even then he was a very good speaker, as Ghassan recalled. 'The director of the school passed away,' he told me, 'and Isa was asked to say a few words at his death. I saw everybody crying.' Shortly after his teaching spell in Kufr Yassif, my father was awarded a scholarship by the Palestinian government to study history at the University of Exeter in Britain. He packed his bags and left Palestine.

14

PEEL AND PARTITION

• • •

The violence between Arabs and Jews became widespread as the Zionists continued to block any move to address Arab grievances. On 15 April 1936, on the road between Tulkarm and Nablus, two Jews were murdered. The following night two Arabs were murdered by Jews, presumably as a reprisal. There were demonstrations and attacks on Arabs at the funeral of one of the Jews in Tel Aviv. Then rumours that Arabs had been killed led to riots in Jaffa in which three Jews were murdered. The Palestine government imposed a curfew on Jaffa and Tel Aviv and a state of emergency was declared.

The Arabs formed the Arab Higher Committee, made up of notables from all communities in Palestine, including Palestinian Arab political parties, and headed by the Grand Mufti. This upsurge of organized nationalism worried the Zionists, who tried to blacken the Palestinian national movement by calling it a 'Nazi' movement. They spoke of 'typical Arab bloodlust', 'Arab fascism and imperialism, and Arab Hitlerism'.[1] Eventually, the Arab Higher Committee called a general strike throughout Palestine. The so-called Arab Rebellion had begun. The Grand Mufti's moderate rivals (including Ragheb Nashashibi) had been removed from senior positions by the British, so now the Mufti's method of violent resistance held sway. Taking a leaf from the Zionist book, bands of Arab militia were formed, arms were smuggled into the country and Jewish colonies were attacked.

The British also became targets. One day a convoy of lorries set out from Haifa to Safad accompanied by an escort of British soldiers. On a mountain road in the Galilee one lorry ran over a mine and was blown to pieces, killing the driver. Further along the road, as the convoy neared Safad, it was ambushed by Arab guerrillas and shots were exchanged for about an hour. No British soldiers were killed but they shot several Arabs.

The road from Haifa to Safad passes near the village of Kufr Yassif, where the Sabbagh family was living at the time. British soldiers came to the village looking for the Arabs who had mined the road. Ghassan was surprised to find his classroom occupied by men from the village, including those hiding from the soldiers. Everyone was ordered to leave the school and assemble on a piece of land nearby. The British soldiers aimed machine guns at the men and children sitting on the ground. They said that if the people who had planted the bomb didn't come forward they would burn every house in the village. No one moved. 'We saw smoke coming out from the houses,' said Ghassan. 'I couldn't tell if the smoke was coming from our house or not because the house behind it was burning as well. I was not so worried about whether they burned the houses or not, our concern was that they not use the machine guns and shoot us. And finally they released us and I walked home. All the houses around our house were burnt but not ours.'

It turned out that a combination of unlikely circumstances had left the Sabbagh house unscathed. Living there at the time was my aunt Georgette, a teacher and therefore an employee of the Palestine government. The soldier who had come to set fire to the house was shown evidence of this, but he said it was not enough to exempt the family from the reprisals. Khalil's wife then showed the soldier a letter from my father in England, with a British stamp on it.

'Madam, I'm sorry,' said the soldier, 'this is not my business. You'd have to talk to the Captain, and he's not around.' The soldier and two or three others then piled furniture up in the middle of the room and were about to set it alight when it turned out none of them had a match. They then tried to borrow matches from the family, without success. 'Then, a miracle happened,' Ghassan told me. 'My mother prayed and said "Please God save us" and the Captain came in to see what was going on. They told him about Isa and he stopped them from burning the house, and put two of them as guards to stop anybody from coming in. I remember that night and the nights that followed, as our house became a camp and many people from the rest of the village came and slept there.'

Isa Sabbagh (*right*) with his father, Khalil, sister Iqbal, and brother Ghassan.

Such actions against Arab communities became commonplace. One British soldier wrote a letter to his fiancée in England, describing a recent day's work: 'Since Wednesday life has been completely hectic. Earlier in the week ... we decided we ... would start a little frightfulness against the villagers, so we arranged with the army to blow up four houses in two villages along the road on Thursday morning ... It took us until 2 o'clock to get the four houses blown up, but everything went off all right. It's a depressing business though, as one has to be frightfully careful to get everyone out of range, and there's an awful feeling of suspense after the time fuse has been lit, in case some half-witted villager may go wandering right up to the house ...'[2]

The police also carried out harsh measures against the Arabs. One British policeman wrote to his family in England: 'What I dislike about this war is that more often than not it is the innocent who suffer. Our hospitals here are filled with women & children maimed & blinded for life .... Life for the police is now all work & no play, even at the best of times Palestine is as dull as ditch water but what with curfews & people walking about with the fear of death on them it's like living in a cemetery.'[3]

A British doctor working in Hebron had to deal with a succession of Arab casualties at the hands of the British, and he was in no doubt where the blame lay: 'I fear wherever one tries to balance the cowardly and cruel dealings of the two sides, there is no doubt which party comes with least credit from the comparison. The rebels fight fairly and chivalrously, and rule with kindness. The British kill the innocent, when no other enemy is near, and loot and rob the poor and destitute.'[4]

As the British tried to clamp down on Arab violence, some of the measures they took attracted the attention of a wider public. The extent of British violence against Palestinian Arabs was not widely publicized at the time, for obvious reasons, but some of the measures the British government took to counter Arab hostility were seized on by Britain's enemies. Italian propaganda broadcasts, joined later by the Germans, began to spread accounts of what they called 'atrocities' carried out by British troops in Palestine. Eventually, these broadcasts were having such an effect that the War Office in London was forced to issue a statement denying that British soldiers and policemen were being brutal. 'Critics fail to realize that the principle of the collective responsibility of a community for crime or disorder committed within its boundaries is fully recognized and understood by the Palestinian Arab. Collective punishment is often the only method of impressing upon a peaceful but terrorized majority that failure to assist law and order may be more unpleasant than submitting to intimidation.'[5]

When this statement justifying British actions was published, a British businessman in Palestine wrote a private letter containing information 'from British Officials who are terrified of being suspected of having "let out" the facts'. He named one official who had 'found himself on the first boat home' after saying things he shouldn't have. Among a long list of abuses by the British, he argued with an official statement about the army's search procedures:

> It falsely implies that when a search is to be made, the
> public are warned in advance and instructed to leave all
> doors unlocked. This is by no means the normal
> procedure. A search of which the populace was
> forewarned would obviously be valueless. The more usual
> procedure is that troops swoop suddenly into a town
> before dawn and impose a 'curfew'. There is no formal
> proclamation of curfew whatsoever. Indeed, most of the
> populace are still asleep in bed at the time of its

imposition.... The sound of firing soon arouses the town
to the knowledge of the curfew. The search then
proceeds. In the bazaars all shops were, of course, locked
and shuttered as they were left the night before. No man,
on pain of shooting, is permitted, still less invited, to leave
his house and proceed to the bazaar to unlock his
premises. The procedure then is for the search parties,
each party headed by men bearing heavy firemen's axes, to
proceed to the business areas and smash open door after
door in street after street, and search. All cupboards and
drawers within the shop are likewise forced and the
search naturally involves complete chaos.

Entire streets of shops have thus been smashed open
and left open, thus providing to the searchers, in regard to
empty tills, rifled safes or missing goods, the official reply
'How can you prove we did it? We left the place open after
we had completed the search, and anyone therefore may
be responsible.'[6]

The writer then describes how the residents are treated when
the army searched a district:

Parties of troops move along street by street and house by
house. Each house as they reach it is cleared of its male
inhabitants, who are passed by military patrols to a large
collecting centre usually located in an open square or
space. Here the inhabitants are required to squat or sit on
the pavement. A little drill is at this stage frequently
imparted. The troops explain through an interpreter that
any man standing up without a previous command to do
so will be shot. The command is then given in English
'Up' – then 'Down' – Up, Down, and then a quicker tempo

'Up-Down-Up-Down'. Anyone not quick enough gets a kick up the backside. Due subjection having been thus established en masse, the male populace is interrogated man by man. 'Where do you live? What is your work?' etc. This goes on till dusk, when the balance still uninterrogated are marched off to a prison camp until the morning. Each man, upon satisfying the interrogators as to his bona fides (i.e., that he is not associated with the rebels), is then and there passed on for 'branding'.

At this formality every man is made to roll up the sleeve of his left arm and is branded on the inside of the upper forearm with an impressed indelible ink stamp, the display of which secures him immunity from arrest throughout the remainder of the search. This branding is carried out irrespective of persons – a man may be a judge of the courts, a doctor, a street scavenger or a newspaper boy.[7]

In London on 13 May 1936, Walter Elliott, Minister of Agriculture in the British Cabinet, got in touch with 'Baffy' Dugdale to tell her that the British government had decided that day to send yet another Royal Commission to Palestine, in the light of the disturbances. This was highly confidential information, but there were several 'gentile Zionists' like Elliott in government who were only too ready to pass on Cabinet secrets if it would help the Zionists in their quest to make Palestine their National Home. Elliott had tried to organize a fight in Cabinet against the decision to send a Commission, but 'all the friends so lavish in assurances had given way'. Aware that Elliott was breaking the code of confidentiality by confiding in her, Dugdale urged him to be cautious.[8] Nevertheless, he continued to be a prolific source of Cabinet leaks to the Zionists.

It was announced that the Commission, under Lord Peel, would visit Palestine as soon as the general strike had been called off. This happened in October after an intervention by the neighbouring Arab states. The Commission's brief (by now wearisomely familiar) was to ascertain the causes of the outbreaks of violence in April, to inquire into how the Mandate was being implemented and to make recommendations for removing any grievances that the Arabs or Jews might have. While the Commission was on its way to Palestine, it received news that the Arab Higher Committee had decided to boycott the proceedings. This meant that much of the time the Commission only heard evidence from Jews and British officials, although they visited several different parts of the country, including Arab centres of population, and in the final days of their hearings they did hear from Arab witnesses.

It appeared that one option being considered was some form of division of the country between Jews and Arabs. Jabotinsky, one of the witnesses, rejected this idea: 'A corner of Palestine, a canton – how can we promise to be satisfied with it? We cannot. We never can. Should we swear to you that we should be satisfied it would be a lie.' But the idea was attractive to some members of the Commission, although one of them, addressing a meeting of Jews in London later, explained there was nothing to worry about. Sir Laurie Hammond told them 'that the National Home in Palestine, if you can get sufficient in that country to meet immediate requirements as a Sovereign Power, will be the first step, in my opinion, towards getting back into the rest of the country. It will take many years, but it will come.'[9]

• • •

It's easy to get the impression that the entire country was steeped in conflict during the late 1930s: Arab against Jew, Jew against Arab, Arab and Jew against the British. But even at times of high political tension life went on much as it always had in towns and villages away from the main centres of conflict. Here, normal friendly relations continued between the Arabs and the Jews.

My uncle tells a story of a family trip that went wrong when he was living in Kufr Yassif. The plan was to drive to a village towards the coast to visit a relative of my grandfather's. Tekla was married by then, to her cousin Fayez, who had borrowed a car for the trip. Another cousin, George, who was to marry Ghassan's sister Iqbal, was to be the driver on this journey. Somehow, the entire family – father, mother, children, cousins – crammed into the car, seven or eight people, and they set off. 'On the way, when we reached Nahariyye,' Ghassan told me, 'the car started going forwards and backwards and forwards and backwards, three or four times and then fell on its side. And it was a Jewish town and so the Jews were on their lands surrounding the main road. They rushed to us – a few of us were slightly injured – and they took us to their homes and offered us tea and cake and whatever they had … They were very, very helpful and very nice. As human beings they are very good people.'

As a child, Azmi Audeh, a carpenter's son from Nazareth, was puzzled about 'the Jewish problem' that his parents and relatives talked about. For instance, he recalled that when his father couldn't find enough fresh fish in the Arab market, 'my Dad used to hold my hand and say let us go down the road to the Jewish vendor and buy from him. The Jewish vendor must have had a great memory because the minute he spotted my Dad, he used to welcome him "Ahlan wa-sahlan ya Abu Nasr," welcome, father of Nasr. He used to lead my Dad inside his shop to a stowed away ice box and have him pick his fish from there. That fish was supposedly a very fresh catch. My Dad seemed always to buy from the Jew whenever he went there. Yes, they used to haggle but he always bought the fish.

The Jew looked exactly like us; had the same skin colour, spoke the same Arabic language, dressed exactly like us, and even had the same nose like us. He seemed to be a very nice man and eager to please. So why was this man a problem? This I could not answer.'[10]

Back in London the Peel Commission was preparing a draft of its report, including a recommendation that Palestine be divided into two states, one Arab and one Jewish. When Weizmann heard of this from one of the Commission members, Professor Reginald Coupland, he told a Jewish group: 'Today we laid the basis for the Jewish state.'[11]

On 22 June 1937 'Baffy' Dugdale met Walter Elliott in the Savoy Grill in London. It was about midnight and Elliott handed her a draft of the Peel Commission report for her to study over the dinner table. It was still being discussed by the Cabinet and would not be published for another fortnight.[12] Weizmann requested an advance copy on 1 July but was refused. 'So you want to strangle us in the dark,' he said melodramatically in a phone conversation with W. Ormsby Gore. This was the 'Billy Gore' that 'Baffy' had wanted to reign in J.H. Thomas's stead and she had succeeded. As expected he had been strongly pro-Zionist up till then and refusing to show Weizmann the advance copy of the Peel report was not at all in his Zionist job description.[13] Although Weizmann knew the gist of the report from Dugdale and others, he had to wait until the rest of the world saw the full Peel Commission report on 7 July.

The Commission began by describing the circle they had been asked to square:

> The Arabs of Palestine, it has been admitted, are as fit to
> govern themselves as the Arabs of Iraq or Syria. The Jews
> of Palestine, it is clear, are as fit to govern themselves as
> any organized and educated community in Europe or

elsewhere. Yet, associated as they are under the Mandate, self-government is impracticable for both peoples. Nowhere, indeed, in all the fields in which the Mandate operates is the deadlock so complete as in this last field. Nowhere is it more manifest that the Mandate cannot be fully and honourably implemented unless by some means or other the national antagonism between Arab and Jew can be composed. But it is the Mandate that created that antagonism and keeps it alive; and, as long as the Mandate exists, we cannot honestly hold out the expectation that either Arabs or Jews will be able to set aside their national hopes or fears and sink their differences in the common service of Palestine.[14]

Chapter 23 of the Peel Commission report, headed 'Conclusion', began with the old English proverb 'Half a loaf is better than no bread'. It then laid out the arguments for a proposal which gave some of the land to the Arabs and some to the Jews – what was called 'partition'. This partition of Palestine – first as an idea and later a reality – has been a crucial factor ever since in the continuing dispute between the Arabs and the Jews. For someone who knows nothing about Palestine it is a deceptively persuasive solution. To people like the Sabbagh family and the rest of the Palestinian Arabs in the 1930s and 1940s it was theft, pure and simple.

The members of my family who lived in Safad or Deir Hanna or Kufr Yassif or Tulkarm belonged to a group who still formed 70 per cent of the population, even in the late 1930s after the massive Jewish immigration permitted by the British. What's more, in the northern part of Palestine, where most of my family lived, Arabs still formed about 90 per cent of the population. And yet, in their wisdom, the Peel Commission (and a succession of other cartographers over the next eleven years) were proposing to hand over Arab communities, including Galilee, to Jewish control.

It was not racism behind the anger of the Palestinian Arabs. They would have resisted equally being put under a government of Welsh, Fijians or Chinese – or even Syrians, Iraqis or Saudis. The Peel Commission, and everyone else who tried to solve the problem, missed the one obvious solution (and it would still work today): persuade the Zionists to accept that in the modern world nations solely defined in ethnic terms are by their very nature undemocratic if they include citizens who are not from that favoured ethnic group, and therefore are deprived of their rights. It might have seemed daringly advanced for the time, but would have been consistent with Woodrow Wilson's post-First World War call – for self-determination for nations previously under Ottoman rule – which was almost immediately ignored by the rest of the Allies.

Soon after the Peel Commission published its report, Judah Magnes, Chancellor of the Hebrew University in Jerusalem, warned of the dangers facing the Jews and the Arabs if partition went ahead. In a debate at a Jewish Agency meeting in Zurich, against a background of heckling and jeering, he said: 'What is the Jewish state that is being offered? It is a Jewish State which, in my opinion, will lead to war, to war with the Arabs.' (This statement generated some laughter in the hall.) 'Perhaps the man who laughed has not been through what happened last year,' Magnes went on. 'I was. My sons were. The sons and daughters of my friends were. I see some of my comrades from Palestine here who were. It is not a laughing matter for them .... Why will it lead to war? In the first place because the Jewish state as it is offered to us contains lands about three quarters of which are in the hands of Arabs.'[15]

• • •

In September 1937 one of the English District Commissioners in charge of the Galilee region was murdered outside the Anglican church in Nazareth. The High Commissioner was convinced it was the work of the Mufti and his supporters and ordered their arrest and the disbanding of the Arab Higher Committee. The Mufti fled to Lebanon disguised as an old woman.

Meanwhile the Zionists had been discussing partition. Some of their leaders were inclined to accept the idea. Weizmann had defended it at the 20th Zionist Congress in 1936. He summarized the present position of the Jews with a Talmudic saying: 'If the jug falls upon the stone, woe to the jug. If the stone falls upon the jug, woe to the jug.'[16] Reluctantly he recommended that the conference accept the idea of partition as a step in the right direction, however unpalatable.

Another Zionist leader who supported partition, but for a different reason, was David Ben Gurion, who had been born in Poland and had moved to Palestine at the age of twenty. He had no desire to share Palestine with its Arab inhabitants, but, as he explained in private correspondence, because 'after we become a strong force, as a result of the creation of a state, we shall abolish partition and expand into the whole of Palestine'. He lived to see the State of Israel do precisely that, thirty years later.

Ben Gurion had lived in Palestine for many years and knew the Arabs well. In a speech at the time, in 1938, he said: 'Let us not ignore the truth among ourselves ... politically we are the aggressors and they defend themselves .... The country is theirs, because they inhabit it, whereas we want to come here and settle down, and in their view we want to take away from them their country.... Behind the terrorism [by the Arabs] is a movement, which though primitive is not devoid of idealism and self sacrifice.'[17] Ben Gurion also confided to a friend: 'Were I an Arab, an Arab with nationalist political consciousness ... I would rise up against an immigration liable in the future to hand the country and all of its Arab inhabitants over to Jewish rule. What Arab cannot do his maths and understand that [Jewish] immigration at the rate of 60,000 a year means a Jewish state in all of Palestine?'[18]

One obvious problem with partition was that however Palestine was divided up, there were always Arabs living in any area given to Jews. Peel called this 'the question of the minorities' and said: 'If the settlement is to be clean and final, this question of the minorities must be boldly faced and firmly dealt with. It calls for the highest statesmanship on the part of all concerned.'[19] The phrase 'clean and final' sounds rather sinister to modern ears, and indeed Peel was suggesting some kind of 'ethnic cleansing' of the Arabs from the Jewish area. He cited the example of an exchange of populations between Greece and Turkey after the First World War. 'Before the operation, the Greek and Turkish minorities had been a constant irritant,' he wrote. 'Now the ulcer has been clean cut out and Greco-Turkish relations, we understand, are friendlier than they have ever been before.'

Like the whole enterprise of making Palestine a Jewish state, population transfer was a mad idea. Mad because, to an outsider, there was no moral or legal justification for this course of action, and it would meet the resistance of every single Arab who would be told to leave his home. But Zionism was its own justification – it often seemed (and sometimes seems) as if anything that was good for Jews was permissible, or at least worth thinking about.* And

---

* There is a Jewish joke which sums up this attitude very well. A class of schoolchildren is asked to write an essay on the elephant. The French child writes an essay entitled 'The Love Life of the Elephant'; the English child writes on 'The Good Manners of the Elephant'; the German child writes about 'The Regimentation of the Elephant'. And the Jewish child's essay is entitled 'The Elephant: Is it Good for the Jews?'

transferring the Palestinian Arabs out of Palestine had been on the minds of the Zionists for a long time. As early as the 1920s, shortly after the Balfour Declaration and when the British were thinking about how to reconcile the conflicting claims of Jews and Arabs in some kind of unitary state, Israel Zangwill was writing: 'We cannot allow the Arabs [90 per cent of the population] to block so valuable a piece of historic reconstruction ... And therefore we must generally persuade them to "trek". After all, they have all Arabia with its million square miles ... There is no particular reason for the Arabs to cling to these few kilometres. "To fold their tents and silently steal away" is their proverbial habit: let them exemplify it now.'[20]

With the backing of the Peel Commission to consider the idea, the compulsory transfer of Palestinian Arabs out of their homeland came to the fore in several Zionist meetings and congresses. Nur Masalha, the Palestinian academic, has made a thorough survey of this topic. He has extracted chilling evidence from archives and reports of the extreme attitudes of many Zionists to the indigenous inhabitants of Palestine. And yet, at the time when the Zionists were putting forward such arguments the Nazi persecution of the Jews in Europe was building to a climax. It is difficult to read the following memorandum put before the 20th Zionist Congress in 1937 without seeing similarities with Nazi documents setting out their arguments for the undesirability of a state in which the Jews were allowed to remain.

> I ... insist upon the compulsory transferring of the whole rural Arab population from the Jewish State into the Arab State. It is a preliminary step to the up-building of the Jewish State. At this stage the statesmen concerned with this question will understand the necessity of this

démarche ... The exchange of land and population, alias
the transferring of the Arab rural population, must be
done with the greatest speed possible. This is a
revolutionary act which has to be finished in the shortest
time. The transferring of the Arabs by such numbers in a
long period shall not have the desired effect of freeing the
country from the heavy burden of a second-class citizen
and cheap producers.[21]

These were not isolated comments. As Nur Masalha has pointed
out,[22] expulsion of the Palestinians from their land had become
respectable among major Zionist organizations. Some Zionists felt
that it might be necessary to consider the morality of the procedure, and did so briefly before coming down firmly in favour:

The matter of population transfer has provoked a debate
among us: Is it permitted or forbidden? My conscience is
absolutely clear in this respect. A remote neighbour is
better than a close enemy. They will not lose from being
transferred and we most certainly will not lose from it. In
the final analysis, this is a political and settlement reform
for the benefit of both parties. I have long been of the
opinion that this is the best of all solutions ... But it never
crossed my mind that the transfer to outside the Land of
Israel would mean merely to the vicinity of Nablus. I have
always believed and still believe that they were destined
to be transferred to Syria or Iraq.[23]

Nur Masalha comments: 'The debates of the Jewish Agency
Executive that June in a sense marked the culmination of a process
that had been unleashed by the Royal (Peel) Commission's investigation and report and more particularly by its elevation of the

transfer solution to real possibility and a respectable option, having now received the imprimatur of an official British body. This process involved unprecedented discussion of the transfer solution and its approval in principle by a majority in the most important Zionist policy-making bodies.'[24]

• • •

I thought about the Zionist idea of 'transfer' (or 'expulsion' as it should be called) while visiting the village of Buqei'a, a pretty place on a hillside in northern Galilee in modern Israel. My cousin Aleef had invited me to stay with his family there. His ancestors had lived in Buqei'a for a couple of hundred years. He took me on a tour of the village. A grandfather had lived in this house, an uncle in that. Down one street was an aunt's house and across from the village square was an old building that once belonged to another branch of the Sabbaghs. In the town centre was the village school, founded by Aleef's great uncle. A little way down from the school was the church, where his grandfather, also called Khalil, had been the village priest. Aleef then drove me down to a fertile valley where the Sabbaghs have had olive groves for generations. 'This is my land,' he said, pointing, 'and that grove belongs to my brother.'

What on earth – I thought to myself – did Zangwill believe about the Palestinian Arabs when he made his remark about them 'folding their tents and stealing away'? Or other Zionists who spoke about 'second-class citizens', 'cheap producers' or 'fellahin'? The idea that the hundreds of Sabbaghs, Khourys and other Palestinian Arab families who had lived and farmed in this area for generations would have 'no particular reason to cling to these few kilometres' was foolish enough. That anything short of terror or force would have caused them to 'trek' and exchange the lush hills and valleys of Palestine for the dry wadis and sand dunes of Arabia was a delusion born of contempt.

Another Zionist, Joseph Weitz, spelt out the rationale for the 'transfer' plan:

> It must be clear that there is no room for both peoples in this country. No 'development' will bring us closer to our aim, to be an independent people in this small country. If the Arabs leave the country, it will be broad and wide-open for us. And if the Arabs stay, the country will remain narrow and miserable ... The only solution is ... Israel without Arabs. There is no room for compromise on this point! The Zionist enterprise so far ... has been fine and good in its own time, and could do with 'land buying' – but this will not bring about the State of Israel; that must come all at once, in the manner of a Salvation (this is the secret of the Messianic idea); and there is no way besides transferring the Arabs from here to the neighbouring countries, to transfer them all: except maybe for Bethlehem, Nazareth and Old Jerusalem, we must not leave a single village, not a single tribe ... There is no other way out![25]

15

'LION-CUB OF ARABDOM'

• • •

My father had set off for England in 1937 on a scholarship from the Palestinian government to study history and geography at the University of Exeter. As the eldest son, he was sorely missed by his family. 'When we got a letter from Isa it was like a holiday at home,' my uncle told me. 'Everybody was happy, especially my father. I remember once he sent us a picture. He was on a boat in London on the River Thames. He had a cigarette in his hand and in the letter he wrote – for the eyes of his father who would read it – *I was just carrying the cigarette – I don't smoke.*' My grandfather Khalil was a chain-smoker, but a Palestinian was not allowed to start smoking until he got married.

Isa was a student at Exeter when the BBC began its first foreign language broadcasting service in Arabic to the Middle East. The Arab Rebellion in 1936 had reflected anti-British feeling among Arabs and the deteriorating situation in Palestine generated antagonism to Britain throughout the Arab world. Around the same time, the Italians set up an Arabic-language radio station to attack Britain in the Middle East because of its hostility to the Italian invasion of Abyssinia in 1935. To counteract some of this propaganda, the British government decided to broadcast its point of view to the Arab world.

The inaugural broadcast of the BBC Arabic Service took place on 3 January 1938. News from Palestine: 'Another Arab from Palestine was executed by hanging at Acre this morning by order of a military court. He was arrested during recent riots in the Hebron mountains and was found to possess a rifle and some ammunition ... A small battle took place yesterday between a police force and an armed band at Safad ... A train travelling in the hills near Jerusalem was fired at, but there were no casualties. The IPC [Iraq Petroleum Company] pipeline was damaged, holes being made in two places. A section of railway track was removed today near Jerusalem, but was discovered before any trains passed over.'[1]

These were not of themselves unusual items for Palestine at the time, but the fact that they were being broadcast throughout the Arab world, by the very nation that was the cause of these events, put the Foreign Office and its diplomats around the Middle East in

Isa Sabbagh experiences life as a student in chilly England.

a flat spin. It was unfortunate to say the least that Sir Reader Bullard, the British Minister to King Abdul Aziz Ibn Saud of Saudi Arabia, was at that moment sitting in a tent with the king to listen to the BBC's inaugural broadcast. Sir Reader recalled the result:

> There was silence in the tent and our party broke up without any talk. When I saw Ibn Saud the next day he spoke of the broadcast. For months, he said, he had refused to listen to the Arabic broadcasts from Jerusalem, because he found them so painful, but he had looked forward to the inaugural Arabic broadcast from London, and had filled his tent with his followers so that they might listen too. 'When the announcer spoke of the execution of that Arab in Palestine,' he said, 'they wept and I wept,' and as he spoke a tear rolled down his cheek and he scrubbed it off with his kerchief. 'Now,' he said, 'as a ruler I know that the first business of a government is to maintain order. I also know that no man has been punished in Palestine by the British for his political opinions, but only for some offence against a law. Nevertheless, if it had not been for the Zionist policy of the British government that Arab would be alive today.'[2]

A Foreign Office official, Rex Leeper, was appalled that the BBC had broadcast the truth. 'Is the BBC to broadcast to the Empire the execution of every Arab [to be condemned] in Palestine?' he asked. 'It seems to me unnecessary, though I suspect that it gives their conscience a warm glow.' In fact, as was to be the case, the BBC's resistance to attempts to censor or slant its broadcasts to the Arab world eventually made it essential listening for everyone with a wireless in the Middle East, as the only source of accurate news about the war. It also turned Isa Khalil Sabbagh, my father, into one of the best-known broadcasters in the Arab world for a decade or more.

He was still studying at Exeter when war broke out. In addition to his main subjects of study, history and geography, Isa was passionate about literature, both English and Arabic. A circular came round from the BBC Arabic Service, which was increasing its staff and looking for Arabic speakers who might be interested in working for them. Isa was the only student from his group who replied, sending a sample script, and he was invited to come to the BBC. He recalled the experience later, as part of a US oral-history project: 'They interviewed me and said they liked the script and then they said, "Right-ho, you're going to broadcast it tonight". I said, "What do you mean 'broadcast it tonight?' I thought I was going to record it and then you broadcast it any time you want it."'

Anyway, he went into the studio at the appointed time and did what he was asked. 'When I emerged from the studio, apparently they had been listening in a room without any glass partition, and they wondered how I had told them during that initial interview that I had never seen a studio, that I had never seen a microphone, etc. I told them that I am a person who values truth and it is true. So, I was asked what was I thinking of when I was reading the script. And I said, "Frankly, now that you mention it, I wasn't reading." I had just been speaking the script which I had learnt by heart, of course, and I was thinking of my friends, my family, and so on. In fact, the script was about strange things in the West. Here is a young Arab man, transplanted into a new society, and of course one observes the comparisons, similarities, differences, etc., and that's what the script was all about. And one fellow shouted, "By Jove, you're a born broadcaster!" I said, "Why, how?" And he said, "Because usually people insist on reading the script, and you say you were speaking it." I said, "Exactly, presumably that's what broadcasting is all about."'[3]

• • •

During the First World War, Palestine had been enemy territory for the British. In the Second World War it remained a focus of German and Italian intrigue. It might even have been a target if the Allies' North African campaign hadn't succeeded in keeping Germany out of Egypt. But the aspect of the war that had the most important impact on the fortunes of Palestine and its people was the Nazi persecution of the Jews. Germany's anti-Jewish policies had begun in the 1930s. First the Nazis sought to expel all Jews from Germany, then came the so-called Final Solution: the mass extermination of European Jews. The growing anti-Semitism of Nazi Germany was used by the Zionists to pressure the British government to step up immigration to Palestine. In spite of the arguments of Weizmann and other Zionists that an exclusively Jewish area in Palestine would be a useful foothold, the Zionist Congress eventually rejected the idea of partition. The Palestinian Arabs were also unwilling to hand over the best areas of their country – which were still populated by hundreds of thousands of Arabs – to the Zionists.

There was yet another government commission in 1938. It annulled the Peel recommendations for partition and was followed in 1939 by a round-table conference at which the Arabs refused to sit in the same room as the Jews – in fact, one group of Arabs refused to sit in the same room as another group. All sides presented entirely irreconcilable demands. Faced with this impasse, the Colonial Secretary Malcolm MacDonald declared that His Majesty's Government intended to relinquish the Mandate and to establish a Palestinian state allied to Britain. He produced a White Paper setting immigration targets for Palestine over the next five years of 10,000 a year, plus an immediate influx of 25,000 refugees, but no further immigration without Arab consent. It also provided for political independence and representative government for Palestine within the next ten years.

For the Zionists it signalled the abandonment of any hope that the British government would help them make Palestine into a Jewish state. But now, according to the White Paper, this had never been the intention of the Balfour Declaration anyway. The White Paper attributed this 'mistaken' belief to 'the vagueness of the phrases employed in some instances [in the Balfour Declaration] to describe these obligations [which] has led to controversy and has made the task of interpretation difficult'.[4] It went on: 'His Majesty's Government believe that the framers of the Mandate in which the Balfour Declaration was embodied could not have intended that Palestine should be converted into a Jewish State against the will of the Arab population of the country.' This would have been news to Balfour and Lloyd George, whose views at a private lunch with Weizmann in 1921 had been recorded by Richard Meinertzhagen in his diary: 'L. G. and A. J. B. both said that by the Declaration they always meant an eventual Jewish State.'[5]

The White Paper continued: 'His Majesty's Government therefore now declare unequivocally that it is not part of their policy that Palestine should become a Jewish State. They would indeed regard it as contrary to their obligations to the Arabs under the Mandate, as well as to the assurances which have been given to the Arab people in the past, that the Arab population of Palestine should be made the subjects of a Jewish State against their will.'[6] But this 'anti-Balfour Declaration' was too little too late.

The Zionists saw it as a betrayal, but it was a bad time to be too anti-British. War with Nazi Germany, where Jews were openly persecuted, meant that Britain needed all the support it could get. Ben Gurion, now the head of the Zionist movement, described the course adopted by the Zionists: 'We shall fight the war against Hitler as if there were no White Paper, and we shall fight the White Paper as if there were no war.'

In Germany the early efforts of the Nazis were directed towards expulsion of the Jews rather than their destruction. Adolf Eichmann ran a unit set up to devise the most efficient methods for getting rid of Jews, initially from German-occupied territories and then from Germany itself. He cared little where they went, so long as they left. With stricter British immigration targets for Palestine, the Zionists lobbied the British government to let in more Jews. During the 1930s, the Grand Mufti, Mohammed Amin al-Husseini, was often accused of trying to further his anti-Zionism through links with the Nazis. In an ironic counterpoint to these accusations, Zionist representatives in Austria sat in Eichmann's office and were treated as honoured clients as they haggled over a thousand passports for Jews to leave Austria and evade the British blockade in Palestine that had been set up to deter illegal immigrants. Thanks to this co-operation between the Security Service of the Nazi Party and the Zionist underground, about 17,000 Jews defied the British and entered Palestine illegally from Austria and Czechoslovakia between January and September 1939.[7]

Even more extraordinary is the fact that an underground group of Palestinian Jews, known as the Stern Gang (after their leader, Avraham Stern), approached the Nazis with the offer of an alliance against Britain.

Stern saw the Arabs as 'beasts of the desert, not a legitimate people'. 'The Arabs are not a nation but a mole that grew in the wilderness of the eternal desert. They are nothing but murderers,' he wrote in 1940.[8] Stern and his group – including Yitzhak Shamir, later a Prime Minister of the State of Israel – believed that the Jews were entitled to the entire territory of biblical Israel, which included areas of Egypt and Iraq, and that all the Arabs should be expelled. The Stern Gang proved to be a thorn in the side of the British (and indeed of more moderate Jews and Zionists) as they carried out a campaign of terror from 1936 to 1948. They were part of what was called the New Military Organization (in Hebrew, the Irgun Zvai Leumi or the Irgun for short). Later, after Stern's death, they reformed as a separate group, using even more extreme measures to attack the British.

In 1941 a representative of the Stern Gang travelled to Beirut and met two Germans, one from military intelligence, the other from the German Foreign Ministry. The Irgun had become convinced that Germany and its allies would win the war and they had drawn up a proposal for collaboration. One of its clauses explained that 'Common interests could exist between the establishment of a new order in Europe in conformity with the German concept, and the true national aspirations of the Jewish people as they are embodied by the NMO [The National Military Organization].' This 'new order in Europe in conformity with the German concept' referred to the Nazi plans for a Europe without Jews. The Irgun proposal spelt this out: 'The establishment of the historic Jewish state on a national and totalitarian basis, bound by a treaty with the German Reich, would be in the interest of a maintained and strengthened future German position of power in the Near East.'

The idea was to help Germany defeat Britain as well as to make Palestine a Jewish state: 'The co-operation of the Israeli freedom movement would ... be along the lines of one of the last speeches of the German Reich Chancellor, in which Herr Hitler emphasized that he would utilize every combination and coalition in order to isolate and defeat England [meaning Britain].'

In laying out what it could offer Germany in the immediate future, the Irgun boasted of its well-established credentials: 'The

NMO, whose terrorist activities began as early as the autumn of the year 1936, became, after the publication of the British White Papers, especially prominent in the summer of 1939 through successful intensification of its terroristic activity and sabotage of English property. At that time these activities, as well as daily secret radio broadcasts, were noticed and discussed by virtually the entire world press.'⁹ (I find it interesting that in this official Irgun document the organization describes its own activities as 'terrorist', with an apparent sense of pride.)

The Irgun reflected the views of an aggressive minority of Zionists opposed to the White Paper and the new British position. But the fact that even a small group of Jews was willing to go to such lengths by helping Nazi Germany solve its 'Jewish problem' in this way shows the nature of the opposition Britain was facing in Palestine as it tried to put the new immigration rules into action.

Many Zionists stepped up their efforts to organize illegal immigration into Palestine from Europe and in some cases this led to tragedy. In October 1940 two ships carrying about 3,500 Jews from Europe arrived at Haifa and most were transferred to a single ship, the *Patria*, moored off the coast. However, they were refused entry, since they had no permits. The British announced that they would be taken to detention camps in Mauritius and their fate decided when the war ended. However, the Haganah, the Jewish defence militia in Palestine, attempted to force the issue by sabotaging the *Patria* with a mine so that it could not sail. Unfortunately the damage to the ship was far greater than intended. Instead of remaining afloat but crippled, the *Patria* sank, taking with it more than 200 Jewish passengers. The survivors were allowed to stay in Palestine on compassionate grounds, but the passengers of a third ship to arrive with about 1,800 Jewish refugees were quickly shipped off to Mauritius.

To discourage illegal immigration, the British government warned that it would subtract the number of illegal immigrants they caught from the quotas set out in the White Paper. They also announced that they would imprison illegal immigrants in a detention camp at Athlit, near Haifa. But the British were in a quandary. The world was slowly waking up to the reality of Nazi anti-Semitism and the British imprisonment of Jews fleeing Nazi persecution could only seem callous. Nevertheless, it appeared to be the only way of dealing with the contradiction embodied in the Balfour Declaration and the Palestine Mandate.

Isa Khalil Sabbagh became one of the most famous broadcasters in the Middle East, and featured often in the publication *Arabic Listener*.

This was one of many dilemmas in the Middle East that my father reported on as he settled into his new job at the BBC. He rapidly rose to become the most recognizable voice on the Arabic Service. He made sure that his family back in Kufr Yassif heard his first broadcast by sending them a telegram (in English, since that was the only language the Post Office could deal with). 'My mother didn't know English,' said my uncle. 'Georgette was in Haifa and Iqbal was still at boarding school, so there was nobody to read the telegram for her. So she took it to the wife of the director of our school – everybody knew that she was educated in English – who looked at the cable and said "Oh, this is from Isa, and there is nothing important there, just to say that he is fine and wishes you all the best." My mother said "OK" and she asked me "Why did he send a cable just to tell us that?" And then, when Georgette came back after three or four days, she read it and said "He was telling us he had a show on the air, but now it's too late."'

Isa had a weekly programme, which he wrote and presented, called *Abu Sham* in which he created the character of a Syrian visitor to London describing what he saw and passing on some of the strange ideas the British had about the Arabs. Only one person in Kufr Yassif owned a radio, so Isa's family would listen to that when he was broadcasting. Later they decided to buy one for themselves. There was no domestic electricity in the village and the radio was powered by heavy, acid-filled accumulators which had to be recharged all the time. Soon the whole village would visit their house at the time of Isa's broadcasts. 'Our home became like a Mecca,' my uncle said.

While Isa was in London his father died. Khalil was only sixty or so, but he had suffered from diabetes (a family trait) and heart disease. It was summer and the family was still living in Kufr Yassif, but Khalil had gone to Haifa with his wife to visit his daughters, Tekla and Georgette. 'One day one of my cousins, Atallah or Riz'allah, came and said that we are needed, we have to go to Haifa,' recalled my uncle. 'And we said "Why should we go to Haifa?" Our father and mother were supposed to come back today. And he said "No, that's why I'm here. They decided to stay longer in Haifa." Well, we accepted it, we didn't understand much about it, but Iqbal was suspicious and said "I'm afraid something's wrong." And they said "Oh, there's nothing wrong." We took a cab, which was very expensive at that time and that's what made Iqbal suspicious. Then we heard the cousin saying to somebody "Please tell the rest of the friends that the funeral might be in Safad." Then we knew that he had passed away and we went on to Haifa. Of course we were crying all the way. He was dead by then. Tekla told me later that he had been feeling fine, but he was in bed and he asked her to cook some spaghetti for him. This was a dish he had never liked in his life. I don't know what made him choose spaghetti, but he said "I would like to have spaghetti for lunch." She said OK, and he said "For the time being, get me a glass of milk." Tekla had a maid but the maid was not permitted to serve him. He wouldn't accept it. His daughter or his wife should serve him but not the maid. Tekla went to the kitchen to fetch a glass of milk. It took her two minutes and when she came back he was already dead. It was a heart attack.'

The family sent a telegram to Isa. Shortly afterwards they listened to a play on the BBC that he wrote and acted in, about a soldier who was blinded in the war and came home to find that his father, to whom he was very close, had died while he was away. 'Isa started crying as the character in the play,' Ghassan said, 'but he really cried on air. For outsiders it was a sad enough story, but for us we knew what it meant.'

To avoid Nazi attempts to put the BBC off the air, it was decided just before war broke out to move some departments far away from London into the heart of the English countryside. One day in August 1939, BBC staff in London were told to report early the following morning with a packed suitcase to a rendezvous point in order to travel by bus to an unknown destination. It turned out to be a Victorian country house called Wood Norton Hall, near Evesham in Worcestershire. It was a large house, once lived in by the Duc d'Aumale, fourth son of Louis-Philippe, the last King of

France. It was – and still is – decorated with *fleurs de lys*, symbol of the French Royal family.[10] Among the departments evacuated to Wood Norton Hall were the Arabic Service, where my father worked, and the Variety Department, where a young woman called Pamela Graydon was a secretary.

The local community was required by law to open their doors to this sudden influx of Londoners and to feed and house them. Many of them were foreigners belonging to the BBC's Monitoring Service. They listened to overseas broadcasts for important information about the enemy's morale, intentions and so on. In addition, there were the staff of the foreign language radio services. Some of the BBC staff worked on a shift system, and one evacuee wrote of cycling back to his billet in the early morning: 'The first rays of the sun just touching the swathes of mist over the river and its water meadows; massed clematis and wisterias on cottage walls; the riot of flowers in front gardens; the dew glistening on row upon fertile row of crops – these were impressions to which not even a weary mind could fail to respond. The night ride to work held yet a different magic: blossom-laden orchards shimmering in the moonlight, a silent glassy river reflecting the stars.'[11]

It was in this romantic environment that the young broadcaster on the Arabic Service fell in love with the beautiful secretary in the Variety Department.

16

LOVE AND WAR

• • •

My mother was a lively and sociable young woman of nineteen or
twenty when she arrived at Wood Norton Hall. Born in Brixton,
south London, she had three brothers and two sisters. Her father
was a larger-than-life character, described by my uncle Alec in the
following terms:

> He was American by birth and came from Harrisburg,
> Pennsylvania. Having once visited the place I can
> understand how he came to leave it. His name was
> William Murray Graydon and those of his forebears I am
> aware of were, like him, literary men. One in particular
> had written a history of the constitution of the United
> States, another a large tome about life in eighteenth-
> century Pennsylvania, and yet another was a well-known
> journalist of his day. This particular talent was
> considerably watered down when it finally surfaced in
> William Murray. His forte was boys' adventure stories
> with titles like 'The Perils of Pekin', 'The Fighting Lads of
> Devon' and 'The Butcher of Cawnpore'.[1]

William Murray Graydon also wrote Sexton Blake stories. He was about fifty-six when he fathered his first child with my grandmother Lilian, who was just nineteen. She was a slight, blue-eyed Irishwoman and William Murray seemed to come and go in her life whenever it was time to father another child. He didn't stay long enough for any of them to remember even seeing him. An entry in a directory called *The Men Behind Boys' Fiction* has my American grandfather coming to England with a wife called Pearl and two children. Her death in the late 1930s or early 1940s 'came as a tremendous shock', it says. Probably not as tremendous a shock as Pearl would have had if she'd known there were six more little Graydons in south London.

All that Alec remembered of his father was a trickle of French banknotes coming in an envelope from Paris, where writers congregated in the 1920s. It was clearly not enough to support six children, so they were sent to two orphanages, one for the boys and one for the girls.

The young English secretary, Pamela Graydon, who caught the eye of Isa Khalil Sabbagh when they were both evacuated by the BBC to Evesham in Worcestershire.

Pamela was not educated to a very high level but she must have shown some spark of native wit and intelligence to get a job at the BBC. Evesham was a long way from the bright lights of London, but the young people who converged on the town provided an interesting social mix. The Chief Constable of Worcestershire was indignant when he found some of them sunbathing in the grounds of Wood Norton at a time when 'normal' people were at work. The BBC had established a club with a bar and dance-floor, sports annex and garden, and bathrooms, for those employees whose lodgings failed to offer such things. As more departments came to Wood Norton, there were gramophone concerts, poetry readings and lectures. Then there were the local country pubs, where strong cider and rhubarb wine helped people forget the war for a while – and also, perhaps, their inhibitions.

I've no idea how my parents met, but there was no shortage of opportunities. I like to think of them walking in the wooded grounds around Wood Norton, where couples often strolled in the evening after work. One BBC employee recalled seeing glow-worms in the grass and listening to nightingales singing while searchlights followed the bombers over Coventry or Birmingham.[2]

For Pamela, a south London girl raised in an orphanage, a hand-some Arab with good English and dark brown eyes might appear irresistible, perhaps reminding her of one of her favourite songs, popular at the time, 'The Sheik of Araby'. For Isa, however, his new surroundings bore little resemblance to the Galilee hills and villages of his homeland. The freer customs of English life were very differ-ent from life in a Palestinian family, where your bride was chosen when you were a child and your father could tell you not to smoke.

The first the Sabbagh family knew about Pamela was when they received a telegram from Isa saying 'Everybody is fine'. It was signed 'Isa, Pamela and Khalil'. Even allowing for the difficulties of communication in wartime, it was an unusual way to break the news of his marriage and the birth of his first child. The family was still mourning the loss of my grandfather, but my aunts stopped wearing black when they received the happy news of my birth. My step-grandmother, however, continued to mourn for another ten years.

According to family tradition, Isa should have married a cousin. There were plenty of candidates, given the many branches of the family tree. It was customary when a girl was born to announce which of her male cousins she would marry. Two sisters in Safad had been picked out for Isa and my uncle Ghassan. Indeed, in one of his radio programmes, Isa had read a poem he had written which was actually intended to be heard by his future bride in Palestine.

When telling me about Sabbagh cousin marriages, Ghassan reeled off a whole lot more from memory: 'Uncle Jamil had only one son and seven daughters. His son Boulos was married to his first cousin Fawziyi who was the daughter of uncle Mikhail. Uncle Mikhail had three girls and five boys. The girls are Samira who married her cousin Rizallah; Fawziyi who married her cousin Boulos; and the third is Faizi who is not married to a cousin but to a son of her cousin, ibn Kurjiyi.'

The author and his mother.

Now Isa had broken with tradition, but that was the least of his worries. After all, he was well informed of events in Palestine. He announced them on the news every day. And he had no idea when he would be able to return to his homeland.

• • •

It was clearly not easy for the British government to put the White Paper recommendations into effect. The violence had increased as the Jews in Palestine organized into militias and the Arabs had also decided that violence was the only way to prevent their land from being taken over. In the early 1940s, Arab resistance to the British had diminished, but there were still occasional skirmishes between them. In February 1940, George Mansur, a Palestinian labour leader, wrote angrily to the Colonial Secretary, Lord Lloyd: 'The Military Authorities pursue a mad policy of hunting and torturing our people. Nine Arab villagers of Allar near Tul-Karem were savagely tortured and brutally beaten. Mohammed Shreim died at the spot and another, Nassan Unaini, was conveyed to the Municipal Hospital of Nablus where he died a week later. The Authorities made their investigations and decided to pay £P250 [250 Palestinian pounds] for each of the families of the deceased. This outrageous incident took place about a month ago when active Arab resistance had stopped.'[3]

Although far from the main theatres of war, Palestine was still subject to occasional air raids from the north. Syria was now under the control of the Vichy French, collaborators with the Germans, and the Italian air force had established bases there from which they sometimes attacked Palestine.

The Sabbaghs got on with life as well as they could. In my father's immediate family the only income came from Georgette's work as a teacher. When she married and stopped work, Iqbal took up teaching instead. Ghassan, now in his teens, passed an exam for the Government Arab College in Jerusalem. Although he was underage he was allowed to take his place among the hundred or so students from all over Palestine. Hasib, Isa's cousin, had gone to the American University of Beirut to study engineering. After graduating he returned to Palestine in 1941 to look for work in construction.

When it came to employment, Arabs in Palestine were often overlooked in favour of Palestinian Jews. This happened even with government projects, as a result of continuing Zionist pressure on the Palestinian government. Hasib first tried to get a job as an engineer in the public works department in Jerusalem, but he was offered a salary lower than that of an unskilled worker. He turned it down and went to Tel Aviv, where he applied to a Jewish firm working for the British military. He was asked to fill in some forms stating the salary he required, so Hasib put down what he knew others were making in similar jobs. He was turned down for having asked for too much. After that he decided not to seek any more work in the public sector and turned to private companies. He invested (and lost) a £500 loan in a small engineering company with two other Palestinian Arabs. Then he went into business for himself, starting as a property consultant to three lawyers, one of whom, Ahmad Shuqayri, became the first leader of the PLO in 1964.

Meanwhile, Isa and Pamela found themselves back in London where the worst of the Blitz seemed to be over. They lived in Hendon, where they had a circle of friends from the London Arab community. Isa played poker with them late into the night. Sadly, married life lost its glamour in wartime London. My parents divorced a couple of years after my birth, although my father stayed in London at the BBC for another five or six years.

My mother continued to work for the Variety Department for most of the war and a few years afterward, living with her mother and brothers and sisters in Clapham. She also worked for the American army in London for a while. I have a photograph of her with 150 American servicemen and women taken in Grosvenor Square. There are a few messages written on the back. Betty Lee wrote: *'To little chick who is slowly but surely turning into a hen.'* Eileen Pengelly wrote, rather cryptically: *'To the girl who never plays squat tag in the asparagus bushes.'* Allen Freeman wrote: *'Bitch or no bitch, I still offer 3 pr of stockings.'* And somewhat failing to enter into the flirtatious spirit of the thing, Lieutenant Colonel J. Foley wrote: *'She is a nice girl. Best of luck.'*

My mother's youngest brother Peter told me that a V2 rocket fell on Clapham, and their flat was damaged. He and his sister Kay struggled out of the rubble and tried to help an elderly woman who lived downstairs and had been trapped by a falling wardrobe. Then there was the sound of sirens and hooting. 'It was the Americans,' said Peter, 'in two jeeps full of American soldiers, with Pam in the middle. They'd heard news of the bomb and come to see if they could help.'

In 2002 I received a letter out of the blue from a woman in Wales who had come across my surname in a radio programme I had written. 'As your name is unusual,' she wrote, 'I wondered if, when you were very young, under five in fact, you attended a day nursery in Clapham. Your mother, if it is you, brought you every morning. She was really stunning, blonde and nearly always wore a "shocking pink" coat. We nurses were very envious. You were a handsome boy with fair curly hair.' My mother had died in 1999. She would have loved this memory from more than fifty years ago.

After my parents divorced, Isa became an important figure in the BBC Arabic Service and he was clearly very popular, judging by the postbag he received from Arab listeners, even during the war. The BBC published a magazine called *Arabic Listener* and scattered through its volumes from 1940 to 1948 are photos of my father, microphone in hand, unruly hair, interviewing a famous person or just looking like a film star himself.

He was also an occasional war correspondent on the Western Front, reporting on the progress of the Allied armies. On one such trip he was in a Liberator military transport aircraft, a type notorious for its problems with leaking fuel tanks and midair fires. 'It was a brand new Liberator,' my father recalled, 'and I discovered a fire in the plane. I saw the sparks and thought, "Good God! Common sense would tell me that there's no place for sparks inside an airplane after take-off." The pilot was a beefy American fellow – very nice, he turned out to be. The sky in England was beautiful, unusually blue, and his co-pilot was whistling away through the window, and I went and tapped him at the back of the neck. "Yeah?" he said. I said "This may not be any of my business, but are sparks actually necessary in an airplane?" He said, "Sparks! Where?" I said, "Down by your right foot." He looked and then he started screaming, "Jack! Get that God-damned extinguisher!" And that was the first time I heard that word: "God-damned". And before I knew it, smoke was filling the whole place. I had three colleagues with me from the BBC. The plane went down and all I know is that when I was revived, I was all wet, lying alongside the plane. Thank God I was alive.'[4]

From time to time the London studios of the Arabic Service were rocked by German bombs. A light would flash in the studio saying DANGER – EVACUATE and the announcer on duty would put on a record of a piece of music that was long enough for him to reach an emergency studio in the basement and pick up the programme as if nothing had happened.

• • •

Nineteen forty-two was an important year for the Zionists. A conference of American Zionists at the Biltmore Hotel in New York decided they could no longer rely on British support to achieve a Jewish state in Palestine. They issued a declaration, stating 'their unequivocal devotion to the cause of democratic freedom and international justice', but they then went on to vote for unlimited Jewish immigration to Palestine. Furthermore they denied the 'moral or legal validity' of the White Paper.

It was effectively a declaration of war against Britain. These American Zionists were eventually joined by other Zionist organizations, as well as Jews already living in Palestine. Their military strength had grown as a result of increased recruitment and arms smuggling. The main Jewish military organization in Palestine was the Haganah. The British had declared it illegal and it was often raided by the British army for attacking Arabs as well as the British. But there were two other smaller and much more vicious organizations known by their Hebrew acronyms: Lehi and Irgun. They were originally the same group – Irgun – but the breakaway Lehi was formed after a disagreement over such issues as targeting the British in Palestine and whether to collaborate with the Nazis.

As the British struggled to restrict immigration, the Jewish extremists attacked British civil and military installations in Palestine. As a result, many of them ended up in prison or were deported. The situation grew nastier by the day and the Zionists with influence over other governments – especially that of the United States – painted Britain in the blackest terms.

American President Franklin D. Roosevelt's knowledge of the Middle East was pretty shaky. He believed what he had been told by the Zionists – that Britain had reneged on a firm promise it had made to hand over Palestine to the Jews. He resolved to look at the

Palestine question in more detail and come up with a solution. In a rambling conversation with a neighbour in 1942, Roosevelt set out his ideas:

> What I think I will do is this. First, I would call Palestine a religious country. Then I would leave Jerusalem the way it is and have it run by the Orthodox Greek Catholic Church, the Protestants and the Jews – have a joint committee run it ... I actually would put a barbed wire around Palestine, and I would begin to move the Arabs out ... I would provide land for the Arabs in some other part of the Middle East ... Each time we move out an Arab we would bring in another Jewish family ... But I don't want to bring in more than they can economically support ... It would be an independent nation just like any other nation ... Naturally, if there are 90 per cent Jews, the Jews would dominate the government ... There are lots of places to which you could move the Arabs. All you have to do is drill a well, because there is this large underground water supply, and we can move the Arabs to places where they can really live.[5]

Astonishingly, after more than twenty years of international debate about the 'Palestine question', the leader of the United States had only a tenuous grasp of Middle East history and geography. He seemed unaware that Islam played a major role in Palestinian society, and thought of Palestinian Arabs merely as nomads who could be deprived of their land and moved anywhere at will, provided there was a well.

• • •

My father's broadcasting career sharpened his love for the Arabic language and he had many opportunities to show off his talents in this area. Most of the presenters and newsreaders in the Arabic Service were Egyptians, and Isa was always correcting their mistakes – he even went to the trouble of making detailed notes, which he showed the director of the department, in a black note-book filled over two months with the time, date, name of broadcaster and subject matter, the mistake and his suggested correction. 'Don't take my word for it,' he told the director. 'Please send it to their own university, Al-Azhar, in Cairo.' Two months later the director called a meeting and announced that he had done exactly that. Al-Azhar had confirmed that the Egyptian broadcasters were making mistakes and congratulated Isa on his corrections. My father was promoted to the most senior rank for a foreigner in the BBC's foreign language services.

Listeners wrote from the Middle East to say that his 'beautiful diction attracts Arab hearts', and one admirer called him, somewhat obscurely, 'the lion-cub of Arabdom'.[6] Isa's fame in the Arab world led to him being brought out to greet distinguished visitors, including Prince Feisal Ibn Saud of Saudi Arabia and his brother Prince Khaled, both of whom later became kings of Saudi Arabia and Isa's good friends.

In Palestine in 1944 the illegal activities of some Palestinian Jews turned to political assassination. On 6 November two members of the Stern Gang killed Lord Moyne, a British minister of state, in Cairo. It was the opening shot in what was called 'The Season', when the more extreme Jews attacked the British. Moderate Jews reluctantly helped the British to track them down and round them up. Lord Moyne's murderers were sentenced to death. At their trial they said they had killed him as a warning to the British not to interfere with future immigration to Palestine.

In May 1945 the Second World War finally ended in Europe, though fighting continued in the Far East until the surrender of Japan in August. In a live broadcast to the Arab world from Trafalgar Square in London, my father referred to the possibility of another war if statesmen failed to learn their lessons from this one. This remark led to him being hauled up before the Director of External Services in the BBC and given a reprimand.

As the Allied armies swept through Europe, the full horror of the organized Nazi slaughter of the Jews came to light when the concentration camps were opened and the survivors liberated. There were hundreds of thousands of them, and as they filled what were called displaced persons camps, the Zionists told the world that there was only one place these people wanted to go.

17

DISPLACED PERSONS

• • •

In the files of the Harry Truman Library in the United States there is a proposal from an organization of American Jews suggesting what might be done with those Jews who survived the Nazi camps. Dated 4 December 1945, it is a reminder that there *were* voices of moderation in the Jewish community at this time.

Lessing J. Rosenwald, the president of the American Council for Judaism, was very critical of the insistence by Zionists that Jewishness was a national as well as a religious characteristic. He insisted that Palestine was 'the homeland of its own citizens only, and not of all Jews'. 'The future of the displaced Jews in Europe continues in uncertainty,' wrote Rosenwald. 'Their plight – with the rigors of winter ahead – remains desperately tragic. Meanwhile, conditions in Palestine have reached a stage alarming to the peace of the world. We have had sabre-rattling, boycott, recriminations, rioting, bloodshed, and threats of still more blood-shed ... It is high time to call a halt to this dangerous course.'[1]

The Council called for a UN Declaration that Palestine should not be Muslim, Christian or Jewish, but a state where people of all faiths could play their part. Immigration procedures should be controlled by representatives of all the inhabitants of Palestine, on the basis of the capacity of the country to absorb new citizens. Then, said the Council, there should be an international commission to devise appropriate institutions for home rule. All of these were sensible suggestions – not that any of them would have been acceptable to the Zionists.

The American Council of Judaism made proposals for dealing with the problem of the displaced Jews. The notion of a Palestine that was not exclusively Jewish should be made known to the surviving Jews. On the basis of such knowledge, a poll should be taken in which they indicated their preferences for where they would like to be resettled. An international commission would then try to organize that resettlement as closely as possible to the preferences of the survivors.

How simple, logical and just it sounds. Indeed, many Holocaust survivors did not want to go to Palestine and would have preferred to emigrate to the United States, Canada or Britain. But those potential havens for the Jews resisted, pushing the entire burden on to the population of Palestine. The Palestinians are the victims of the victims, said Edward Said. The Palestinian Arabs were in no way responsible for the Holocaust, but some of the survivors of that atrocity victimized them by denying them self-government. The Palestinian Arabs paid a heavy price for the evils of Nazism.

Zionist emissaries visited the displaced persons camps to 'invite' the Jews to come to Palestine. While they hoped to find homes for the Holocaust survivors, they were also trying to bring about the National Home against the will of the British by increasing the proportion of Jews in Palestine as quickly as possible. There was less value to Zionism in settling the Jews in other countries, and so threats and intimidation were sometimes used to persuade European Jews to opt for Palestine. Astonishingly, in 1938, as news of the Nazi camps began to leak out, Ben-Gurion had observed:

'If I knew that it was possible to save all the Jewish children of Germany by transporting them to England, and only half by transferring them to the Land of Israel, I would choose the latter, for before us lies not only the numbers of these children but the historical reckoning of the people of Israel.'[2]

Jewish immigration to Palestine was orchestrated by many Zionist groups in the camps. They provided invaluable aid to the survivors, but were also recruiting new immigrants for the National Home in Palestine. A British general, Sir Frederick Morgan, spoke out about this topic and was subjected to a barrage of Jewish criticism in Britain and America. The World Jewish Congress stated officially that 'General Morgan's allegation of "a secret Jewish force inside Europe aiming at a mass exodus to Palestine" is fantastically untrue.' But a modern researcher, Peter Grose, has confirmed that Morgan was right and there was 'an organized plan, operating in defiance of civil and military occupation authorities, aimed at transporting the surviving Jews out of Europe, whether they were in a condition to want it or not, to Palestine'.[3]

In spite of Zionist efforts to persuade them, only 10 per cent of the three million Jews left in Europe ended up settling in Palestine.[4] An American envoy to the camps, Earl Harrison, reported to US President Harry S. Truman: 'Palestine is definitely and pre-eminently the first choice.'[5] A few months later, David Niles, a White House aide and a committed Zionist, admitted that Harrison did not have the necessary evidence to support this statement. The picture was far more complex than Harrison had picked up in one brief visit. Many Polish Jews who wanted to return to Poland and other groups who were anti-Zionist refused to bow to Zionist pressure to settle in Palestine.[6] 'What if Canada, Australia, South America, England and the United States were all to open a door to some migration?' asked Morris Ernst, a prominent

Two midwives of the State of Israel, President Harry Truman and Chaim Weizmann.

non-Zionist Jew in New York. 'Only a minority of the Jewish DPs [displaced persons] would choose Palestine.'[7]

American intelligence reports also revealed that many German-Jewish refugees who had fled the Nazis by escaping to Palestine wanted to return to Germany now that the war was over. In the British House of Commons, Ernest Bevin, the Foreign Secretary of the new Labour government, asked if it was really right 'that the Jews should be driven out of Europe'. Even Winston Churchill, a staunch Zionist for the last thirty years, said that 'the idea that the Jewish problem could be solved or even helped by a vast dumping of the Jews of Europe into Palestine is really too silly to consume our time in the House this afternoon'.[8] Nevertheless, the official Zionist agencies in Britain and the United States continued to insist that the remnant of Europe's Jews wanted to live in Palestine and that this was the only solution to their tragic situation.

There were good reasons why some Jews might not have wanted to go. Having lived in, and survived, a country at war, they were now being asked to go to another country that was, to all appearances, also at war. There were also much more attractive places to live than the hot, dusty, impoverished country of Palestine. In addition, many of the Jews who had suffered persecution in Europe were intellectuals or professionals and didn't want to respond to Zionist pressure to become farmers or labourers in Palestine. They knew that in the US or Canada they could continue with their old occupations rather than face further unnecessary disruption. To divert European Jews to Palestine, Jewish communities in the US, Canada and Australia – where many of the European Jews really wanted to go – had been asked by the Zionist organizations to refrain from lobbying their governments to let them in. In fact, it would have required heavy lobbying to persuade the American government to increase their immigration quotas. All through the war, as the news leaked out of the Nazi horrors, America set its face against making special efforts to offer sanctuary to Jews.

The year before the sinking of the *Patria*, the United States had refused entry permission to 900 Jewish refugees from Germany on a ship called the *St Louis*. Instead, they sent the *St Louis* back to Germany, to the terrible situation they had tried to flee. Early in the war, the United States had also rejected a Swedish proposal that they should take 20,000 Jewish children from Germany, as well as refusing to open up Alaska to Jewish immigration. A postwar US army memorandum warned against allowing Jews even into the American zone of occupied Germany, saying that 'every Zionist-indoctrinated Jew who arrives in the American zone is an unconscious asset to Moscow'. It was a reflection of a mindset that had blamed the Russian Revolution on Russian Jewry.

About the same time as the Labour party swept to power in Britain in 1945, Harry S. Truman became President of the United States, after the sudden death of Roosevelt. Unfortunately, Truman's understanding of Palestine was as inadequate as Roosevelt's. When a group of ambassadors from the Middle East tried to brief him on the nuances of the Palestine situation, Truman dismissed them. 'I am sorry, gentlemen, but I have to answer to hundreds of thousands who are anxious for the success of Zionism. I do not have hundreds of thousands of Arabs among my constituents.'[9]

The new governments in Britain and the United States brought with them an era of yet more inquiries, commissions and investigations into the Palestine situation. An Anglo-American Committee of Inquiry visited Palestine in 1946 at a time when Jewish terrorist activities were increasing against the British. On 23 April an Irgun force attacked a British police station and kidnapped one of the occupants. Two days later, the Stern Gang killed seven British paratroopers. 'Despite their official condemnation of terrorism,' wrote A. J. Sherman, 'the Jewish community were virtually united in refusing to reveal the whereabouts or identities of terrorists ... British police and troops, baffled and frustrated by this display of solidarity, were infuriated by the disparity between the Jewish Agency's public pronouncements and their knowledge, gleaned from having broken the Agency's cypher, that there was in fact coordination between the Agency's officials and senior officers in the Haganah, if not both Irgun and the Stern group.'[10]

Ben-Gurion was one of the witnesses before the Anglo-American Committee of Inquiry. He was asked whether the Jewish Agency and the Haganah supported the acts of sabotage being carried out against the British police and army. He lied and emphatically denied any connection with such acts.[11]

The Committee returned from the Middle East with a set of recommendations for unrestricted immigration and a bi-national state. The British government rejected the idea. Then came the Morrison-Grady plan, devised by Herbert Morrison, Deputy British Prime Minister, and an American Ambassador, Henry

Grady. It recommended immediate entry of 100,000 Jewish refugees and the federalization of Palestine, with a small Jewish enclave and a larger Arab one. The British and American governments accepted these recommendations, but the Zionists rejected them.

In June 1946 the British Foreign Secretary Ernest Bevin upset the Americans by saying that the reason they wished to see 100,000 Jews in Palestine was because they 'did not want too many Jews in New York'.[12] This uncomfortable truth merely added to the strain between the British and US governments over Palestine. In turn, the Americans criticized Britain for restricting Jewish immigration to Palestine. The British MP (and Zionist) Richard Crossman was outraged. 'Why should these people from a safe position across the Atlantic lambast my country for its failure to go to war with the Arabs on behalf of the Jews?' he asked. 'America was not prepared either to receive the Jews from Europe or to risk a single American soldier to protect them in Palestine.'[13]

All this time the Zionist extremists in Palestine were stepping up their pressure with a series of ever more hideous terrorist attacks on the British administration and its army, which was only trying to keep order. In one week in November 1946, nineteen people (eleven British and eight Arabs) were killed in Palestine by land mines and suitcase bombs laid by Jewish terrorists. Two months later, they attacked in five different cities, using bombs, machine guns and flame throwers. In the same month, a Haganah spokesman proudly announced that more than 200,000 Jews had immigrated illegally into Palestine in the last fifteen months.

There were three separate Jewish paramilitary organizations all trying in their own ways to attack the British. The largest was the Haganah, a well-regimented, well-supplied force which carried out such anti-British operations as liberation of interned immigrants from the Athlit camp, bombing of the country's railroad network, and sabotage operations on British police stations. It also assisted with the organization of illegal immigration. They liked to be seen as more ethical than the other two illegal paramilitary groups, the Irgun and the Stern Gang, although in fact the Haganah usually refrained from terrorism for political rather than ethical reasons, seeing it as bad for their public relations to be killing soldiers and civilians in cold blood.

• • •

When the Second World War ended, my father returned to Palestine for the first time in nearly ten years. It was not a pleasant place to be. A visiting United Nations Commission described the situation: 'The atmosphere in Palestine today is one of profound tension. In many respects the country is living under a semi-military regime. In the streets of Jerusalem and other key areas barbed wire defences, road blocks, machine-gun posts and constant armoured car patrols are routine measures. In areas of doubtful security, Administration officials and the military forces live within strictly policed security zones and work within fortified and closely guarded buildings. Freedom of personal movement is liable to severe restriction and the curfew and martial law have become a not uncommon experience.'[14]

One day my uncle Ghassan, a customs officer in Haifa, received a phone call from Isa who had just arrived in Palestine and was staying in Jerusalem. Isa explained that he would be coming to Haifa on a certain day at a certain time, using a certain taxi company. The family was overjoyed and the news spread quickly. At the appointed hour a large crowd gathered outside the offices of the taxi company. By then, Isa was famous throughout the Middle East, and so in addition to close family members there were more distant relatives and many well-wishers. 'Something like two, three, four, five hundred people were there – God knows how many,' Ghassan told me. 'The traffic stopped and everything. We went to the taxi cab company to meet Isa and take him home.' Unfortunately my father wasn't there. He'd been called away on a BBC assignment at the last minute, but he did get to Haifa the following day, to be greeted by a smaller crowd. 'Only a couple of hundred,' Ghassan said.

Isa's cousin Hasib was now a successful businessman in Haifa. By 1945 he had established himself and set up an engineering company, the Consolidated Contractors Company, with several partners. In spite of many vicissitudes – the first of which would be the disappearance of Palestine – he is still at the head of the company today, controlling an annual turnover of $1.4 billion.[15]

The King David Hotel in Jerusalem, after being bombed by
Jewish terrorists in 1946, killing 91 people.

Political efforts and government inquiries were getting nowhere
and the situation in Palestine was going from bad to worse, despite
the mass arrests of suspected terrorists. In London the political
Zionists still had their supporters in Parliament. In the House of
Commons in July, Richard Crossman said: 'No Jew anywhere can
be won over to support the Government by the arrests of thousands
of their brothers. It is impossible to crush a resistance movement
which has the passive tolerance of the mass of the population.'[16]
This could equally apply to the situation in Palestine today.

Jewish weapons and arms dumps were discovered; more ships
laden with illegal immigrants arrived at Haifa and were turned
away; there were curfews and mass arrests in Jewish areas; land
mines exploded under official vehicles; and bombs were directed
against British targets outside Palestine. In February 1947 the
British government asked the Jewish Agency to call on the Jewish
community to cooperate with the police and army to bring the
terrorists to justice. On behalf of the Jewish Agency, Golda Meir
publicly rejected this request. Meir, Menachem Begin, head of the
Irgun, Yitzhak Shamir and Ben-Gurion all eventually became
Prime Ministers of the State of Israel. In that position, they were
outraged that some Palestinian Arabs should resort to terrorism.

On occasion the Haganah coordinated their activities with the
Irgun and the Stern Gang; most notably when the Irgun blew up
the King David Hotel in Jerusalem, then used as the British headquarters. The first plan devised by the Irgun (led by Menachem
Begin) was considered by Haganah too ambitious. They changed
their minds after the British raided Jewish Agency headquarters
and arrested many of the leaders. Documents were discovered by
the British army which revealed the secrets of Haganah-Irgun
collaboration so long denied by Ben-Gurion. These documents
were taken back to the King David Hotel. Now the Haganah were

eager to destroy them before they could be analysed in any detail.

Two days after the raid, at the end of June 1946, Begin received the go-ahead from the Haganah command. Three weeks later, using milk churns full of explosives smuggled into the hotel's basement, the terrorists destroyed an entire wing of the building, killing ninety-one people – British, Arabs and Jews – and injuring many more. 'We particularly mourned the alien civilians whom we had no wish to hurt,' said Begin in his memoirs, 'and the fifteen Jewish civilians, who had so tragically fallen.' Haganah and the Irgun denied responsibility for the deaths and injuries. They said that the British should have evacuated the hotel after a telephoned warning about fifteen minutes before the explosion. But the British received such warnings every day and there was nothing to distinguish this one from just another hoax call.

As so often happens, this terrorist act planted dragon's teeth. In the 1980s the *Washington Post* carried an interview with a Palestinian Arab serving an eighteen-year jail sentence in Israel for terrorism offences. His father had been killed in the Jewish terrorist attack on the hotel in 1947.[17]

Ernest Bevin, the British Foreign Minister, made one last attempt to save the deteriorating situation early in 1947, with yet another plan for Palestine. It proposed an extension of British control for another five years, after which Palestine would become independent. A further 100,000 Jewish immigrants would be allowed and a joint Arab-Jewish advisory council would be set up. Arabs and Jews rejected the plan. In the face of mounting Jewish terrorism in Palestine, the British government requested a special session of the General Assembly of the United Nations. The UN was only two years old, the successor to the League of Nations, whose acceptance of an unworkable Mandate had been one reason for the problem in the first place. It was about to face its first major test.

18

UNSCOP AND ROBBERS

• • •

One September morning in 2003 I visited the Citadel in Acre, the former fortress of Daher al Omar. Now it is an Israeli tourist attraction. In the well-kept grounds there were a group of Jewish schoolchildren, a small band of Japanese visitors with a guide, and a gardener watering the flowerbeds. The building was normally open as a museum, although only a small part dealt with pre-twentieth-century history. Its main offering to visitors is the Museum of 'Heroism', with displays praising the activities of anti-British Jews in the 1940s.

It turned out that the Citadel was closed for renovations, but a helpful member of staff told me they had kept open the room with the gallows used by the British for executions. A young woman in a dark blue uniform led me up a ramp and into an inner courtyard. We went through a strong metal door and up some steps. There was an ante-room with photos on the wall of nine Jews, described as 'martyrs', who had been hanged in the room next door. The room itself had a noose hanging from the ceiling, artfully lit to produce a sinister shadow on the wall. Below the noose was a wooden floor with an open trapdoor to a stone floor five or six feet below. There was an Israeli flag in one corner and a fake flame lamp near the trapdoor.

I asked my guide about the nine 'martyrs' whose pictures were in the next room.

'Why are they "martyrs"?' I asked. 'Didn't they murder people?'

'No, no!' she said, outraged at my suggestion. 'None of them murdered anyone.' Then she paused, and added as an after-thought, 'Well, one of them killed an Arabic person ...'

The Jews who attacked the British and Arabs in Palestine in the 1940s were emulated by later generations of terrorists, including members of the PLO, Hamas, the Al-Aqsa Brigade and al-Qaeda.* Like the Irgun and the Stern Gang, these groups do not think of their victims in the same light as themselves, with the same humanity and the same rights. Just as the victim of the terrorist hanged in Acre was seen as a legitimate target because he was only 'an Arabic person', so the people killed in the atrocities on 11 September 2001 were considered legitimate targets because of their 'otherness' from the Islamic fanatics who carried out the deed. But there is a second aspect of modern terrorism that harks back to Jewish terrorism in the 1940s: the belief that it will work, that it will bring about change. Events in Palestine in the late 1940s prove that relentless and atrocious acts have led governments to 'give in to terrorism', even after they have said they won't.

In 1947, as part of its discussions about what to do with Palestine, the United Nations General Assembly considered whether the future status of Palestine and the problem of the Jewish refugees were linked. One European delegate protested at this idea: 'It must be manifest to everybody that the only effect of linking together these two problems is to render more difficult the

---

* It is worth noting that the first ever hijacking of a civilian airliner was carried out by the Israeli government in 1954. In an attempt to gain the release of two Israeli spies captured by Syria, Israel brought down a Syrian airliner and held its innocent passengers as hostages.

Daher al Omar's Citadel in Acre, later used by
the British as a prison for Jewish terrorists.

solution of each. It is evident that the appalling tragedy of the homeless Jews in Europe makes it much more urgent to find a solution to the question of Palestine, as long as Palestine is considered to be the only place where Jewish refugees can find a home. This problem of Jewish homelessness can only be eased if the Member States will grant Jewish refugees a temporary or a permanent home.'[1]

One of the Arab delegates said: 'The Arabs of Palestine are not responsible in any way for the persecution of the Jews in Europe. That persecution is condemned by the whole civilized world, and the Arabs are among those who sympathize with the persecuted Jews. However, the solution of that problem cannot be said to be a responsibility of Palestine, which is a tiny country and which had taken enough of those refugees and other people since 1920 … Any delegation which wishes to express its sympathy has more room in its country than has Palestine, and has better means of taking in these refugees and helping them.'[2]

But such clear thinking had no effect. Early in 1947, the General Assembly voted to send one more committee out to Palestine to make definitive recommendations for how the Palestine problem should finally be dealt with, and in the committee's brief the issue of the Jewish refugees was firmly linked with Palestine.[3] The United Nations Special Committee on Palestine (UNSCOP) consisted of eleven delegates from among the member states of the UN. They set off in spring 1947 to visit Palestine and Europe, armed with 'the widest powers to ascertain and record facts, and to investigate all questions and issues relevant to the problem of Palestine'.

The Palestinian Arabs refused to meet yet another committee. It seemed to them that the committee was founded on the premise that some way had to be found to get as many European Jews as possible into Palestine. The Arabs still made up two thirds of the population, despite massive immigration over the last decade, not all of it legal. The Zionists saw it as yet another opportunity to press their claim that they had a 4,000-year-old right to the land.

David Ben-Gurion criticized the British for failing to hand over Palestine to the Jews and announced that 'we are entitled to Palestine as a whole'. The British government responded by pointing out to UNSCOP that, as the Balfour Declaration had mandated, it *had* established a 'national home' in Palestine, where a huge number of Jews now lived. 'The denial of this fact, the concealment of the truth and the failure to recognize that there was ever any reason for granting the most extreme Jewish demands in the face of bitter opposition from the inhabitants of the country must appear to all impartial observers as at least a gross self-deception.'[4]

When Chaim Weizmann appeared before the committee, he warned the members that it would not be easy for the Jews to accept the sort of partition recommended in the 1939 White Paper. He and the Zionists had rather hoped for a territory eight times larger.[5] In fact, he had earlier explained to one of Churchill's private secretaries that he felt some kind of partition would be acceptable, since 'it was possible to take two bites at the cherry. So long as sufficient elbow room was given at the start, he did not see why all the burden should fall on the present generation and why one could not look to the possibility of future expansion *by some means or other.*'[6]

While UNSCOP was in Palestine, the Irgun kidnapped two British sergeants and held them hostage. They wanted to persuade the British not to execute three Irgun members who had been found guilty of terrorist offences by a British military court. Two UNSCOP members managed to evade the British police and visit Menachem Begin, the leader of the Irgun. When one of them pointed out that the British sergeants had nothing to do with the sentencing of the Irgun members, Begin merely said, 'They are soldiers of an army invading our soil.'[7] One of these UNSCOP members was Ralph Bunche, a black American. After hearing the Zionists' arguments, he confessed that his own feelings as a black man had been awakened in 'emotional identity'. As he was leaving Begin's hideout, he said something that the terrorist leader (and future Israeli Prime Minister) never forgot: 'I can understand you. I am also a member of a persecuted minority.'[8]

The British executed the Irgun men and Begin's organization murdered the two British sergeants, booby-trapping the body of one of them to try to kill the rescuers. Appalled by this event, British police ran amok in Tel Aviv in retaliation, killing five Jews and committing other acts of violence. No British policeman or soldier was prepared to identify the culprits and no criminal charges were subsequently brought.[9]

In Britain, the regular deaths of British soldiers and administrators in Palestine horrified a war-weary public who wondered why Britain was still in Palestine. 'Why should British soldiers continue to be exposed to this kind of killing?' asked *The Economist* magazine. 'Why should the British community bear the cost?... The cost of Palestine to Britain is incalculable.'[10] 'By February 1947,' writes Ilan Pappe, 'Britain had had enough.' There were other pressures on the British government. 'A particularly hard winter in 1946–7 and a harsh American attitude towards Britain's debt to the United States, created an economic crisis in Britain that served as an incentive for a limited process of decolonization, mainly in India and Palestine.'[11]

Meanwhile, UNSCOP members heard complaints from a Palestinian Jew called Levitsky about the British, in particular the emergency regulations they had brought in to try to fight Zionist terrorism. The UNSCOP commission reported Levitsky's complaint: 'What do you think of a country in which a military commander can place any person or family under police supervision for a year if he suspects that a weapon has been discharged in their premises? He can do even more – he can order their deportation, confiscate their home, even sentence them to death. He can order the destruction of any house in any street in which a shooting occurs.' He went on: 'And these are not uncommon at all ... I know of hundreds of such cases – families ejected, furniture thrown out on the street, houses destroyed, simply because weapons have been discovered in them.' 'As I listened,' wrote the UNSCOP member detailing Levitsky's grievances, 'I grew more and more indignant until I could scarcely contain myself.'[12] He would no doubt have been equally indignant to discover that all of these measures were to be used by the government of Israel against Palestinians.

The UNSCOP committee also visited displaced persons camps in Europe. A Zionist official at one of them said that he considered all European Jews to be 'Palestinian citizens in exile', therefore Palestine should be treated as having a Jewish majority – a sort of majority-in-waiting.[13] A rabbi working in the camps told him of the difficulties he had had persuading other countries to take Jews who wanted to settle there. 'I have peddled my wares through many capitals of the world,' he said, 'and while I have not found a lack of sympathy, I have gotten no results.'[14] However, UNSCOP found evidence that the people running the camps were also colluding with the Zionist groups that were organizing illegal immigration to Palestine. A journalist asked one of the International Refugee Organization officials about a group of children who had gone missing from the camp and turned up on an illegal immigrant ship. The official replied that the children had gone on a picnic and never returned.

'Isn't it rather unusual to allow them to go off on picnics by themselves? I mean, aren't security precautions taken. Doesn't a member of your staff go along?'

The official nodded. 'We sent along one of our staff,' she said. 'He did not return, either.'[15]

After their intensive tour of Palestine and post-war Europe the UNSCOP committee gathered to discuss their recommendations. It was not an easy task.

To the Palestinian Arabs, of course, the issue was simple, as they constantly tried to explain. They still formed a large majority in Palestine, yet they were the only indigenous population in the former Ottoman empire not to be granted independence. They hoped the UNSCOP commission would find the best way to reconcile the interests of all the inhabitants of Palestine in a fair and equitable form of government. They had been willing to accept as much since the end of the First World War. Most modern nations have citizens who are members of minority groups. Most national governments try to treat all citizens equally and come down hard on any form of institutionalized bias in favour of one group over another. Any departure from this ideal situation is condemned by the international community. Indeed, that is what the human rights movement was set up to monitor and identify.

It would have been possible at any time between 1917 and 1947 to devise a form of democratic government for Palestine. It is wrong to say (as was often said at the time) that the Arabs and the Jews were irreconcilable and therefore had to be given separate states. Unfortunately, this is how the UNSCOP commission saw it. 'The basic conflict in Palestine is a clash of two intense nationalisms,' they reported. 'There are now in Palestine some 650,000 Jews and some 1,200,000 Arabs who are dissimilar in their ways of living and, for the time being, separated by political interests which render difficult full and effective political co-operation among them, whether voluntary or induced by constitutional arrangements.'[16]

This reads as if it is a balanced description of the two communities and their interests, but it fails to recognize that the 650,000 Jews are dissimilar from the Arabs only because most of them came from and imported an alien culture. The small proportion of Jews who had lived in Palestine for centuries were very similar to the Arabs, apart from in their religious practices. In this respect, they were no more dissimilar to the Arabs than the Arab Christians were to the Arab Muslims, and no one ever suggested that the 10 per cent Arab Christians should govern Palestine over the 90 per cent of Muslims and Jews.

The Zionists sought an entirely Jewish state; the Arabs did not ask for an entirely Arab state. They had lived for centuries with Palestinian Jews among them. They could even have lived

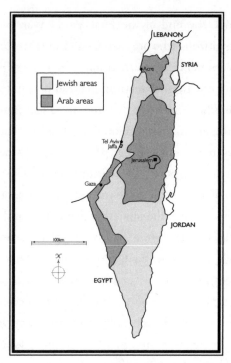

The Jewish state proposed by the UN partition plan would have a population that was half Jewish, half Arab and would place half a million Arabs under Jewish rule.

peacefully with a reasonable number of immigrant Jews in the 1920s and 1930s if those Jews had merely wanted to live in a demo-cratic Palestine. But they were Zionists. They wanted to live in a Jewish Palestine with a predominantly European culture.

The accounts given by UNSCOP members in their memoirs and the commission's final report, show that most of them never grasped this point. They assumed the Palestinian Arabs would accept no solution that allowed Jews to live in Palestine. In fact, the only solution they would not accept was complete Jewish control over part or all of Palestine, where many hundreds of thousands of Arabs were living. Unfortunately, that was the only solution the Zionists would accept.

The UNSCOP commission was no more successful in dealing with the problem than any of the other groups of well-meaning but often naive Westerners who had visited Palestine in the previous thirty years. Their 'solution' was the partition of Palestine into two different states: a Jewish state and an Arab state. Such a plan was almost as difficult to implement as it would be to partition Britain into one territory for people with red hair and another territory for the rest. Although there were exclusively Jewish communities in Palestine, there were no large swathes of Jewish-occupied territory. As the UNSCOP members sat down with their maps and coloured pencils they began to realize that they faced an impossible task. Here's how one member of UNSCOP described the process, with the different committee members' names in bold:

> **Fabregat** wanted the Jewish State to include the whole of Galilee, the Negev west of Beersheba, and a large indentation connecting the coastal plain with Jerusalem. The Jewish part of Jerusalem would become part of the Jewish State. He proposed that Jaffa should be an enclave in the Arab State.
>
> **Rand** thought Jerusalem and its environs should be an international city, part neither of the Jewish nor the Arab State.
>
> My position [**Jorge Garcia-Granados**] was the same as Rand's, but I did not agree to his idea of a free city of Jerusalem, keeping that as a future bargaining asset.
>
> **Lisicky** thought the Jewish State should include the Negev and all the rest, but believed that we should permit the General Assembly to decide the fate of Western Galilee.

Garcia Salazar was ready to give the Jews the whole of Galilee, but not the Negev.

Sandstrom at the beginning had more or less shared this plan, then later appeared somewhat dubious about Western Galilee.

Blom more or less was influenced by Sandstrom's opinion and had not yet expressed himself clearly.[17]

Garcia-Granados went on to describe some merely 'technical difficulties': 'First, Galilee had a large Arab population and a small Jewish one; and was the only really fertile land in Palestine. The Jews had established a number of settlements there, showing their ability to develop this area, and it would be most suitable for their immigration ... some of us felt that if Galilee was given to the Arabs, the tremendous investments the Jews had made in the coastal part of Western Galilee, and all their plans for its continued development, would vanish.'[18] So much for the 'tremendous investments' the Palestinian Arabs had made over several centuries in farming, village and town development, religious life and so on, much of which could vanish if Galilee was given to the Jews.

'If a Jewish state were set up,' wrote Garcia-Granados, 'it would be essentially an industrial state, and its effect on this entire part of the world would be most significant. Its impact on the backward economy of the neighboring Arab countries would help transform them from semi-feudal, semi-colonial nations into modern progressive ones. We knew, of course, that whether good or bad, the Arab political leaders were against all this; and that if we finally recommended any form of Jewish independence, which was later accepted by the General Assembly, bloodshed might result. But this would pass, I felt. It must pass.'[19] Nearly sixty years later, the bloodshed continues.

UNSCOP's final recommendation came in two parts: a majority of members recommended partition; a minority recommended a federated state of Jews and Arabs. This latter solution would have posed similar problems when it came to drawing up the map, but at least it envisaged a shared Arab and Jewish government.

The partition option went forward for discussion at the UN General Assembly. Two states were envisaged: a Jewish state in an area inhabited by 498,000 Jews and 497,000 Arabs (including 90,000 Bedouin); and an Arab state with 725,000 Arab inhabitants and 10,000 Jews. Because of its complex religious and cultural situation, Jerusalem was to be placed under an international trusteeship, controlled by the United Nations.

In the area that was to be handed over to Jewish control, only about 6 per cent of Jews owned the land. It seemed they were getting a bargain, but David Ben-Gurion, the Zionist leader, wasn't happy: 'Together with the Jews of Jerusalem, the total population of the Jewish State at the time of its establishment, will be about one million, including almost 40 per cent non-Jews. Such a [population] composition does not provide a stable basis for a Jewish State. This [demographic] fact must be viewed in all its clarity and acuteness. With such a [population] composition, there cannot even be absolute certainty that control will remain in the hands of the Jewish majority ... There can be no stable and strong Jewish state so long as it has a Jewish majority of only 60 per cent.'[20] Once again, the aims of the Zionists were made clear. Somehow or other, sooner or later, Palestine would have to become an entirely Jewish state. The UNSCOP recommendations were therefore reluctantly accepted by the Zionists. The Palestinian Arabs rejected them.

They now had to be put before the UN General Assembly and it needed a two-thirds majority of those voting to be formally passed.

My father was to witness the vote when he was sent to the UN General Assembly. It took place in a converted skating rink in Lake Success, New York. He never wrote or spoke about covering the UN debates over Palestine for the BBC's Arabic Service, but it must have been an extremely difficult time for him. He was required to be an objective observer, but what he was observing with growing certainty was the dismemberment of the country of his birth.

19

THE UN VOTE, 29 NOVEMBER 1947

• • •

In the months leading up to a final UN decision on Palestine, the Palestinians became increasingly dependent on the BBC for accurate information. The Mandatory government of Palestine (which came under the auspices of the Foreign Office) imposed severe censorship on news about discussions on Palestine in the corridors of power. Even though the BBC Arabic Service was given more freedom about what it could and could not broadcast, occasionally an edict, in the form of 'advice', came from a government department worried about the effect of some particular news story.[1]

The UNSCOP recommendations were published on 8 September 1947. Most Zionists saw partition as the best way forward under the circumstances, although some Jews warned against it. For instance, Dr Judah Magnes wrote a prophetic letter to the *New York Times* in which he said that 'partition would not stop the terrorist activities of Jewish groups, and that having secured partition through terror, they would attempt to secure the rest of the country for the Jews in the same way'.[2]

Three weeks later, the British government announced that it had decided to end the Palestinian Mandate. In October it gave a deadline of six months, after which it would vacate the country if no settlement had been reached. Over the next two months in Palestine, both the Jews and the Arabs set about organizing militias to instigate or defend against the violence that seemed to be inevitable.

Events at the UN reached a climax in November 1947. The UNSCOP recommendation for partition was put before an ad hoc committee of the General Assembly. It received a cautious vote in favour (25 votes for, 13 against, with 17 abstentions). Thirty countries were either against it or unwilling to express a view. Some of them argued that the UN had no legal power to impose partition on the Palestinian Arabs. After all, they did not want it and they had never been formally consulted. The twenty-five votes in the ad hoc committee were enough to secure a referral to the General Assembly, but now a two-thirds majority had to vote in favour to validate the decision.

It has often been said that the Jewish state in Palestine was the result of an outpouring of goodwill towards the Jews from all the nations of the world. Here is a typical example from a Jewish website: 'The UN vote to partition Palestine in November '47 was in a certain way "permission" from the world to re-establish [*my italics*] a Jewish State.'[3]

Setting aside the dubious use of the word 're-establish', it's the use of the word 'world' that is so deceptive in trying to convey what happened at Lake Success in 1947. The UN was only three years old and, as the events showed, its decisions were already far from the genuine expression of world opinion that would be desirable in such an organization, if it were ever possible. But in fact, as has happened over the last fifty years, what nations thought – or said they thought – was influenced far more by self-interest and hardly at all by a genuine consideration of the issues and an attempt to arrive at a just solution to one of the world's most intractable problems. In the prevailing atmosphere of cynicism today about the UN as a genuine forum of world opinion, it's not often realised how, even during its earliest years, the organization was prey to being manipulated by special interests. There has rarely been such blatent use of threats and bribery to rig the General Assembly vote as the activites of the Zionists in Palestine, Europe and America in 1947. And once they had won over the United States, the outcome was a foregone conclusion.

There were fifty-six nations with a vote at the UN in 1947. The United States and the Soviet Union, for their own political reasons, would support partition, and Britain decided to oppose it. Five Arab states and three others with large Muslim populations also opposed it. As for the other forty-five, it was difficult to predict which way they would go.

David Niles, a Zionist member of the White House staff who was to have considerable influence on President Truman, once revealed just how far some officials in the American government were prepared to go to support the Zionists. It was believed that the eleven Latin American states would vote as a bloc, and that they would be influenced by pressure from Spain. General Franco, the Fascist dictator of Spain, was seeking membership of the UN and Niles argued that even if liberal Americans were uncomfortable supporting Spain's application, 'Letting Spain into the UN means nothing, but if we support it, that will assure us of eleven votes for partition.'[4]

One member of the Zionist delegation, Abba Eban, showed how little the final vote had to do with a considered assessment of the arguments. 'Here was the Jewish people at the threshold of its greatest transition, and yet there was a danger that everything would be lost through utterly marginal circumstances in countries ostensibly external to the issue.'[5] They had to find a way to influence those marginal circumstances.

'To whom would the Liberian delegates really listen?' asked Peter Grose in his book about Israel and America. 'Could anyone reach the Philippines delegation via friends in Manila? How was Haiti leaning on Tuesday? Accosting delegates at every turn, in the lounges at Lake Success, in the diplomatic dining rooms of Manhattan, the Jewish Agency teams deployed all the techniques of persuasion that Weizmann himself had perfected in Balfour's London a generation before. Their arguments were tailored to the interests and emotions of each particular interlocutor. To the diplomats from the Netherlands, the representatives from Jewish Palestine stressed economic development, praised Dutch efforts at reclamation at home. "We propose to conquer the wilderness in the same way you conquered the ocean," argued [David] Horowitz. To the Ethiopians, by contrast, the Zionist team stressed ancient history, the Queen of Sheba, the ties of Ethiopia with the land of Israel in biblical days.'[6]

David Horowitz, a member of the Zionist delegation, also recalled: 'The telephones rang madly. Cablegrams sped to all parts of the world. People were dragged from their beds at midnight and sent on peculiar errands. And, wonder of it all, not an influential Jew, Zionist or non-Zionist, refused to give us assistance at any time. Everyone pulled his weight, little or great, in the despairing effort to balance the scales to our favour.'[7]

'We [are] in no sense of the word to coerce other delegations to follow our lead,' warned President Truman, objecting to efforts to make America support partition and persuade others to do so. 'I do not think I ever had as much pressure and propaganda aimed at the White House as I had in this instance,' he wrote later. 'The persistence of a few of the extreme Zionist leaders – actuated by political motives and engaging in political threats – disturbed and annoyed me.'[8] Although Truman supported a state of Israel, he was not always well-disposed towards Jews: 'I fear very much that the Jews are like all underdogs. When they get on top they are just as intolerant and as cruel as the people were to them when they were underneath. I regret this situation very much because my sympathy has always been on their side.'[9]

One of the Zionists working hard to fix the vote was Michael Comay, in charge of the Jewish Agency's New York office. He described in a letter how the Agency finally managed to change President Truman's mind: 'Greece, the Philippines and Haiti – three countries completely dependent on Washington – suddenly came out one after another against its declared policy [partition]. We stalled off a decision, and over Thanksgiving Day, which was a holiday, an avalanche descended upon the White House while some newspapers openly accused officials in the State Department of sabotage. The President, we learned, became very upset and threw his personal weight behind the effort to get a decision ... It was only in the last 48 hours, i.e. on Friday and Saturday, that we really got the full backing of the United States.'[10]

In the closing hours of the UN General Assembly session, the various members of the UN had given their views and indicated how they would vote. The head of the Philippines delegation, General Carlos Romulo, explained in a speech that the Philippines would vote against partition and gave his reasons why: 'Whatever the weight we might choose to assign to the arguments of the one side or the other, it is clear to the Philippine Government that the rights conferred by mandatory power, even if subsequently confirmed by an international agreement, do not vitiate the primordial right of a people to determine the political future and to preserve the territorial integrity of its native land. We hold that the issue is primarily moral. The issue is whether the United Nations should accept responsibility for the enforcement of a policy which … is clearly repugnant to the valid nationalist aspirations of the people of Palestine. The Philippine Government believes that the United Nations ought not to accept any such responsibility.'[11]

Romulo was ordered home immediately by President Roxas of the Philippines. The President had received what he called a 'high-pressure telegram' warning of the adverse effect that a vote against partition would have on Philippine–American relations. Specifically, there was a financial aid package pending in Congress and the Philippines was dependent on US support while it rebuilt its war-destroyed economy. It was unwise to do anything that might annoy America. Just to make certain, the political Zionists tracked down a Jewish friend of the Philippine President in England and, although it was the middle of the night, they asked him to phone Manila and tell the President how to vote.[12] The Philippines eventually voted for partition, despite having publicly announced that it was 'repugnant to the valid nationalist aspirations of the people of Palestine'.[13]

The small African state of Liberia had also decided to vote against partition, but the Zionists leapt into action. In spite of Truman's ban on coercing UN members for their votes, David Niles realized that Liberia's economy was dominated by the investments of the Firestone Rubber Company. He asked the owner of the company, Harvey Firestone Jr, to threaten the President of Liberia with withdrawal of his investment unless Liberia voted for partition.[14] Firestone was persuaded to do so because American Jews threatened to boycott Firestone tyres if he didn't.[15]

Another small country that initially objected to partition was Haiti. The Haitian President received a message through the American consul in Haiti that the White House wanted him, 'for his own good', to change his country's vote. He did.[16]

Some bigger nations were also subjected to intense lobbying. The French vote, for instance, could have gone either way. France had traditional links with Arab North Africa, but it also had an emotional attachment to the Jewish cause. Weizmann sent a telegram to the former French Prime Minster Leon Blum. 'Does France wish to be absent from a moment unfading in the memory of man?' he asked. Blum's intervention led to the American financier Bernard Baruch telling the French delegate to his face that a French vote against partition would mean the end of all American aid to France. France voted for partition.[17]

Two other pieces of evidence among many indicate the prodigious effort made to rig the vote in favour of a Jewish state. There are reports in State Department files that one Latin American delegate was given $75,000 in cash to change sides; another turned down $40,000, but was ordered by his government nevertheless to vote for partition. The pro-Arab Cuban ambassador suspected the $40,000 went instead to whoever gave the order.[18]

News of these frantic attempts by the Zionists to get their way soon leaked out to the supporters of the Palestinian Arabs. The Lebanese delegate to the General Assembly addressed his fellow members on the topic and urged them to vote according to their consciences: 'My friends, think of these democratic methods, of the freedom in voting which is sacred to each of our delegations. If we were to abandon this for the tyrannical system of tackling each delegation in hotel rooms, in bed, in corridors and anterooms, to threaten them with economic sanctions or to bribe them with promises in order to compel them to vote one way or another, think of what our Organization would become in the future. Should we be a democratic organization? Should we be an organization worthy of respect in the eyes of the world? At this supreme juncture, I beg you to think for a moment of the far-reaching consequences which might result from such manoeuvres, especially if we yielded to them.'[19]

The Syrian delegate also protested: 'You see to what extent their influence [the Jews] has extended here. In the United States, they are one to thirty, whereas in Palestine they are one to three. Living in this democratic country, they have extended their influence into all circles.' At this there were hisses from Zionists in the gallery. 'They have even extended it to the centre of the United Nations,' the Syrian delegate continued, 'and intimidate speakers by hissing at them. This is the proof that they are dominating people here even though they are one to thirty in this country.'[20]

There were many in the US government who balked at the joint US-Zionist pressures. James Forrestal, Secretary of Defense, wrote in his diary: 'The method that had been used to bring coercion and duress on other nations in the General Assembly bordered on scandal.'[21] Another US official, Sumner Welles, the former Under-Secretary of State, later wrote: 'By direct order of the White House, every form of pressure direct or indirect was brought to bear by American officials upon those countries outside the Muslim world that were known to be either uncertain or opposed to partition.'[22]

Faced with the knowledge of this concerted Zionist campaign, there were feeble efforts by the Arabs to counteract the effects of it, but they had neither the resources nor the will of the Zionists. The occasional example I have come across suggests that their hearts were not in it and they had little chance of success. Jorge Garcia-Granados, the Guatemalan delegate to the UN and pro-Zionist, was approached one day by a group of Arab delegates. They asked him what he would do if his government instructed him to change his position and vote against partition. 'I tell you it will not happen,' he replied, 'but if you want to know what I would do in that impossible case, I would resign before I would act contrary to my convictions.' 'Well,' came the reply, 'you may have to resign because we are working very hard on your government.'[23]

Gideon Rafael, a junior member of the Jewish Agency delegation, also gave another (unverifiable) example of Arab lobbying: 'A female diplomat representing one of the smaller countries was charmed out of her political directives by the ardent wooing of a handsome Arab diplomat and reportedly vowed to cast her vote against partition contrary to her instructions. Urgent representations were made to her foreign ministry and a new delegate, male, was sent to replace her.'[24]

The populous Arab town of Nazareth was handed over to Israel after 1948.

Saturday, 29 November 1947, was the day of the vote. A basket with the names of the fifty-six member states was set in front of the General Assembly president. The first name picked was Guatemala and the voting began. It took only three minutes, but, said one Jewish observer, 'it seemed to me to stretch the length of the Jewish exile'.[25] When the voting was over, the resolution had been carried by a vote of 33 for, 13 against, and 10 abstentions.

However, the pro-partition votes were only two more than was necessary. If the Philippines, Liberia and Haiti had not been pressured to change their votes, the resolution would not have been passed.

What had the General Assembly actually voted for? Did the assembled nations of the UN really comprehend what partition meant? 'The plan was a masterpiece of gerrymandering,' wrote the American author Richard H. Curtiss. 'It awarded 56.4 per cent of the country to the Jews, who comprised 33 per cent of the population and owned less than 6 per cent of the land ... Even after partition, the Jewish portion would contain a very large number of Arabs, a certain recipe for trouble, while the Arab portion would contain almost none of the Jewish population. Despite virtually unanimous opposition to the plan from State and Defense Department experts on the Middle East, President Truman put United States support behind it.'[26]

On 29 November 1947, Palestine, the Arab nation that had stretched from Syria to Egypt – with ancient towns like Haifa, Jaffa, Acre, Safad, Tiberias and Jerusalem – was consigned to oblivion. Many of the Palestinians who lived there were told that they were no longer Palestinians, they were now citizens of a new Jewish state to be called Israel.

In Jerusalem, Yitzhak Sadeh, a senior Haganah leader, had followed the voting at the UN. 'If the vote is positive, the Arabs will make war on us,' he had said, 'and if the vote is negative, then it is we who will make war on the Arabs.'[27] As it turned out, the vote was positive but the Haganah still set out to make war on the Arabs.

20

THE END OF HISTORY

...

It has been said that the Palestinians never miss an opportunity to miss an opportunity. But what opportunity was missed in 1947? What could they have done to prevent the subsequent events, known ever since as al-Nakba, the Arabic word for 'catastrophe'? It is difficult to imagine an alternative history in which nearly 500,000 Palestinians in the area allocated to the Jews (including entire towns and villages) meekly accepted partition, allowing strangers with a different culture, a different language and a different religion to control their lives.

Had the Palestinian Arabs had more foresight, they might have retained more of their homes and land. But accurate foresight doesn't always help. In the fifty years of Zionism leading up to 1947, many people had warned that if the rights of the inhabitants of Palestine were ignored it would lead to resistance, violence and bloodshed. These warnings were dismissed or ignored. If all the Arabs had passively acquiesced in their fate and accepted a new status as citizens of a Jewish state, it would have been more difficult for Israel to expand its borders, take over Arab land and expel hundreds of thousands of Palestinians. But they would still have done it. As we've seen, the Zionist leaders saw the areas they were allocated in the partition plan as a starting point for a Jewish state, not as the final boundaries. As the Israeli historian Ilan Pappe has observed: 'It was clear to the Zionist leadership that without the uprooting of the local population it would be impossible to implement the dream of a Jewish nation-state.'[1]

In all likelihood world opinion would have been hostile to such displacement if it had happened to a peaceful, unresisting Palestinian population, rather than one which saw partition as an injustice and tried to resist it. But as the later history of Israel has shown, world opinion has never been a major influence on its actions. Sooner or later, the leaders of the new Jewish state would have used force to expand it and to change its population structure. With nearly half its population Arab, Israel would not have been a Jewish state. And a Jewish state was what they had wanted for fifty years.

The news of the UN vote in November 1947 was greeted with dancing in the streets by Jews and incredulity and anger by Arabs. A three-day strike was declared, accompanied by street clashes between Arabs and Jews. On 2 December six Arabs and eight Jews were reported killed. An Arab cinema, the Rex, was burned down by Jews in Jerusalem. Arabs then set fire to Jewish shops. On 13 December the Irgun killed at least sixteen Arabs and injured sixty-seven more in bombings in Jerusalem and Jaffa, where a hundred Arab houses were destroyed.[2]

At the end of December the Arabs of Haifa signed a ceasefire with the Haganah. Arabs were beginning to leave the city in fear, although they were urged not to by their leaders. What happened next has been described by Benny Morris, Professor of History at Ben-Gurion University in Israel:

Late on the morning of 30 December, Irgun gunmen threw bombs into an Arab crowd milling about the gate of the Haifa Oil Refinery. Six died and some 50 were injured. Immediately, a mob of Arab refinery workers, reinforced by Arabs who had survived the bombing, attacked their Jewish co-workers with sticks, stones and knives. Altogether, 39 Jews were murdered and 11 seriously injured in the hour-long pogrom. The Haganah massively *retaliated [my italics]* on the night of 31 December 1947–1 January 1948, raiding the villages of Balad al Sheikh and Hawassa, in which many of the refinery's workers lived. The raiding units' orders were to kill 'maximum adult males'. The raiders penetrated to the centre of Balad al Sheikh, fired into and blew up houses, and pulled out adult males, and shot them. According to the HGS, 'the penetrating units ... were forced to deviate from the line agreed upon and in a few cases hit women and children' after being fired upon from inside houses.[3]

Here the cycle of violence was initiated by the Jews, but Morris does not call the Arab response a 'retaliation'. The first 'retaliation' he mentions is the Haganah killing men, women and children. Apparently they were 'forced to deviate from the line agreed upon', but it is unclear who forced them and how. Morris also calls the Arab attacks a 'pogrom', although this is incorrect because it was not a government-organized attack on the Jews. If any attack fitted the definition of a pogrom it was the officially authorized murder of dozens of innocent residents of Balad al Sheikh and Hawassa, some of whom (according to the Yishuv's Defence Committee) had actually protected Jews in the refinery.

The Jewish violence was shared between the Haganah and the two terrorist organizations, the Irgun and the Stern Gang. The Haganah presented itself as more disciplined and discriminating than the terror gangs, claiming to hit only the 'guilty', although it did extend its violence to more innocent targets in 'areas already marked by Arab-initiated violence'. Morris says 'the Haganah also on occasion *inadvertently* employed terror, as in an attack on Jerusalem's Semiramis Hotel in January 1948.'[4] Twenty-two men, women and children were killed when the Haganah bombed the hotel.

By early 1948 the Haganah's attacks on innocent civilians became less inadvertent as they hit deliberately at Palestinian traffic and villages, in retaliation for attacks on Jews by Arabs. Within ten days of the UN vote, an order went out to one Haganah brigade to 'harass and paralyse' Arab traffic on a particular road. One unit of the brigade ambushed two vehicles with Molotov cocktails, wounding six Arabs who then burnt to death in the fire. Morris, who tells this story, believes that the commander of the unit was Ariel Sharon, yet another future prime minister of Israel. 'The ambushers,' the commander explained, 'recalled previous Arab attacks on Jewish convoys and were filled with "hatred".'[5] 'Only strong, massive, retaliatory action, it was felt, would overawe and pacify the Arabs,' wrote Morris, 'But the reprisals often hit the innocent along with the guilty, bred anger and vengefulness and made additional Arab communities amenable to the Husseinis' militant nationalist appeals, despite great initial reluctance to enter the fray.'[6]

The British High Commissioner, still in tenuous command of the country, also thought that the Jewish actions were triggering the violence they claimed to be trying to stop. He called some of the Jewish attacks 'an offence to civilization'.[7] Although the British were still nominally in control there was a sense in which they increasingly let the two sides 'slug it out'. They had experienced a decade of British deaths in Palestine and were reluctant to add to the death toll. Even so, although the British could no longer be accused of thwarting the Jewish National Home, Jewish terrorists still targeted the British army from time to time. Eleven British officers died in an Irgun bomb attack on the officers' club in Jerusalem in March. At the beginning of April the British announced that they would evacuate Palestine on 15 May.

• • •

There was one final act in the drama of the Palestinians in Palestine. It was a foregone conclusion that there would now be a Jewish state in much of pre-1948 Palestine. The outrage of the Arab countries surrounding Palestine had led to threats of war to prevent partition. When partition seemed inevitable, the Arab armies prepared for the date in May when the British would leave, in order to defend against the possibility that the new state would immediately try to expand its borders into the areas allocated to the Arabs in the partition plan.

But in addition to their dissatisfaction with the boundaries of their state-to-be, the Jews had another worry – the dilution of the Jewishness of the state by hundreds of thousands of Arabs who had the right to live in their own homes under the UN resolution. Ideas of 'population transfer' that had cropped up in Zionists' diaries and conversations and even, eventually, in the Peel report, now took on an attractive reality.

In the years 1947–9 about 700,000 Palestinian Arabs left their homes in Palestine never to return. Over the years, Israel has presented this mass departure as having nothing to do with any Jewish intentions to expel them. In 1961, as reported in *The Times*,

Ben-Gurion 'denied in the Knesset yesterday that a single Arab resident had been expelled by the Government since the establishment of the State of Israel and he said the pre-State Jewish underground had announced that any Arab could remain where he was. He said the fugitives had fled under the orders of Arab leaders.'[8] Indeed, according to a recent Jewish account, Ben-Gurion 'urged the Arabs to remain, promising that they would not be harmed'.[9] Simha Flapan, a Jewish historian, summarizes the official Israeli position as 'that Israel was not responsible for the exodus and in fact did everything in its power to stop it'. He says that this claim is 'found in all official Zionist history and propaganda and all Israeli information publications'.[10]

Here's a current version of how and why the Palestinians left, from an American website:

> In 1948, when six Arab armies invaded the Jewish state in order to destroy it on the very day of its birth, broadcasts by the advancing Arab armies appealed to the resident Arabs to leave their homes so as not to be in the way of the invaders. As soon as the 'quick victory' was won, they could return to their homes and would also enjoy the loot from the Jews, who would have been driven into the sea. It didn't turn out quite that way. Those Arabs who, despite the urgings of the Jews to stay and to remain calm, foolishly left, became refugees. Those who decided not to yield to those blandishments are now, and have been for over 50 years, citizens of Israel, with all the same rights and privileges as their Jewish fellows.[11]

Almost every word of this is untrue, as has been shown over the years by many historians, Jews, Arabs and others, drawing on Israel government archives. The flight of the Arab refugees was a cause, not a result, of actions taken by the Arab countries surrounding Palestine. It began months before the Arab armies crossed the borders of Mandate Palestine. These armies did not invade to 'destroy [Israel] on the very day of its birth' but advanced into the territories allocated to the Palestinian Arabs to restore order, prevent them being invaded by the Israelis and stop the expulsions. Detailed research over the last fifty years has failed to find any broadcasts telling the Arabs to leave their homes. On the contrary, the only relevant Arab broadcasts appealed to them to stay. In contrast, there were very few Jews who urged the Arabs to stay, but there was a concerted military and political effort to get rid of them, – 'cleansing' was the word used in official documents. And although it is beyond the scope of this book, those who stayed do not have 'all the same rights and privileges as their Jewish fellows'. They are now very much second-class citizens in a racially defined state.

Chaim Weizmann became the first president of Israel. He had participated in every step of the planned takeover of Palestine as it had unfolded over the previous forty years, including the need to expel the Palestinians, yet he made a breathtakingly cynical remark about the flight of the refugees. It was, he said 'a miraculous clearing of the land: the miraculous simplification of Israel's task'.[12] This statement further confirms that 'Israel's task' was to achieve a Palestine without Arabs.

For the truth about the Arab exodus, we have to thank Benny Morris, among other Israeli 'new historians'. He has no doubt that there was a deliberate policy (formed by the Haganah) of expulsion using violence. It began while the UN was still considering what to do about the Palestine question in 1947, and continued as official government policy after the establishment of Israel.

During the closing years of the Mandate, the Haganah, the Irgun and the Stern Gang had focused their attacks on the British.

Increasingly, however, they had turned to Arab targets as a soften-
ing-up process for the war that both sides foresaw. As early as
August 1947, three months before the UN vote, the Haganah had
attacked and blown up a farmhouse lived in by a prosperous Arab
family of orange growers, killing twelve people in the house,
including a mother and six children.[13] This attack marked the inauguration of a policy to destroy houses and kill Arabs and their
families who were said to be resisting the Jewish takeover of their
land.[14] As the months passed, the criteria for inflicting terror on the
Arabs became less to do with targeting alleged 'militants' and their
families and more to do with 'cleansing' whole areas of Palestine
that had a large Arab population. Within hours of the UN vote,
there were signs that some Arabs were leaving their homes,
although the intention was a temporary absence rather than permanent exile.

In anticipation of further increases in violence, the better-off
Arab families – in areas next to Jewish neighbourhoods in Jaffa and
Jerusalem, for example – were packing their bags to go and stay
somewhere more peaceful until the violence blew over. Civilians
were being killed randomly and some areas were becoming dangerous places to bring up a family. Many of the wealthier
Palestinians had friends or relatives in other parts of Palestine or in
Syria or Egypt. They felt that a short stay away would be a sensible
precaution.

It wasn't long before the Jewish forces and Zionist leaders saw this
natural caution on the part of a few Arabs as something to be
encouraged. In Tel Aviv, next to Jaffa, one Haganah officer suggested
that the reservoir in Jaffa be put out of commission so that the Arabs
would be forced to leave for lack of water. When he visited
Jerusalem in February, David Ben-Gurion observed that there were
no 'strangers', as he called the Arabs. 'What has happened in

Jerusalem ... could well happen in great parts of the country – if we [the Yishuv] hold fast ... And if we hold fast, it is very possible that in the coming six or eight or ten months of the war there will take place great changes ... and not all of them to our detriment. Certainly there will be great changes in the composition of the population of the country.'[15]

Every military operation had a dual purpose. One was to achieve a military objective, such as the prevention of attacks from some Arab militia group. Until May, the Arab resistance to Jewish hostilities was in the hands of a not very effective Arab Liberation Army, sponsored by the Arab League, and various groups of Arab irregulars. The second purpose behind the Jewish military operations was to force the departure of ordinary Arabs from their homes for long enough to destroy their houses or villages and deny them the right of return, sometimes infecting the wells with bacteria to ensure this.

Morris gives many examples of Arabs being expelled from their homes. First it was a trickle, and then, as things took a nastier turn, a flood. When the village of Mansurat al Kheit was attacked by the Haganah in January 1948, dwellings were burnt, farm animals killed and the raiders were under orders to eliminate anyone who resisted. As a response to Arab attacks on traffic, a village to the north, al-Husseiniya, was attacked in mid-March, a number of houses blown up, and several dozen Arabs killed – including men who had come from Iraq to help resist Jewish attacks, and women and children. The *mukhtar* or head man of the village, having been told he would not be harmed, was executed by the Jewish forces.[16] At the end of February, Jewish agents set off a car bomb in a garage they said was being used to make weapons. Dozens of Arabs were killed and wounded. The Haganah often used mortars to attack ordinary Palestinians in their houses. On 5 March five occupants of a house in Haifa, including a woman and her two children, were killed. The panic caused by such attacks on the town led to dozens of families leaving the city every day.

It is in these early attacks that a third aim becomes evident. Not only were the Jewish forces trying to achieve military objectives, and to expel Arabs, they were also hoping that the news of their brutality would spread and precipitate Arab flight without any need for actual expulsions. The most notorious example of this terrorism was the massacre at Deir Yassin on 9 April 1948. There are few knowledgeable people (apart from a dwindling band of Irgun and Lehi veterans) who would now deny that this was a deliberate massacre of innocent civilians. It was designed to show other Palestinian Arabs what would happen if they stayed in their towns and villages.

Deir Yassin was a small village on the outskirts of Jerusalem which was not involved in any anti-Jewish activity. The village elders had opposed an attempt by Arab irregulars to recruit men from the village to fight the Jews. They had also refused to allow the village to be used by the irregulars to attack a nearby Jewish base – and had their sheep slaughtered in revenge. They had even signed a non-belligerency pact with their Jewish neighbours. It is difficult to see what more they could have done to convince the Jews of their peaceful intentions. But they were Arabs, living in a land that the Jews wanted for themselves.

On the morning of 9 April about 130 Jews from the Irgun and the Stern Gang, supported by machine-gun cover from the official Jewish militia, the Haganah, attacked the village and in a full day of fighting destroyed houses and killed the inhabitants as they tried to flee. Those who couldn't flee (including women and children) were rounded up, taken to a nearby quarry and murdered. 'The conquest of the village was carried out with great cruelty,' wrote one Jewish observer. 'Whole families – women, old people, children – were killed. Lehi members tell of the barbaric behaviour of the Irgun towards the prisoners and the dead. They also relate that the Irgun men raped a number of Arab girls and murdered them afterwards.'[17]

Another Jew, a Haganah intelligence officer, reported: 'In the quarry ... I saw the five Arabs they had paraded in the streets of the city. They had been murdered and were lying one on top of the other ... I saw with my own eyes several families [that had been] murdered with their women, children and old people, their corpses were lying on top of each other ... The dissidents were going about the village robbing and stealing everything: chickens, radio sets, sugar, money, gold and more ... Each dissident walked about the village dirty with blood and proud of the number of persons he had killed. Their lack of education and intelligence as compared to our soldiers [i.e., the Haganah] was apparent ... In one of the houses at the centre of the village were assembled some 200 women and small children. The women sat quietly and didn't utter a word. When I arrived, the "commander" explained that they intended to kill all of them. [But] in the evening I heard that the women and children had been transported and released in Musrara.'[18]

The leader of the massacre, Menachem Begin, described the Arab casualties as 'troops' in his account of Deir Yassin, and boasted that in the following days 'the Arabs began to flee in terror, even before they clashed with Jewish forces'.[19] Doris Katz, a member of the Irgun, later dismissed the massacre, saying that Deir Yassin was 'an Arab village near Jerusalem which the IZL [the Irgun] had conquered rather too thoroughly, giving rise to exaggerated reports of massacres of women and children and general brutality'.[20] She also wrote: 'Even if the accusation were true, in this age when an atom bomb was used to bring horrible death to tens of thousands of defenceless men, women and children and when its use was justified as a military expedient in that it saved thousands of American and British lives, then any outcry against Deir Yassin was sheer and utter hypocrisy.'[21]

'The massacre and the way it was trumpeted in the Arab media added to the pressure on the Arab states' leaders to aid the embattled Palestinians and hardened their resolve to invade Palestine,' writes Benny Morris. 'However, the most important immediate effect of the massacre and of the media atrocity campaign that followed was to trigger and promote fear and further panic flight from Palestine's villages and towns.'[22]

For decades after these events, the story of the Deir Yassin massacre was related by Arabs to illustrate how innocent civilians were targeted by the Jewish militias. Initially the story was dismissed by Israel as propaganda, but gradually the weight of emerging evidence has been too great to deny. Those who wish to minimize its significance have said that it was one of those unfortunate but isolated events that occurs in the heat of battle. But recent researchers have refuted that line and revealed other massacres solely designed to inflict terror. According to the former director of the Israeli army archives, 'in almost every village occupied by us during the War of Independence, acts were committed which are defined as war crimes, such as murders, massacres, and rapes'.[23] Uri Milstein, the authoritative Israeli military historian of the 1948 war, goes one step further, maintaining that 'every skirmish ended in a massacre of Arabs'.[24]

Meron Benvenisti, the former deputy mayor of Jerusalem, described several other massacres in villages around the town of Safad. 'These atrocities,' he writes, 'which fifty years later are regarded as libel, invented by the enemies of Israel, and whose retelling is perceived as an example of the rewriting of history by revisionist historians – were, at the time they took place, known to ministers in the Israeli government, military commanders, and even the general public. The government set up commissions of its own, but the work of these bodies came to naught because soldiers and officers refused to testify against their comrades in arms.'[25]

These activities were part of a specific Jewish plan to expel the Arabs, as described by the Israeli historian Ilan Pappe:

> They were cautious enough not to write it, although there was this 'plan D' (Dalet), that reveals enough of the systematic expulsion. The idea was prepared by the Jewish military forces in March 1948. In that plan, they defined a very important principle: any Arab village or neighbourhood that would not surrender to the Jewish forces, that would not raise the white flag, would be uprooted, destroyed and the people expelled. I think they knew well that there was very little chance of more than five or six villages surrendering. Why should they surrender, especially after Deir Yassin in April and the big fright in the Arab community? In fact, only four villages put up a white flag. All the rest were potentially an object of expulsion. I must add that a few other neighbourhoods did raise a white flag but it didn't help them … All this is very clear. We have to remember that the UN partition plan of November 1947 would have left an equal number of Jews and Arabs in the Jewish state. This contradicted the idea of a Jewish state. So they had to make sure that as few Arabs as possible were still there. And that's what happened.[26]

As 15 May neared – the date on which the British had said they would leave Palestine – the Haganah stepped up its efforts to capture as many of the villages and towns of the Palestinian Arabs as possible. This led to what Morris describes as a 'massive demographic upheaval [which] caught ... the Arab states largely unawares and caused great embarrassment: It highlighted the Palestinians' weakness and the Arab states' inability, so long as the Mandate lasted, to intervene. At the same time, it propelled these states closer to the invasion about which they were largely unenthusiastic. There is no evidence that the Arab states and the Arab Higher Committee wanted a mass exodus or issued blanket orders or appeals to flee.'[27]

At this stage, the armies of the other Arab states who were to invade Palestine held back from military action to preserve the area allocated to the Arabs. But the Haganah made strenuous efforts to occupy as many as possible of the Arab cities in Palestine. They took Jaffa on 28 April, the Arab quarters in the New City of Jerusalem on 30 April, Beisan on 8 May, Safad on 10 May and Acre on 14 May 1948. In contrast, the Palestine Arabs did not seize any of the territories reserved for the Jewish state under the partition resolution.[28]

In Tiberias, a town in which Jews and Arabs had traditionally lived together in friendship, the Arab quarter was bombarded by mortars. In an attempt to cut off the city from neighbouring Arab towns, the Haganah took over a hilltop village called Khirbet Nasir ad Din and killed twenty-two Arabs, including women and children. The rest of the inhabitants fled to Tiberias with news of the massacre, creating panic among the Arabs there. One Jewish National Fund official wrote in his diary: 'I cannot justify this action by the Haganah. I don't know whether there was justification for the assault and the killing of so many Arabs. The flight of the women and children of the village in panic made a bad impression on me.'[29]

Safad was another important target for the Haganah. There were about 10,000 Arabs living in the town and only 1,500 Jews. Nevertheless, under the UN partition plan it was to be put under Jewish rule in the Jewish part of Palestine. On 16 April the British evacuated the town. Yigal Allon, one of the senior officers in the region, later explained what happened next:

> We regarded it as imperative to cleanse the interior of the
> Galilee and create Jewish territorial continuity in the
> whole of Upper Galilee. The protracted battles reduced
> our forces, and we faced major tasks in blocking the
> invasion routes. We, therefore, looked for a means that
> would not oblige us to use force to drive out the tens of
> thousands of hostile Arabs left in the Galilee and who, in
> the event of an invasion, could strike at us from
> behind....I gathered the Jewish *mukhtars*, who had ties
> with the different Arab villages, and I asked them to
> whisper in the ears of several Arabs that giant Jewish
> reinforcements had reached the Galilee and were about
> to clean out the villages of the Hula, [and] to advise them,
> as friends, to flee while they could. And the rumour
> spread ... that the time had come to flee. The flight
> encompassed tens of thousands. The stratagem fully
> achieved its objective, and we were able to deploy
> ourselves in face of the [prospective] invaders along the
> borders, without fear for our rear.[30]

Manufactured rumours only worked, of course, because of the increasing toll of actual Jewish military actions.

Orders were given that three villages in the Galilee should be attacked, their inhabitants expelled and their houses blown up. A Catholic priest conducting a service in one of the villages described what he saw and heard: 'When I just finished blessing the bread there was a terrible explosion in Tabigha. We rushed out and saw pillars of smoke rising skyward. House after house was bombed and torched, then matters proceeded toward the Jordan. All was bombed, the tents and the huts were burned. All day there were explosions, and smoke and fire were visible: in the evening the "victors" returned with trucks loaded with cattle. What they couldn't take they shot ... The mother of Big Awad and Old Dahan were killed.'[31]

In Safad itself, the Haganah terrorized the Arab inhabitants with mortar bombs, one of which was lobbed into a market place and killed thirteen Arabs, mostly children. On 1 May the Jewish army conquered two villages near Safad, to prevent them being used as Arab bases. They took dozens of prisoners and expelled women, children and old men who tried to stay in their homes. A day or two later the prisoners were murdered in a gully between the villages and Safad.

Across the valley, the inhabitants of Safad watched the destruction and mayhem, and got the message: to leave before the same thing happened to them. Thousands of refugees (including a dozen or more of my relatives) streamed out of Safad towards Syria and Lebanon. But Safad wasn't entirely in Jewish hands for another ten days. There was fighting between the Jews and Arab militias, and Arab reinforcements were called for, pushing their way on roads towards the town through hordes of refugees. The British army, days away from leaving the country for good, did nothing to prevent the Jewish onslaught on Safad, and the town fell on 11 May.[32] To make doubly sure that the town remained entirely Jewish, the leaders of Safad's Jewish community appealed to the new Israeli government to prevent any Arabs from returning and to bring in thousands of Jews to live in the Arabs' houses. If this couldn't be

The next day I went to Barclays, which was open, and withdrew £20,000 in cash. On the way home, I dropped by the Municipality, where I was greeted in a friendly way by my Jewish friends who were at their posts. They urged me to stay in town, joking that they needed me for protection against the Arab armies. I said I had come to collect money to help my family, given their situation since the fall of Safad, and had to return to Beirut. I left Haifa for the last time on 14 May. When we got into Beirut harbour on 15 May, security people came on board and said that all the women and children could disembark in Beirut, but that the men had to return to where they had come from. It was a government order that had to be obeyed without exception.

I immediately started trying to contact my Lebanese friends and, in no time, had reached Hamid Frangieh, who was Foreign Minister at the time. Frangieh wrote a letter to the security forces on official stationery, which was presented to the security people at the harbour, instructing them to allow all the passengers on that particular ship to disembark. So, because of me, scores of other males were able to go ashore in Beirut on 15 May.[35]

Four days after Safad fell, the last British soldier left Palestine and the State of Israel was declared. In the words of one historian, 'the British had not so much transferred power as abandoned it'.[36]

21

PALESTINE LOST

• • •

Safad in 2004 was a very different town from Safad in 1948, when the Arab population fled. I visited on Saturday, 16 October 2004, and it was deserted. There seemed to be more cats on the streets than people. A Jewish Sabbath turns a very devout community like Safad into a ghost town. Occasionally, a black-coated figure would flit across an alleyway. Between the houses there were views down to the Sea of Galilee. On the left of the vista were the Golan Heights and the Syrian border and on the right the town of Tiberias.

At the top of the hill I stood outside an old Turkish fort. It had been used by the British as a prison and was now a community centre. In the distance, a man walked towards me. He wore a red shirt and jeans and no skullcap. It was David, my Jewish guide and a resident of Safad. Unlike the vast majority of Israelis, David's family had lived in Palestine for eleven generations – as long as the Sabbaghs. What's more, he had imbibed the attitudes of his mother, a left-wing Jew who had lived in Safad when five sixths of the population were Arabs, and had many friends among the Christians and Muslims. As we walked around the town, David told me stories his mother had passed on to him about the old days and the events of 1947–8. She had been appalled by the Zionist plan to take Palestine from the Palestinian Arabs.

I had found this unusual man on the internet. On a Safad message board, among requests from American tourists about where to hire a car or how to get to Safad from Ben-Gurion airport, was one from a Jew seeking information about his family. David had replied and said that he knew much about the history of Safad families, and had taken an MA on the topic. I wrote out of the blue and asked him if he knew anything about my family. He replied within seconds and said that he knew about the Sabbaghs of Safad from 1267 – 'the time of Baybars the Mameluke' – until 1948.

In fact, David lived and breathed the history of Safad. He was a history teacher as well as a guide, but had stopped teaching at a nearby college because of the racism of the local Jews towards Arabs who tried to study there. Facts poured out of him as we walked the streets of the old city, which had originally been divided into Christian, Muslim and Jewish quarters. Many of today's inhabitants are recent immigrants and when I did hear conversation it was more often Russian than Hebrew.

There were many fine old stone houses, some now derelict, others renovated as gift shops or galleries. David explained how, after the Arabs left and were prevented from returning, their houses were sold for as little as $100 (about $800 or £400 in today's money) to Jews who claimed to be artists, in order to transform the area into a tourist attraction. Judging by what was on display in those houses that were still trying to survive as art galleries, the definition of 'artist' had been somewhat stretched.

One house was occupied by a Russian painter and his wife. His works covered the whitewashed walls of the main room, high-vaulted and cool. Mingled with rather good expressionist portraits and snow-covered scenes of his homeland, were more tourist-

oriented paintings – brightly coloured scenes of Safad and the surrounding landscape. The man's eyes lit up when we walked into
his gallery, but he was disappointed to learn that we only wanted to
look at the building because David had identified it as one of the
Sabbagh houses. When I tried to take a photograph, the painter's
wife snapped 'No pictures!'

David described how this house was mentioned in a book by
Mahmoud Abbas, known as Abu Mazen, and shortly to be
President of Palestine. Abu Mazen had been born and raised in
Safad, and remembered this very house as having an extremely old
olive tree in the centre of one of the rooms. Sure enough, the
stump of the tree was still there. This memory triggered a story
from David about how Abu Mazen had got in touch with him from
Ramallah at the time of the Oslo Peace Agreement (when it
looked as if it might be possible for Palestinians to visit Israel) and
asked if he would guide him around the city fifty years after he had
left it. David agreed to do this, but changed his mind when the
news got out and his wife found a dead cat on the doorstep. *This
will happen to your children too, if Abu Mazen visits Safad'*, said
an accompanying note. In fact, in 1994, Abu Mazen did visit the
town, incognito.

David told me another story showing the hostility of the
newcomers to the former inhabitants. 'At the time of Oslo, a
Palestinian Arab who used to live in Safad called me from Ramallah
and said that he wanted to know what had happened to his family's
house. I looked into the matter and found that the house still
existed and was lived in by a lawyer. The man asked me if I'd see
whether the lawyer would sell it. In fact, the lawyer agreed to a price
and the sale was made. But shortly after the news of the sale got
out, the house mysteriously burnt down one night, and the Israeli
police were never able to find how it happened.'

Although several generations of Sabbaghs lived in Safad, my grandfather eventually moved to the town of Tulkarm. It was here that my father was raised and educated. However, several of my father's cousins had lived in Safad and David took me to their houses: elegant stone buildings cascading down a steep hill, a church and belfry built into the top floor of one of them. I peered through a crack in the wooden gate to see a cool, tree-shaded courtyard.

As we walked through the sleepy town, David pointed out numerous small signs of what it had once been. Several shops in the high street still bore plaques with Arabic quotations and the date of construction. Beneath the shabby rolled-up awning of one building he pointed out some half-concealed Arabic writing showing that it had once been an Arab restaurant.

We criss-crossed the town, passing a fourteenth-century Arab mausoleum where Muslim notables of the town were buried. Nearby were the remains of a sixteenth-century mosque. Both were crumbling, and the mausoleum was full of rubbish. In Israel, it seems, the only history worth investigating (and sometimes fabricating) is Jewish history; the only antiquities worth preserving are Jewish ones. Like Daher al Omar's mosque in Tiberias, the Safad mosque and mausoleum had been vandalized and had fallen into disrepair. Old Jewish buildings fared better. In spite of the down-at-heel nature of the town, with 10 per cent unemployment and a moribund tourist industry, there is $80 million available (half of it coming from the government) to restore synagogues, revitalize the 'artists' colony (the old Christian Arab quarter) and restore the old cemeteries.

One cemetery not up for restoration is on a hillside on the edge of town. There were once five Arab cemeteries in Safad, but four have been destroyed. The fifth contains tombs of some of my ancestors and relatives. I asked David if we could go and see them, but a high barbed-wire fence surrounded the area. David told me the land had been sold to a friend of Ariel Sharon's son to turn into a wildlife park. Indeed, the only sign of life visible through the fence was a solitary bedraggled ostrich, free to roam the cemetery and peck at the tombs and gravestones.

Aleef Sabbagh in front of one of the former Sabbagh homes in Safad. The Arabic inscription has been defaced by Jews who took over the town.

When the State of Israel was declared in 1948, my uncle Ghassan was living over the border from Safad, in Syria. He told me of the memorable night of 14 May when the British finally handed over Palestine to the mercies of the UN partition plan. 'There was a small shop owned by a very clever man,' he said. 'He went to Damascus, where there were thousands of Palestinians and brought huge maps of Palestine to follow the progress of the fighting. He put a piece of glass on the table and the maps under it, and everybody would pass by to see where the Arab armies are now – "the Iraqis are here", and so on. He bought a radio too and everybody would listen to the news, and the only radio station at that time was the BBC. And on 14 May 1948 everybody was listening that night to the news and they kept announcing that Isa Khalil Sabbagh was going to say a word at twelve midnight, at twelve midnight, at twelve midnight, and everybody was waiting. Everybody wanted to know what Isa was going to say at midnight. And then finally he came on the radio and said: "God help the Arabs at this moment. It's an historical moment, the British reign is over; Palestine is liberated and long live the Arabs and long live Palestine." And everybody started clapping, and of course I had to buy coffee for everybody and it cost me a lot. At that time, to pay one Lebanese piastre for a cup of coffee at a time when you had no income any more, it was really something.'

'God help the Arabs' was right.

My father's cousin, Elias, was living in Haifa when the State of Israel was declared. He tried to get back to his family in the village of Deir Hanna and make his way from there to Lebanon. But his efforts to find a truck in Haifa were fruitless. The whole of northern Palestine was in chaos with many Arabs trying to flee in the face of Jewish attacks. 'I was alarmed and confused,' Elias told me, 'and then I met a friend who told me there might be a small cargo boat that transported people from Haifa to Beirut. After paying a large sum of money to the owner, I boarded the boat with just a few pounds in my pocket. When the boat left Haifa there were another twenty passengers on board. It took a day and a half to travel to Beirut, 140 kilometres to the north.' When the passengers became hungry the crew of four refused to give them any food. 'A fight took place,' Elias said, 'and we managed to get all the food that was left in the kitchen.' In Beirut, Elias met his brother Fayez, who was married to Tekla, my aunt. They were eventually joined by Ghassan and his mother, brother and sister.

Ghassan had spent some time in Syria after 15 May, without a job. 'We had no income,' he said, 'and I never even thought of working at that time because we believed we'd be going back to our own homes. Nobody would hire you for a month or two or three.' Ghassan was eventually reunited with other members of the family in Beirut. A friend of his in Syria had gone to Beirut and was returning on a bus when through the window he saw Abdallah, the son of Khalil's brother Hanna. Abdallah asked if he knew where Ghassan was and the friend wrote Ghassan's address on a piece of paper and threw it out of the bus.

'The slip of paper went in the air, and Abdallah followed it,' said Ghassan, 'but our friend didn't know whether he caught it or not. When he came back he said "I saw one of your cousins." He didn't know his name. Then about a week later we received a registered letter from Abdallah and he told me that they were in Lebanon, and so I got a visa from the Syrian government and I went to Lebanon and I saw Abdallah and Georgette. The next day I was eating breakfast and I saw Uncle Mikhail and his son Faiz in Beirut, and they told us that they were in Rameish. So I said "OK, if every member of the family is in Lebanon, I should go to Lebanon."'

Khalil's brother Mikhail (Elias's father) was still in Palestine. When he heard that his family was in Beirut, he tried to visit them. But of course, the border was closed between the new state of Israel and its Arab neighbours. 'He risked his life,' said Elias, 'by hiring people smugglers, riding a horse at night and sleeping in caves during the day. He was a great and a wise man. He could stay with us only for a week, and the purpose of the journey was to provide us with money so we could survive until we found jobs.'

Palestinian society was now falling apart. There was barely an area of Palestine that was not either under Israeli control or threatened by Israeli plans for expansion. Although the Palestinian Arabs had been under attack by the Jews for some time before the state of

Israel was declared, the official proclamation triggered the first Arab–Israeli war. As a result of the UN deciding that much of Palestine should now be a Jewish state, the regular armies of Egypt, Transjordan, Syria, Lebanon, and Iraq invaded Palestine to protect and defend the Palestinian Arabs and to attack the army of the State of Israel, which had given every indication of its intention to acquire the areas allocated to the Arabs in the partition plan and to expel Palestinian Arabs from areas under its control.

From 15 May 1948 until a final ceasefire on 7 January 1949, a series of carefully planned campaigns by the Israeli army picked off the Arab armies one by one and expanded de facto control beyond the borders of the area the Jews had been allocated under the UN partition plan. The fighting was accompanied by more and more planned expulsions from Palestinian Arab areas that came under Israeli control.

The occasional Israeli voice was raised against the wisdom of this behaviour. At a Cabinet meeting on 16 July, Aharon Zisling, the Agriculture Minister, made an extremely accurate prophecy: 'We are embarking on a course that will most greatly endanger any hope of a peaceful alliance with forces who could be our allies in the Middle East ... Hundreds of thousands of Arabs who will be evicted from Palestine, even if they are to blame, and left hanging in midair, will grow to hate us ... If you do things in the heat of the war, in the midst of the battle, it's one thing. But if, after a month, you do it in cold blood, for political reasons, in public, that is something altogether different.'[1]

As the fighting intensified, the UN tried to mediate between the two sides and to come up with some kind of proposal that would settle the dispute peacefully. Count Folke Bernardotte, head of the Swedish Red Cross, was appointed to the task and there were high hopes that he would obtain the trust of both Jews and Arabs.

He had negotiated with Heinrich Himmler in 1945 to release more than 20,000 prisoners from Nazi concentration camps, including 6,500 Jews.

Bernardotte's first achievement was to get both sides to sign a truce on 11 June, although in contravention of the terms of the truce, the Israelis used this time to gather additional arms and train more soldiers.[2] The Jewish underground fighters even announced that 'The Fighters for Freedom of Israel [Lehi] will not regard itself as bound by any ceasefire order anywhere, anyplace, anytime.'[3] (On his first briefing in Israel, Bernardotte had been told by senior Israelis that 'the State of Israel was now in a position to take full and complete responsibility for the acts committed by the Stern Gang and members of the Irgun.'[4] This turned out to be nonsense.) The Arabs violated the truce too, but the Israelis had more to show for it. The truce collapsed a few days later and the fighting resumed.

Bernadotte and his small UN team worked away at a range of proposals for a permanent settlement, which they tried out cautiously on both sides. The Israelis rejected anything that might curb their ambitions to take over as much of Palestine as possible. In particular, they objected strongly to a suggestion that Jerusalem should be an Arab city with some kind of safeguards for other faiths. They said it was unreasonable to give the Arabs control of Jerusalem because there were 100,000 Jews living there and only 65,000 Arabs. Bernardotte pointed out that 'If we agree with that principle, the basic premise of Israel itself is undermined. There is only one place in that state, namely the capital, Tel Aviv, where the majority of the population is Jewish.'[5]

Bernardotte was troubled by the growing refugee problem and he wanted guarantees from the Israelis that the Palestinians would be allowed to return to their homes after the war. He was shocked when he visited a refugee camp in Ramallah.

I have made the acquaintance of a great many refugee
camps; but never have I seen a more ghastly sight than
that which met my eyes here at Ramallah. The car was
literally stormed by excited masses shouting with Oriental
fervour that they wanted food and wanted to return to
their homes. There were plenty of frightening faces in
that sea of suffering humanity. I remember ... a group of
scabby and helpless old men with tangled beards who
thrust their emaciated faces into the car and held out
scraps of bread that would certainly have been considered
quite uneatable by ordinary people, but was their only
food. Perhaps there was no immediate danger of this
camp becoming a breeding ground of epidemic diseases
that would spread all over Palestine. But what would
happen at the beginning of October, when the rainy
season began and the cold weather set in?[6]

The right of return for refugees was rejected by the Israelis. The
whole point of the expulsions was to make it possible for Israel to
be a state with the largest possible proportion of Jews. Why would
they ever agree to let the Arabs back once they had got rid of them?
Anger against Bernardotte grew among the Israelis, and nowhere
more strongly than among the Irgun and the Lehi. Even
Bernardotte's humanitarian deal with Himmler to save concentration camp victims was turned on its head, and rumours were
spread of his 'friendship' with the Nazi.

A plot was hatched – led by the future Israeli Prime Minister
Yitzhak Shamir – to kill Bernardotte as an enemy of the Jews. On 16
September Bernardotte put the finishing touches to a report for
the UN in which he said that no 'just and complete' settlement was
possible, if the right of return for the Palestinian Arabs was not

recognized. 'It would be an offence against the principles of elemental justice if these innocent victims of the conflict were denied the right to return to their homes while Jewish immigrants flow into Palestine and, indeed, at least offer the threat of permanent replacement of the Arab refugees.'[7] The following day, a four-man Stern Gang team waited in a jeep in a street in Jerusalem for Bernardotte's car to approach. They blocked the road and stopped the UN convoy with Bernardotte's official car in the middle. Two assassins shot out the tyres of the escort cars, and a third fired several times into Bernadotte's car, killing him outright.

Judah Magnes, the rector of Jerusalem's Hebrew University offered this tribute in the *New York Times*: 'Count Bernardotte had come closer than any other man to bringing Jews and Arabs to an understanding.... He had done more to advance the cause of peace and conciliation in Palestine than all other persons put together.'[8]

The children of Palestinian refugees are a generation who have lived in camps their entire lives, banned by Israel from returning to family homes in Palestine.

The expulsion of Palestinians from their homes accelerated in July 1948. During a quiet period after the truce, the inhabitants of Ramleh and Lydda, two towns with a combined population of 50,000–70,000 Arabs, felt reasonably safe from Jewish attack.

They were outside the area allocated to the Jews in the partition plan and were near the heavily populated Arab West Bank. As a result, thousands of refugees from areas already under Jewish control flooded into the two towns and the surrounding areas, creating problems of employment, food supply and accommodation.

The Israelis wanted to advance beyond these two towns to acquire as much territory as possible, so they had to make a decision about how to treat the inhabitants. 'Clearly,' said Yitzhak Rabin, commander of one of the Israeli Defence Force (IDF) brigades, 'we could not leave Lod's [Lydda's] hostile and armed populace in our rear, where it could endanger the supply route to Yiftach (another brigade) that was advancing eastward.' In fact, that was an option. When the German army advanced across France it didn't expel all the French people. They continued to live in their homes under a hostile occupying force. However, it would serve two aims if the Palestinians could be expelled from their towns: it would remove the 'hostile and armed populace' (although it is unlikely that all 50,000 of them were armed), but it would also remove 50,000 Arabs from what was intended to be an expanded Jewish state.

Yigal Allon, another commander, asked Ben-Gurion, 'What is to be done with the population?' and the Prime Minister of Israel waved his hand in a gesture which said, according to Rabin, 'Drive them out!' 'Allon and I held a consultation. I agreed that it was essential to drive the inhabitants out,' Rabin said later. '"Driving out" is a term with a harsh ring,' he admitted. 'Psychologically, this was one of the most difficult actions we undertook.'[9]

The Israeli army began operations against Lydda on 9 July. These were, says Benny Morris, 'designed to induce civilian panic and flight'. They succeeded. A combination of bombing and shelling was followed by ground raids, led by Moshe Dayan. One of

Dayan's troopers later described the scenes:

> [My] jeep made the turn and here at the ... entrance to
> the house opposite stands an Arab girl, stands and
> screams with eyes filled with fear and dread. She is all
> torn and dripping blood – she is certainly wounded.
> Around her on the ground lie the corpses of her family.
> Still quivering, death has not yet redeemed them from
> their pain. Next to her is a bundle of rags – her mother,
> hand outstretched trying to draw her into the house. And
> the girl understands nothing ... Did I fire at her? ... But
> why these thoughts, for we are in the midst of battle, in
> the midst of conquest of the town. The enemy is at every
> corner. Everyone is an enemy. Kill! Destroy! Murder!
> Otherwise you will be murdered and will not conquer the
> town. What [feeling] did this lone girl stir within you?
> Continue to shoot! Move forward! ... Where does this
> desire to murder come from? What, because your friend
> ... was killed or wounded, you have lost your humanity
> and you kill and destroy? Yes! ... I kill everyone who
> belongs to the enemy camp: man, woman, old person,
> child. And I am not deterred.[10]

Thousands of refugees, new and old, left the two towns,
expelled by the Israelis as a part of their policy of 'cleansing' the
area. Morris quotes descriptions of the exodus by Jewish eye-
witnesses:

> A multitude of inhabitants walked one after another.
> Women walked burdened with packages and sacks on
> their heads. Mothers dragged children after them ...
> Occasionally, [Israel Defence Force] warning shots were

heard ... Occasionally, you encountered a piercing look
from one of the youngsters ... in the column, and the look
said: 'We have not yet surrendered. We shall return to
fight you.' ... The town looked like after a pogrom. [The
word is used correctly this time.]

One Israeli soldier recorded his vivid impressions of
the refugees' thirst and hunger, of how 'children got lost'
and of how a child fell into a well and drowned, ignored,
as his fellow refugees fought each other to draw water.
Another soldier described the spoor left by the slow
shuffling columns, 'to begin with jettisoning utensils and
furniture and in the end, bodies of men, women and
children, scattered along the way'. Quite a few refugees
died on the road east – from exhaustion, dehydration and
disease – before reaching temporary rest near and in
Ramallah. Arab Legion OC [Officer Commanding] John
Glubb, ... wrote that 'nobody will ever know how many
children died'.[11]

'Great suffering was inflicted,' Rabin admitted later. But the
sufferers he was referring to were his men, not the Palestinians
they were expelling from their family homes. 'Soldiers ...
includ[ing] youth movement graduates, who had been inculcated
with values such as international fraternity and humaneness. The
eviction action went beyond the concepts they were used to.
There were some fellows who refused to take part in the expulsion action. Prolonged propaganda activities were required after
the action to remove the bitterness of these youth movement
groups, and explain why we were obliged to undertake such a
harsh and cruel action.'[12]

• • •

Today the town of Nazareth is Israel's largest Arab city, but it nearly wasn't. In July 1948 news reached Nazareth of the expulsions from Lydda and Ramleh and the inhabitants of Nazareth suspected they would be next. The appearance of hundreds of refugees from towns and villages to the west was an omen.

Azmi Audeh, the son of a carpenter in Nazareth, recalled the events of July 1948 in a memoir.

> More than 2,500 people came to the village of Saffuriya, which is only six miles from Nazareth, seeking refuge. During the night of 15 July 1948 three Israeli planes bombed Saffuriya. They flew over the village and dropped barrels filled with explosives, metal fragments, nails and glass. They shocked the whole village, broke windows, doors and killed innocent civilians. The following day on 16 July 1948 the shelling and artillery bombardment of the village continued and the mass exodus of civilians began pouring into Nazareth. By the end of the day, the village

750,000 Arabs lost homes, possessions and wealth as a result of the policy of 'ethnic cleansing' carried out by the Jewish armies and administration in 1947–8.

was captured by the Israelis and was emptied of its inhabitants. Nazareth became surrounded from the south, the west and the north by Israeli soldiers.[13]

To escape from the anticipated onslaught, Audeh's family sought sanctuary in a nearby convent. They waited there all night, listening to the Israeli attacks, and the following morning Audeh's father set off back into town to see what had happened.

> We all sat down in the basement agonizing about what would happen to Dad. The picture that tortured my brain was that of what I had heard previously about the behaviour of the wild, savage and vicious Jewish soldiers at Deir Yassin and other Arab villages and towns. I imagined my Dad lying in a pool of blood, defenceless, being stabbed to death by a Jewish soldier. The picture became so vivid in my mind that it tormented me no end. Time seemed to crawl so slowly that one minute appeared to take as long as one hour. I felt as if my brain was going to explode, with me entrapped in this basement, unable to do or accomplish anything. It was a feeling of hopelessness, a feeling of defeat, a feeling of being beaten down and a feeling of failure.

> I was awakened from this trance, with a commotion around me, and with my Dad's voice, asking us all to hurry up and follow him back home. We all leapt up and followed him after thanking the nuns and the convent. We reached home and found it in shambles. Everything of value had been stolen by the Jewish soldiers while the rest of the furniture was smashed into pieces. The shock of seeing our home in this situation was too much for my Mom to bear. She almost collapsed, but then she knelt

down and kissed the ground and thanked God that all of us were safe. Thus, on 17 July 1948, Nazareth fell into the hands of the Jews and a new life under a new occupier began.[14]

Decades later the story of how Nazareth's Arabs were saved from expulsion was told by Peretz Kidron, a writer who had been asked to ghost-write the memoirs of Ben Dunkelman, a brigade commander given the task of dislodging Arab forces from the Galilee region. After reaching Nazareth by an undefended rear road, Dunkelman experienced hardly any resistance before the town capitulated. The town's leaders said that they would not resist the Israeli army if Dunkelman and his soldiers promised not to harm the civilian population. An agreement was signed to this effect.

Two days later, Dunkelman was ordered by his immediate superior, Haim Laskov, to expel all the inhabitants, about 15,000 Arabs, Muslims and Christians. 'I was shocked and horrified,' said Dunkelman in the original draft of his memoir. 'I told [Laskov] I would do nothing of the sort – in view of our promises to safeguard the city's people, such a move would be both superfluous and harmful. I reminded him that scarcely a day earlier, he and I, as representatives of the Israeli army, had signed the surrender document in which we solemnly pledged to do nothing to harm the city or its population. When Haim saw that I refused to obey the order, he left.'

Twelve hours later, Dunkelman was ordered to withdraw his brigade from Nazareth to make way for another unit and he was replaced as military governor of the town. 'I felt sure that this order had been given because of my defiance of the evacuation order,' Dunkelman said. 'But although I was withdrawn from Nazareth, it seems that my disobedience did have some effect. It seems to have given the high command time for second thoughts, which led them to the conclusion that it would, indeed, be wrong to expel the inhabitants of Nazareth. To the best of my knowledge, there was never any more talk of the evacuation plan and the city's Arab citizens have lived there ever since.'

This story only emerged many years later. Dunkelman insisted it be removed from the final version of his memoir. Appalled by the story, Kidron kept a copy, which he later published. Unfortunately, there weren't many officers like Dunkelman in the Israeli army, and over the following months a succession of towns and villages were 'cleansed' of their Arab inhabitants.

In his definitive study, *The Birth of the Palestinian Refugee Problem Revisited* (2004), Benny Morris presents authenticated stories of expulsions, massacres and rapes that for years were dismissed by the Israeli government as PLO propaganda. In a newspaper interview, Morris was asked how many Israeli acts of massacre were perpetrated in 1948. He was able to give a very precise answer:

> Twenty-four. In some cases four or five people were executed, in others the numbers were 70, 80, 100. There was also a great deal of arbitrary killing. Two old men are spotted walking in a field – they are shot. A woman is found in an abandoned village – she is shot. There are cases such as the village of Dawayima [in the Hebron region], in which a column entered the village with all guns blazing and killed anything that moved. The worst cases were Saliha (70–80 killed), Deir Yassin (100–110), Lod (250), Dawayima (hundreds) and perhaps Abu Shusha (70). There is no unequivocal proof of a large-scale massacre at Tantura, but war crimes were

perpetrated there. At Jaffa there was a massacre about
which nothing had been known until now. The same at
Arab al Muwassi, in the north.

About half of the acts of massacre were part of
Operation Hiram [in the north, in October 1948]: at
Safsaf, Saliha, Jish, Eilaboun, Arab al Muwasi, Deir al
Asad, Majdal Krum, Sasa. In Operation Hiram there was
an unusually high concentration of executions of people
against a wall or next to a well in an orderly fashion. That
can't be chance. It's a pattern. Apparently, various officers
who took part in the operation understood that the
expulsion order they received permitted them to do these
deeds in order to encourage the population to take to the
roads. The fact is that no one was punished for these acts
of murder. Ben-Gurion silenced the matter. He covered
up for the officers who did the massacres.[15]

Unbelievably, Morris, who has done much in recent years to
validate the horror stories told for decades by Palestinians, then
went on in the newspaper interview to defend the expulsion of
700,000 Palestinians from their homes. 'A society that aims to kill
you forces you to destroy it,' he said. 'When the choice is between
destroying or being destroyed, it's better to destroy.'

'There is something chilling about the quiet way in which you
say that,' replied the interviewer.

'If you expected me to burst into tears,' said Morris, 'I'm sorry to
disappoint you. I will not do that. There are circumstances in
history that justify ethnic cleansing. I know that this term is completely negative in the discourse of the twenty-first century, but
when the choice is between ethnic cleansing and genocide – the
annihilation of your people – I prefer ethnic cleansing.'[16]

It is difficult for me to see the members of my family – my father's brothers and sisters, his cousins and their parents – as potential perpetrators of genocide. I would not describe the resistance of the Palestinians to domination by European Jews or expulsion from their homes as genocide. And it is the case that by the second half of 1948, when many of the expulsions were carried out, Israel was no longer seriously threatened by the crumbling Arab armies, who had no coordinated strategy and were outnumbered in most types of armaments – which Israel was receiving from Europe and America by the shipload. 'At each stage of the war, the IDF significantly outnumbered all the Arab forces arrayed against it,' writes Avi Shlaim, Professor of International Relations at St Antony's College, Oxford, 'and by the final stage of the war its superiority ratio was nearly two to one.'[17]

Many Israelis today – and many others who read only Zionist accounts – still do not know the true story of how the Palestinians lost their land, and some Israelis, who do know, argue that the myths that surround the birth of Israel should be actively promoted. Shlaim quotes two recent articles by Israeli writers. 'They would like school history books to continue to tell only the heroic version of Israel's creation. In effect, they are saying that in education one has to lie for the good of the country. Patriotism, it would seem, remains the last refuge of the scoundrel.'[18] In fact this is no more than an echo of a remark years before by Yitzhak Shamir, who publicly stated that 'it is permissible to lie for the sake of the Land of Israel'.[19]

• • •

In June 1948 the novelist Arthur Koestler wrote an account of travelling through Palestine. He observed with some objectivity the vicissitudes of Palestine in a time of war, but then lapsed into anti-Arab racism:

A few villages along the [coastal] road are still populated
by Arabs. Some of them are even working in the fields;
and a little withered Arab woman is selling oranges to
Jewish soldiers out of a basket on her back. War is
Hecuba to her and she is Hecuba to war. But not for long.
A few weeks later some Arab lads will start sniping from
these villages at Jewish trucks on the road; the Jewish
army will herd the villagers together, dynamite their
houses, and put the young men into concentration camps;
while the old ones will tie a mattress and a brass coffee-
pot on the donkey, the old woman will walk ahead leading
the donkey by the rein and the old man will ride on it,
wrapped in his kefiye, and sunk in solemn meditation
about the lost opportunity of raping his youngest
grandchild.[20]

Another Jew who made racist observations of Arab life in
Palestine at this time was Doris Katz, a member of the Irgun. She is
described in the introduction to her book *The Lady was a Terrorist*
as 'a sensitive and cultured woman'. She and a number of other
Irgun members took over an Arab village called Yehudiah:

The village was one of the largest and richest in the
country, by Arab standards. By European standards it was
nothing more than a cluster of mud-baked hovels, set
unevenly in rough-hewn, steep, winding streets, with here
and there a stone house belonging to some local notable.
Some of these notables must have had tidy-sized
stockings stuck away somewhere. Their houses were
furnished with magnificent carpets and drapes and
excellent furniture. They obviously made up for their lack
of toilet and washing facilities by the liberal use of

expensive perfumes which they bought by the litre, or
even by the gallon, if the size of their perfume bottles was
any gauge.[21]

Towards the end of 1948, Joseph Weitz of the Jewish National
Fund, a man who had pushed very hard for a policy of Arab expulsion, wrote in his diary an account of the land he and his fellow
Zionists had coveted for decades and was now cleansed of most of
its Arabs:

> The Galilee is revealed to me in its splendour, its hidden
> places and folds, its crimson smile and its green softness
> and its desolation. I have never seen it like this. It was
> always bustling with man and beast. And the latter
> predominated. Herds and more herds used to descend
> from the heights to the valleys of the streambeds, their
> bells ringing with a sort of discontinuous sound, which
> vanished in the ravines and hid among the crevices, as if
> they would go on chiming for ever. And the shepherds
> striding after them like figures from ancient times,
> whistling merrily and driving the goats toward the trees
> and bushes to gnaw at them hungrily; and now the picture
> has disappeared and is no more. A strange stillness lies
> over all the mountains and is drawn by hidden threads
> from within the empty village.
>
> An empty village; what a terrible thing! Fossilized lives!
> Lives turned to fossilized whispers in extinguished ovens;
> a shattered mirror; mouldy blocks of dried figs and a
> scrawny dog, thin-tailed and floppy-eared and dark-eyed.
>
> At the same time – at the very same moment – a
> different feeling throbs and rises from the primordial
> depths, a feeling of victory, of taking control, of revenge,

and of casting off suffering. And suddenly the whispers vanish and you see empty houses, good for the settlement of our Jewish brethren who have wandered for generation upon generation, refugees of your people, steeped in suffering and sorrow as they, at last, find a roof over their heads. This was our war.[22]

Weitz hoped that the war was nearly over, and that the 'fossilized whispers in extinguished ovens' (an unfortunate phrase) would dwindle to silence, but the Zionism that had dominated his thinking and actions and those of his colleagues had played them false. It had misled them into believing that their takeover of the territory of the Palestinian Arabs would bring about a peaceful Jewish State of Israel. More than fifty years of history have shown how wrong they were.

EPILOGUE

On 20 October 2004 I sat at a long table in a building in the centre of Ramallah and spoke with Yasser Arafat. Short and pale, his wide eyes staring through horn-rimmed spectacles, he sat behind a wall of gifts presented to him by visitors from around the world: a sculpture of a dove of peace, two bronze horses rearing up on their hind legs, a model of a hawk, a crucifix – even though he was a Muslim. On the table was a large pile of papers, and there were more documents scattered across a reading stand in front of him. He was recovering from what had been described as 'flu', although rumours circulated that week of a much more serious illness.

I was with two friends, a Palestinian diplomat and his wife, and we were the first visitors Arafat had seen for several days. Instead of the traditional kiss on both cheeks, he welcomed us by kissing our shoulders, so as not to pass on his 'flu'. His hands were soft and discoloured in patches, but there was little sign of the tremor that had been reported as a symptom of Parkinson's disease.

When I asked Arafat if he remembered my father, he replied 'Of course, of course.' He asked after my cousin Hasib in London (who had recently suffered a stroke). My Palestinian friend and his wife enquired about Arafat's health, presented him with a box of Belgian chocolates and relayed some political news from Europe. At one point in our conversation, Arafat said, apparently inconsequentially: 'You know, the best marble comes from Beit Jala [a village near Bethlehem], the best marble in the world.' Three weeks later, on 11 November, he was dead. And a few days after that, to scenes of mass grief, he was buried in a grave surrounded by marble from Hebron, not Beit Jala.

During his long career, Arafat had seen the world's view of the Palestinians change from a barely recognized population of refugees in the 1950s to a people who had a history, a nationality and a justified grievance. That recognition came about partly as a result of Arafat himself, and partly – it has to be said – because of Israel's treatment of the Palestinians.

• • •

But I have stopped my personal history of Palestine in the year 1948, the last year in which the real Palestine – the territory that had been known as Palestine by its inhabitants for hundreds of years – could be said to exist. Much has happened since then to increase the hardship suffered by the Palestinian Arabs who used to live in the towns and villages of Palestine and now live in camps in Jordan, Lebanon, Gaza and the West Bank.

Four months after the State of Israel was established, Ben-Gurion proposed a major military offensive to capture the West Bank (then a part of Jordan). But in an uncharacteristic burst of statesmanship, six ministers voted against this plan and Ben-Gurion failed to get a majority. He described this decision as a cause for 'mourning for generations to come'.[1]

Meanwhile, the Arab countries surrounding Israel kept up the pressure – both diplomatic and military – to force Israel to redress the injustice it had meted out to the Palestinians. Israel's neighbours – Egypt, Jordan and Syria – each had cause to suffer from Israel's continued bellicosity, as well as having to stand by while Palestinian Arabs in Israel were subjected to harsh treatment. In 1956 Israel invaded Gaza (then under Egyptian control) and headed for the Suez Canal in collusion with Britain and France, who resented Egyptian President Gamal Abdel Nasser's nationalization of the canal. International outrage led to the operation being aborted and Israel, Britain and France were forced to withdraw their forces. But Israel's government still 'mourned' the 1948 decision not to invade the West Bank, and tension continued to build up between Israel and its Arab neighbours.

In 1967 the Six Day War began with Israel's pre-emptive strike on Egypt's air force and army, and its capture of Gaza and the Sinai. Then Israel invaded Jordan, capturing Jerusalem, the West Bank and the Golan Heights (a part of Syria). In the process, another 275,000 Palestinian refugees were created. From then until now – in spite of the declared illegality of Israel's occupation of Palestinian land, and its continued breaching of international law as applied to its treatment of civilians in occupied territory – Israel has continued to hold and control Palestine and Palestinians.

Those events, from 1948 to the present, are in the foreground of most of what we know about the Israelis and the Palestinians these days. This has concentrated the world's attention on 'the Arab-Israeli dispute', in which the primary issue is who did what to whom in and around the State of Israel. But it has also pushed into the background the major and original injustice: the takeover of Palestine by the Zionists.

For Israel's supporters this is how it should be. They argue that what happened fifty or a hundred years ago is no longer relevant. It is time for the Palestinians to put all that behind them and learn to live with the fact that Israel exists. There is no turning back. There is no possibility of 'pushing the Jews into the sea', as some Arabs suggest. It's a tough world and the Palestinians must accept their losses and move on.

Raymonda Tawil, a Palestinian journalist and activist who was born in Acre and now lives in the West Bank, has an answer to such arguments. She describes a conversation she had with an Israeli soldier in the office of the Military Governor of Ramallah, nearly thirty years after the Israeli takeover of Palestine.

> 'You Palestinians,' the soldier said. 'You ought to give up. Accept the situation. You're finished.'
>
> 'What do you mean, "finished"?' she said. 'You say we should give in? Accept the situation? When the Jews were in the ghettoes, did *they* give in? Did they "accept the situation"? No, they didn't. Well, neither will we. You say no one likes us, no one is on our side. But who liked *your* people? Who was on the side of the Jews? No one! But the Jews fought. Even when everyone around was trying to annihilate you. Well, we Palestinians are just like you Jews. We don't want to be victims. We want to be able to defend ourselves. The whole world denied the existence of the Jewish people – but it does exist. I respect your fight for survival and dignity. You should respect ours!'[2]

It was the Zionists who insisted that the twentieth-century map of the Middle East be redrawn according to the state of affairs that existed – or that the Zionists claimed to exist – some 3,000 years ago. If the Zionists could fall back on Old Testament history to claim Palestine, surely the Palestinians have an even greater right to claim back the land they owned much more recently, for the last few centuries? Unfortunately, at least in Western political circles between 1900 and 1948, the Old Testament myths were believed and the hard facts were ignored.

Jews have been persecuted in many different countries over the centuries, culminating in the horror of the Nazi concentration camps. The Zionists argued that they would continue to be persecuted for as long as they remained stateless and had no nation of their own. However, this does not make it acceptable to deprive other people of their rights. And if persecution is an argument for being given a nation, the Palestinians are currently being perse-cuted by Israel. There is also the uncomfortable fact that most Jews today who choose to live in Britain, America or Europe do not believe it is necessary for them to live in an exclusively Jewish state in order to be free from persecution.

The Palestinian writer Afif Safieh has written:

> If I were a Jew or a Gypsy, the Holocaust would be the
> most horrible event in History. If I were a Black African it
> would be Slavery and Apartheid. If I were a Native
> American, it would be the discovery of the New World by
> European explorers and settlers that resulted in near total
> extermination. If I were an Armenian it would be the
> Ottoman-Turkish massacres. And if I happen to be
> Palestinian, it would be the Nakba-Catastrophe. No one
> people has a monopoly on human suffering. It is not
> advisable to try to establish a hierarchy of suffering.
> Humanity should consider all the above as morally
> repugnant and politically unacceptable. And humanity is
> increasingly beginning to express its adhesion to the
> principle that there is only one mankind and not different
> kinds of men and women.[3]

Unfortunately, successive Israeli governments, and many of their citizens, seem to believe that Palestinian Arabs are 'different kinds of men and women', and this has led to continuing injustice in their attitude to Palestinians, both in Israel and outside. After 1948 the Israelis continued the policies they had adopted during the Arab–Israeli War to expel as many Arabs as possible from the areas they controlled, while trying to claim more territory from the areas allocated to the Palestinian Arabs.

They also refuse to take any responsibility for the Palestinian refugee problem. Before the revelations of Benny Morris and other Israeli historians, the Israelis publicly denied having caused the problem, and therefore made no effort to solve it. Of course, the first rulers of Israel were fully aware of what they had done as soldiers a few years before, but for thirty years or more they were able to persuade the world, and indeed many of their own citizens, that the Palestinian Arabs made themselves refugees.

This is bad enough, but I have met Jews who have even foggier ideas about where the Palestinian refugees came from. At a lunch party in London a few years ago, hosted by Jewish friends, most of the guests, apart from me and my wife, were Jewish. One of them, a pleasant, middle-aged woman, started discussing the Palestinian refugees. She did not know that I was Palestinian and complained that the Palestinian refugee problem had been hijacked by anti-Semites. 'It's unfair the way people use the Palestinian refugees to attack Israel,' she said. 'You never heard about them before Israel was established.' It took me a moment to realize the depth of her ignorance. She apparently believed that the Palestinian refugees, like the poor, had always been with us, but once Israel had come into being they had become a stick with which to beat the Jews.

'Refugees' is such an evocative word these days. Because of what the Palestinian refugees have become, it is difficult to think of them as anything other than sad, deprived and inadequate. And yet, when I hear my family's stories of the exodus from Safad, for example, I see a very different group of people. These people – like Hasib's sister, Su'ad, whose clothes were shredded on the journey – came from a prosperous Palestinian town. Among them were lawyers and doctors, shopkeepers and teachers, café-owners and waiters, children, young married couples, old men and women. Not only were they made homeless and stateless, but most of them became bankrupt. Their houses were usually taken over by Jews, who took possession of the furniture, fittings, jewellery, cash and cherished mementoes. People in Britain, Europe or America may not be able to imagine what it is like to be a Palestinian, but all you have to do is visualize how you would feel if, at a few hours' notice, you had to walk out of your house, leaving everything behind that you couldn't carry, and walk dozens of miles to another country, and never return.

Nevertheless, millions of the refugees' descendants have settled in new lands and re-established themselves in different societies, often very successfully. Su'ad, who walked from Safad to Beirut as a teenager, ended her days living within a stone's throw of Kensington Palace in London, in the house of her brother Hasib, who made a fortune from the company he started in Haifa in 1945. My father died after a successful career in the US Diplomatic Service. I too have made a successful career as a writer and television producer. Cousins and children of cousins are doctors, engineers, draftsmen, psychologists and teachers in Europe, America and Australia. But that's not the point.

As the new State of Israel began to establish itself, it found that (despite all its efforts) it had a small population of Palestinian Arabs (about 10 per cent of the original inhabitants), including some members of my family. My father's sister Georgette, for example, a teacher married to her cousin Abdallah, stayed behind in Haifa. Her son grew up in Israel and married a Jewish girl. Israel is often described as 'the only democracy in the Middle East', yet the attitude of most Israelis to the Palestinian Arabs can only be described as racist.

Arabs are also Semites. In this context one might even speak of Jewish anti-Semitism, that is, a prejudice against Arabs. My Jewish guide at the Acre Citadel, who dismissed a victim of Jewish terrorism as 'just an Arabic person', was anti-Semitic. And in September 2003 the young immigration officer in the arrivals area when I flew to Israel betrayed similar prejudices.

She picked up my British passport, saw my un-English name and assumed I was Jewish.

'Where will you be staying in Israel?' she asked.

'The American Colony hotel in Jerusalem,' I said.

She looked puzzled. 'But that's an Arab hotel.* Why do you stay there? What's wrong with all the Jewish hotels in Jerusalem?'

'I stay there because I like it,' I said.

'You like *Arabs*?' she said, a note of disgust in her voice.

Imagine a British immigration officer saying to a Jewish visitor: 'But that's a Jewish hotel. Why do you stay there? What's wrong with all the British hotels in London?'

'I stay there because I like it.'

'You like *Jews*?'

A modern Jewish writer has characterized the current Israeli approach to the Palestinians as 'OK, we've suffered; you've suffered, let's talk.' But he goes on to write: 'To which we have to say, "No, it's not 'we've suffered, you've suffered, let's talk,' it's 'We've suffered and we've caused you to suffer – NOW let's talk."'[4]

Underlying this sentiment is one stark fact. The biggest step Israel could take to move the peace process forward would be to apologize. The Zionist takeover of Palestine and expulsion of its Arab inhabitants was a glaring injustice to the Palestinians, inflicted upon them by people who became the government and

---

* Actually it's owned by a Swedish company, but most of the staff are Arabs.

citizens of Israel. What hurts and angers Palestinians almost as much as the loss and destruction of their homes, the massacre of their relatives, the uprooting of their olive groves and the constant flouting of their civil liberties is that Israel will not acknowledge this original injustice.

To say 'we cannot accept historical responsibility for the creation of the problem' prompts the question 'whose responsibility was it?' Many histories of the State of Israel and Palestine devote more space than I do here to 'what the Arabs did wrong', both before and after 1948. The usual intention is to shift some of the blame for the loss of their country on to the Palestinian Arabs. We are told of the violence some Arabs carried out, their refusal to participate in various legislative councils or to accept any form of partition of their land, the talks some of their leaders had with the Nazis, the incompetence of their military enterprises, and so on, and so on.

These facts are presented as some kind of counterweight to the injustice embodied in the Balfour Declaration and the British Mandate. The argument goes that if the Palestinian Arabs had done A, B or C, they might not be as badly off as they are today, and therefore they have to accept some share of the blame for their fate. This is rather like saying that a man who is beaten up by robbers is partly to blame for his injuries if he resists, and therefore, presumably, the robbers should get a lighter sentence. If he had handed over his wallet after a punch in the face they wouldn't have had to break his arms and legs.

The fact is the Palestinians did nothing to cause their own fate. Did the Palestinians slaughter and expel themselves? Did they compel Jews from Europe to flock to Palestine and buy up land? Did the Palestinians lobby the British government to give away a land that didn't belong to them?

Obviously, few politicians in Israel today were directly involved in the takeover of Palestine (although Sharon was, as were most of the early Israeli Prime Ministers). And Israelis living in a fashionable house formerly owned by an Arab family are not directly responsible for the theft of that house. But they should at least accept that its original inhabitants are absent not by choice, but because they were brutally expelled and forbidden to return.

All right-thinking people react strongly against anyone who tries to play down the responsibility of Nazi Germany for the massacre of six million Jews. But modern Germany has made strenuous efforts, including massive financial reparations, to accept responsibility for what happened to the Jews. It is time for the State of Israel to do the same with respect to the Palestinian Arabs, and to set in motion an honest and open-minded dialogue about how to rectify this most intractable and glaring injustice.

FURTHER READING

The best recent overall survey of the history of Palestine I have come across is the multi-authored *A History of Israel and the Holy Land*. Like all Judaeo-centric books about the history of the area, the editors are uncomfortable using the name 'Palestine' in the title, even though it is in the titles of the chapters covering the period from AD 633 to 1948, since that is what the book is really about. Once you get past the introduction by Shimon Peres, it even deals reasonably objectively with the tenuous connection between the Bible and verifiable historical events. There is also a good range of photographs and illustrations of key artefacts and sites.

There are two books which deal with the misuses of Bible texts and biblical archaeology to create a mythical history of the Jewish people and to suppress the history of the Palestinians. Philip Davies's *In Search of 'Ancient Israel'*, although written for students, is a very approachable and often lively summary of recent academic analysis of the biblical texts that shows the limitations of using them as historical narratives. Keith Whitelam's *The Invention of Ancient Israel* complements Davies's book by describing how the true history of pre-Christian Palestine has been obscured by the creation of a history of ancient Israel.

From Haven to Conquest, edited by Walid Khalidi, is a selection of eighty readings from often hard-to-find texts about Zionism and the Palestine problem, with a short section on pre-Balfour Declaration texts and good coverage of the Mandate period and events leading up to the UN vote. There are two books which deal in more detail with these events. One, *Nisi Dominus*, is by Nevill Barbour and was published in 1946 at the height of British discussions about how to deal with the poisoned chalice of Palestine. The other, *Palestine: The Reality*, by J. M. N. Jeffries, is an extraordinary book for two reasons. First, it is a rich mixture of detailed reportage and passionate polemic about the events of the 1920s and 1930s when the Zionists manipulated the British by intervening at every point when it looked as if the rights of the Palestinian population might actually be paid some attention by the government. Second, unlike most books that have fallen out of print because they were of interest at a particular time and have been superseded, it has disappeared from view in the second-hand market and is only obtainable from a few libraries. Apart from this book, most out-of-print books are likely to be found via www.abebooks.com.

Among modern books on the events before and after the de-Arabization of Palestine, *The Birth of Israel*, by Simha Flapan, and *A History of Modern Palestine*, by Ilan Pappe, both Israeli scholars, give balanced accounts of the events of the last hundred years in Palestine.

Professor Benny Morris's work, *The Birth of the Palestinian Refugee Problem Revisited*, makes it impossible to doubt any longer the version of the story told by Palestinians about their expulsion from Palestine in 1947–8. Professor Morris's detailed research in Israeli archives is thorough, objective and shocking.

Finally, for the connoisseur, *The Rise of Israel*, a thirty-nine-volume set of documents covering the Zionists' sixty-six-year-long project to make Palestine a Jewish state, is a gruesome and enthralling treasure chest of letters, memos and reports, all presented in facsimile, to establish the precise methodology by which the idea of a few Zionists in 1892 led to the development of the state of Israel.

Michael Avi-Yonah (ed.), *A History of Israel and the Holy Land*, Continuum, New York, 2001

Neville Barbour, *Nisi Dominus*, George G. Harrap, London, 1946

Michael J. Cohen, Isaiah Friedman and Aaron S. Klieman (eds), *The Rise of Israel*, Garland Publishing, Inc., New York, 1987

Philip Davies, *In Search of 'Ancient Israel'*, Sheffield Academic Press, 1992

Simha Flapan, *The Birth of Israel*, Pantheon Books, New York, 1987

J. M. N. Jeffries, *Palestine: The Reality*, Longmans, Green and Co, 1939

Walid Khalidi (ed.), *From Haven to Conquest*, The Institute for Palestine Studies, Washington, 1987

Benny Morris, *The Birth of the Palestinian Refugee Problem Revisited*, Cambridge University Press, 2004

Ilan Pappe, *A History of Modern Palestine*, Cambridge University Press, 2004

Keith W. Whitelam, *The Invention of Ancient Israel*, Routledge, 1996

NOTES

References to websites, in < > brackets, were correct at the time of writing, but in the fast-moving world of the internet addresses can change or sites disappear. If material quoted in the book no longer appears to be retrievable, the reference can usually be retrieved by typing specific quotes into www.Google.com.

PROLOGUE
1. James Boswell, *Life of Johnson*, Oxford University Press, 1983, p. 333.
2. See, for example, <http://www.valleyadvocate.com/gbase/News/content.html?oid=oid:76538>

I ANCIENT PALESTINE
1. <http://www.fodors.com/miniguides/mgresults.cfm?destination=jerusalem@80&cur_section=fea&feature=30001>
2. J. M. N. Jeffries, *Palestine: The Reality*, Longmans, Green and Co., 1939, p. 11.
3. Philip Davies, *In Search of 'Ancient Israel'*, Sheffield Academic Press, 1992, p. 148.
4. Niels Peter Lemche, *On the Problems of Reconstructing Pre-Hellenistic Israelite (Palestinian) History*, Department of Biblical Studies, The University of Copenhagen. *Journal of Hebrew Scriptures*, Vol. 3, 2001.
5. <http://www.fodors.com/miniguides/mgresults.cfm?destination=jerusalem@80&cur_section=fea&feature=30001>
6. Davies, *In Search of 'Ancient Israel'*, p. 59.
7. G. W. Bowersock, *Palestine: Ancient History and Modern Politics* in *Blaming the Victims*, edited by Edward Said and Christopher Hitchens, Verso, 1988, pp. 182–4.
8. Golda Meir, quoted in article by Sarah Honig, *Jerusalem Post*, 25

November 1995.

9. Quoted from Istakhri and Ibn Hawkal, in Guy Le Strange, *Palestine Under the Muslims*, Palestine Exploration Fund, 1890.

10. Edward Said, *The Question of Palestine*, Vintage, 1992, pp. 10–11.

11. Haim Gerber, 'Palestine and Other Territorial Concepts in the 17th Century', *International Journal of Middle East Studies*, 30 (1998), pp. 573–650.

12. Mosshe Sharon in Michael Avi-Yonah (ed.), *A History of Israel and the Holy Land*, Continuum, New York, 2001.

13. Beshara B. Doumani, 'Rediscovering Ottoman Palestine: Writing Palestinians into History', *Journal of Palestine Studies*, XXI/2 (Winter 1992), pp. 9–10.

14. <http://www.palestinefacts.org/pf_early_palestine_zionists_impact.php>

15. Nevill Barbour, *Nisi Dominus*, George G. Harrap, 1946, p. 32.

16. K. J. Asali (ed.), *Jerusalem in History*, Scorpion Publishing, 1989, p. 231.

17. Tudor Parfitt, *The Jews in Palestine 1800–1822*, Royal Historical Society/Boydell Press, 1987.

2 'THE FIRST KING OF PALESTINE'

1. Constantine de Volney, *Travels Through Syria and Egypt*, Vol. II, G. G. J. and J. Robinson, 1788, pp. 130–2.

2. Ibid., p. 91.

3. De Volney, *Travels Through Syria and Egypt*, Vol. I, pp. 390–1.

4. De Volney, *Travels Through Syria and Egypt*, Vol. II, p. 229.

5. Richard Pococke, *A Description of the East and Some Other Countries*, Printed for the Author by W. Bowyer, 1745, Vol. II, p. 69.

6. De Volney, *Travels Through Syria and Egypt*, Vol. II, pp. 92–3.

7. Ibid., p. 94.

8. Amnon Cohen, *Palestine in the 18th Century*, The Magnes Press, 1973, p. 16.

9. Ahmad Hasan Joudah, *Revolt in Palestine in the Eighteenth Century*, The Kingston Press, 1987, pp. 37–8.

10. Cohen, *Palestine in the 18th Century*, p. 130.

11. Ibid., p. 86.

12. De Volney, *Travels Through Syria and Egypt*, Vol. I, pp. 126-7.
13. Cohen, *Palestine in the 18th Century*, p. 88.
14. Ibid.

3 DAHER'S DECLINE

1. Constantine de Volney, *Travels Through Syria and Egypt*, Vol. I, G. G. J. and J. Robinson, 1788, p. 157.
2. Thomas Philipp, *Acre*, Columbia University Press, 2001, p. 41.
3. Sauveur Lusignan, *A History of the Revolt of Ali Bey Against the Ottoman Porte*, James Phillips, 1784, pp. 150–1.
4. De Volney, *Travels Through Syria and Egypt*, Vol. II, pp. 114–15.
5. Philipp, *Acre*, p. 47.
6. De Volney, *Travels Through Syria and Egypt*, Vol. II, pp. 124–6.
7. Ibid., pp. 130–2.
8. Ibid.

4 PALESTINE IN THE NINETEENTH CENTURY

1. Stuart A. Cohen, *English Zionists and British Jews*, Princeton University Press, 1982, p. 5.
2. W. M. Thomson D. D., *The Land and the Book*, T. Nelson and Sons, 1861, p. 273.
3. Laurence Oliphant, *Haifa or Life in Modern Palestine*, Harper and Brothers, 1886, pp. 68–71.
4. Ibid.
5. Quoted in 'Herzl Hinted at Napoleon's "Zionist Past"', *Ha'aretz* magazine, 26 April 2004.
6. Abel Manna, *The Notables of Palestine at the End of the Ottoman Period, 1800 – 1918*, House of Palestine, 1986, pp. 236–7.
7. *Arabian Nights: Supplemental Nights*, Vol. 3, introduction by Richard Burton, privately printed by the Burton Club, 1888, pp. xiv–xv.
8. Robert Irwin, *The Arabian Nights: A Companion*, Allen Lane, The Penguin Press, 1994, pp. 57–8.
9. Thomson, *The Land and the Book*, p. 278.
10. Michael Asaf, 'Hayahasim Bin Arabim Veyihudim Bearetz Yisrail 1860–1948' (in Hebrew), *Culture and Education*, 1970, p. 160, quoted in Mustafa Abbasi, 'The Arab Community in Safad,

1840–1918', *Jerusalem Quarterly File*, <http.www.jqf-jerusalem.org/2003/jqf17/safad.pdf>

11. Thomson, *The Land and the Book*, p. 470.

12. Beshara B. Doumani, 'Rediscovering Ottoman Palestine: Writing Palestinians into History', *Journal of Palestine Studies*, XXI/2 (Winter 1992), p. 7.

13. Beshara Doumani, *Rediscovering Palestine*, University of California Press, 1995, pp. 26–7.

14. Laurence Oliphant, *Haifa or Life in Modern Palestine*, Harper and Brothers, 1886, pp. 115–16.

5 TRAVELLERS' TALES

1. Beshara B. Doumani, 'Rediscovering Ottoman Palestine: Writing Palestinians into History', *Journal of Palestine Studies*, XXI/2 (Winter 1992), p. 8.

2. Mark Twain, *The Innocents Abroad*, Dover Publications, 2003, p. 535.

3. Samuel Katz, *Battleground: Fact and Fantasy in Palestine*, Bantam Books, 1973, pp. 90–115.

4. <http://www.palestinefacts.org/pf_early_palestine_zionists_impact.php>

5. Aaron Berkowitz, *The Four Returns*, <http://www.aarons-advocates.org/afour-ret.html>

6. Meir Abelson, <http://www.acpr.org.il/ENGLISH-NATIV/issue1/Abelson-1>

7. Rabbi Adam Stock Spilker, *Cultivating Ahavat Tziyon / Love of Zion*, Mount Zion Temple, Kol Nidre 5764 / 5 October 2003.

8. Joseph Katz, 'Origins of the Arab–Jewish Conflict', <http://www.eretzyisroel.org/~peters/depopulated.html>

9. *Jewish World Review*, <http://www.jewishworldreview.com/cols/charen041202.asp>

10. Walid Khalidi, *All that Remains*, Institute for Palestine Studies, 1992, p. 472.

11. Israel Zangwill, 'The Return to Palestine', *New Liberal Review*, 2 (Dec. 1901) p. 627.

12. Justin McCarthy, *The Population of Palestine*, Columbia University Press, 1990, p. 10.

13. Theodor Herzl, *Excerpts from His Diaries*, Scopus Publishing Company, Inc., 1941, entry for 3 September 1897.

14. Eliezer ben-Yehuda and Yehiel Michal Pines, quoted in Benny Morris, *Righteous Victims*, Vintage Books, 2001, p. 49.

15. <http://www.capmag.com/article.asp?ID=2136> Footnote says: 'The essay has apparently not been translated into English, but besides the Hebrew (in *Kol Kitve Ahad Ha'am*) there is a German translation, on which the translation above was based.' Ahad Ha'am, *Am Scheidewege: Gesammelte Aufsätze*, Vol. 1, Judischer Verlag, 1923, pp. 86–8.

16. 'Letters from Palestine' (1891), from *The Complete Works of Ahad Ha'am* (in Hebrew), Dvir, 1949, p. 24.

17. Israel Zangwill in speech to Zionist group in Manchester, quoted in Nur Masalha, *Expulsion of the Palestinians*, Institute for Palestine Studies, 1992, pp. 7–10.

18. Avi Shlaim, *The Iron Wall*, W. W. Norton, 2000, p. 3.

19. A facsimile of this letter, written to David Wolffsohn on 6 May 1904, is available on the internet at <http://www.jafi.org.il/education/herzl/timeline7.html>

6 BIBLE STORIES

1. Paul Goodman (ed.), *The Jewish National Home*, J. M. Dent and Sons Ltd, 1943, p. 12.

2. Ze'ev Herzog, *Ha'aretz* magazine, 29 October 1999.

3. Philip Davies, *In Search of 'Ancient Israel'*, Sheffield Academic Press, 1992, pp. 51–2.

4. Keith W. Whitelam, *The Invention of Ancient Israel*, Routledge, 1996, pp. 122–4.

5. Niels Peter Lemche, *On the Problems of Reconstructing Pre-Hellenistic Israelite (Palestinian) History*, Department of Biblical Studies, The University of Copenhagen. *Journal of Hebrew Scriptures*, Vol. 3, 2001.

6. Davies, *In Search of 'Ancient Israel'*, p. 64.

7. Whitelam, *The Invention of Ancient Israel*, pp. 147, 164.

8. Ibid., pp. 23, 29.

9. Edmund Leach, 'Anthropological approaches to the study of the

Bible during the twentieth century', in E. Leach and D. A. Aycock (eds), *Structuralist Interpretations of Biblical Myth*, Cambridge University Press, 1983, quoted in Whitelam, *The Invention of Ancient Israel*, p. 162.

10. Davies, *In Search of 'Ancient Israel'*, pp. 41, 112.

11. John Bright, *A History of Israel*, SCM Press, 1979, p. 179.

12. Whitelam, *The Invention of Ancient Israel*, p. 173.

13. Davies, *In Search of 'Ancient Israel'*, p. 64.

14. Whitelam, *The Invention of Ancient Israel*, p. 163.

15. *Bamachane* magazine, 18 March 1969, quoted in <http://artscapeweb.com/masada.html>

16. See Nadia Abu El-Haj, *Facts on the Ground*, University of Chicago Press, 2001, p. 116.

17. Ze'ev Herzog, *Ha'aretz* magazine, 29 October 1999.

18. Davies, *In Search of 'Ancient Israel'*, p. 30.

19. H. Shanks, *Biblical Archaeology Review*, 17 (1991), pp. 62–8.

20. Quoted in Edward W. Said, *The Question of Palestine*, Vintage, 1992, p. 79.

21. W. F. Albright, *From the Stone Age to Christianity*, Doubleday, 1957, pp. 280–1.

7 BALFOUR AND FRIENDS

1. J. M. N. Jeffries, *Palestine: The Reality*, Longmans, Green and Co., 1939, p. 193.

2. Elie Kedourie, *In the Anglo-Arab Labyrinth*, second expanded edition, Frank Cass, 2000, p. 100.

3. O. S. Edwardes, *Palestine: Land of Broken Promises*, Dorothy Crisp & Co, 1946, p. 15.

4. *The Letters and Papers of Chaim Weizmann*, Series A, Letters, Vol. VII, Israel Universities Press, 1975, pp. 79, 112.

5. Jeffries, *Palestine: The Reality*, p. 149.

6. Footnote to quotation: 'No "suzerainty", the right of a nation to control another's international affairs, had yet been awarded since the War was not over, but the Zionists hoped that Britain would be made suzerain of Palestine.' Jeffries, *Palestine: The Reality*, p. 149.

7. Stuart A. Cohen, *English Zionists and British Jews*, Princeton

University Press, 1982, p. 234.

8. Ibid., p. 15.

9. *Hansard*, House of Commons, 10 July 1905.

10. *The Letters and Papers of Chaim Weizmann*, p. 81.

11. Tom Segev, *One Palestine Complete*, Abacus, 2000, p. 119.

12. Letter from Presidents of Board of Deputies of British Jews and of the Anglo-Jewish Association, *The Times*, London, 24 May 1917.

13. Ibid.

14. *The Letters and Papers of Chaim Weizmann*, p. 419.

15. Quote from *Der XIIte Zionisten Kongress*, Judische Verlag, Berlin, 1922, quoted in Nevill Barbour, *Nisi Dominus*, George G. Harrap, 1946, p. 63.

16. Quoted in Barbour, *Nisi Dominus*. Original source N. M. Gelber, *Hatsharat Balfur Vatoldoteha*, Jerusalem, 1939, p. 162.

17. Quoted in Barbour, *Nisi Dominus*. Original source Gelber, *Hatsharat Balfur Vatoldoteha*, p. 175.

18. Quoted in Barbour, *Nisi Dominus*. Original source Gelber, *Hatsharat Balfur Vatoldoteha*, p. 198.

8 A LETTER TO LORD ROTHSCHILD

1. *Palestine: Statement of Policy*, Cmd. 6019, His Majesty's Stationery Office, 1939.

2. Arthur Koestler, *Promise and Fulfilment: 1917–1949*, Macmillan, 1949, p. 4.

3. Address delivered at London Zionist Conference, 21 September 1919, quoted in *Zionist Policy*, British Zionist Federation, 1919.

4. Samuel Landman, 'Secret History of the Balfour Declaration', *World Jewry*, 1 March 1935.

5. Ibid.

6. J. M. N. Jeffries, *Palestine: The Reality*, Longmans, Green and Co., 1939, p. 156.

7. *The Letters and Papers of Chaim Weizmann*, Series A, Letters, Vol. VII, Israel Universities Press, 1975, pp. 86–7.

8. Isaiah Friedman (ed.), *The Rise of Israel*, Vol. 8, Garland Publishing, Inc., New York, 1987, p. 28.

9. Ibid., p. 26.

10. Ibid., p. 36.
11. Ibid., p. 41.
12. Ibid., p. 39.
13. Moshe Smilansky, quoted in Benny Morris, *Righteous Victims*, Alfred A. Knopf, Inc., 2001, p. 43.
14. H. Sacher, *A Jewish Palestine: The Jewish Case for a British Trusteeship*, Zionist Organization, London, 1919, p. 17, quoted in Tom Segev, *One Palestine Complete*, Abacus, 2000, p. 119.
15. Edwin S. Montagu, *The Anti-Semitism of the Present Government*, PRO, Cab. 24/24, 23 August 1917.
16. Blanche Dugdale, 'Its Origin', in Paul Goodman (ed.), *The Jewish National Home*, J. M. Dent, 1943, p. 4.
17. Jeffries, *Palestine: The Reality*, pp. 167–8.
18. 31/10/1917 Minutes of War Cabinet, National Archives, London, Cabinet Papers, 24/4, quoted in Friedman (ed.), *The Rise of Israel*, p. 138.
19. Nevill Barbour, *Nisi Dominus*, George G. Harrap, 1946, p. 65.
20. P. Goodman (ed.), *Chaim Weizmann*, London, 1945, Chapter XIV, quoted in Barbour, *Nisi Dominus*, p. 65.
21. Jeffries, *Palestine: The Reality*, p. 174.
22. Ibid., p. 178.
23. Maurice Samuel, *What Happened in Palestine*, The Stratford Company, 1929, pp. 148, 170.
24. Richard Meinertzhagen, *Middle East Diary 1917–1956*, Thomas Yoseloff, 1959, p. 9.

9 PICKING UP THE PEACE

1. O. S. Edwardes, *Palestine: Land of Broken Promises*, Dorothy Crisp & Co, 1946, p. 18.
2. J. M. N. Jeffries, *Palestine: The Reality*, Longmans, Green and Co, 1939, p. 178.
3. Frances E. Newton, *Fifty Years in Palestine*, Coldharbour Press, 1948, p. 130.
4. Richard Meinertzhagen, *Middle East Diary 1917–1956*, Thomas Yoseloff, 1959, p. 12.
5. Memorandum by Kinahan Cornwallis, Director of the Arab Bureau in

Cairo, on the (Zionist) Commission on 20 April 1918, quoted in Doreen Ingrams, *Palestine Papers 1917–1922*, John Murray, 1972, p. 28.

6. Quoted in Isaiah Friedman (ed.), *The Rise of Israel*, Vol. 10, Garland Publishing, Inc., 1987, p. 14.

7. Ibid., pp. 16–17.

8. Letter from Muslim-Christian Committee of Jaffa to Military Governor, Storrs, quoted in Friedman (ed.), *The Rise of Israel*, Vol. 10, pp. 41–2.

9. Weizmann to Clayton, quoted in Friedman (ed.), *The Rise of Israel*, Vol. 10, p. 95.

10. Quoted in Friedman (ed.), *The Rise of Israel*, Vol. 10, p. 37.

11. Sykes to Ormsby-Gore, quoted in Friedman (ed.), *The Rise of Israel*, Vol. 10, p. 27.

12. Quoted in Friedman (ed.), *The Rise of Israel*, Vol. 10, p. 38.

13. Letter from Jabotinsky to Weizmann, quoted in Friedman (ed.), *The Rise of Israel*, p. 49.

14. Quoted in Friedman (ed.), *The Rise of Israel*, pp. 50 –1.

15. Quoted in ibid., pp. 52 –3.

16. Secret 'Memorandum on British Commitments to King Hussein' prepared for the inner group at the Peace Conference in 1919. Robert John found a copy in 1964 among the papers of the late Professor Wm. Westermann, who had been adviser on Turkish affairs to the American Delegation to the Peace Conference. Quoted in Robert John, 'Behind the Balfour Declaration: Britain's Great War Pledge To Lord Rothschild', *The Journal for Historical Review*, 6/4 (Winter 1985–6), p. 389 <http://www.ihr.org>

10 MANDATE

1. Richard Meinertzhagen, *Middle East Diary 1917–1956*, Thomas Yoseloff, 1959, pp. 24–5.

2. Ibid., pp. 24–5.

3. J. M. N. Jeffries, *Palestine: The Reality*, Longmans, Green and Co., 1939, p. 267.

4. National Archives, London F.O. 608/99. Minutes of an informal meeting held on 21 March 1919, quoted in *The Rise of Israel*, Vol 10, Garland Publishing Inc., 1987, pp. 221–25.

5. Izzat Tannous, *The Palestinians*, I. G. T. Company, 1988, p. 182.

6. Jeffries, *Palestine: The Reality*, p. 259.

7. Quoted in ibid., p. 249.

8. Ibid., p. 257.

9. Ibid., p. 266.

10. Quoted in ibid., p. 293.

11. Ibid., p. 301.

12. Ibid., pp. 236–40.

13. 'Unless the Lord Build the House They Labor in Vain Who Build It: The Palestine Mandate', *The Weekly Review*, 2 May 1946.

14. Meinertzhagen, *Middle East Diary 1917–1956*, p. 52.

15. Ibid., p. 58.

16. Jeffries, *Palestine: The Reality*, p. 359.

17. Ibid.

18. Ibid., p. 367.

19. Ibid., p. 393.

20. Theodor Herzl, *A Jewish State*, translated by S. D'Avigdor, D. Nutt, 1896, pp. xii, 102.

11 INTO THE 1920s

1. Quoted in Paul Goodman (ed.), *The Jewish National Home*, J. M. Dent and Sons Ltd, 1943, Chaim Weizmann, Introduction, p. xiv.

2. Arthur Koestler, *Promise and Fulfilment: Palestine 1917–1949*, Macmillan, 1949, pp. 34–5.

3. Maurice Samuel, *What Happened in Palestine*, The Stratford Company, 1929, pp. 76–7.

4. Quoted in Mordechai Bar-On, *In Pursuit of Peace*, United States Institute of Peace, 1996, p. 12.

5. Tom Segev, *One Palestine Complete*, Abacus, 2000, p. 140.

6. Report of Palin Commission, 7 July 1920, quoted in Aaron S. Klieman (ed.), *The Rise of Israel*, Vol. 18, Garland Publishing, 1987, p. 81.

7. Report of Palin Commission, 7 July 1920, quoted in Klieman (ed.), *The Rise of Israel*, Vol. 18, pp. 8–9.

8. Quoted in Klieman (ed.), *The Rise of Israel*, Vol. 18, p. 5.

9. J. M. N. Jeffries, *Palestine: The Reality*, Longmans, Green and Co., 1939, p. 371.

10. Bernard Wasserstein, *Herbert Samuel: A Political Life*, Clarendon Press, 1992, p. 243.

11. Bernard Wasserstein, *The British in Palestine*, Royal Historical Society, 1978, pp. 16–17.

12. Quoted in Avi Shlaim, *The Politics of Partition: King Abdullah, the Zionists, and Palestine, 1921–1951*, Oxford University Press, 1990, p. 54.

13. Koestler, *Promise and Fulfilment: Palestine 1917–1949*, pp. 33–4.

14. Quoted in Klieman (ed.), *The Rise of Israel*, Vol. 17, pp. 16, 22, 27.

15. Leonard Stein, *The Truth About Palestine*, Zionist Organization, 1922.

16. Sami Hadawi, 'Bitter Harvest', quoted in *The Origin of the Palestine–Israel Conflict*, 3rd edn (including Intifada 2000), published by Jews For Justice in the Middle East, <http://www.cactus48.com/ truth.html>

12 HOSTILE ACTS

1. Tom Segev, *One Palestine, Complete*, Abacus, 2000, p. 357.

2. Mary-Jane Deeb and Mary E. King (eds), *Hasib Sabbagh: From Palestinian Refugee to Citizen of the World*, Middle East Institute, University Press of America, 1996, p. 2.

3. Segev, *One Palestine, Complete*, p. 304.

4. Douglas V. Duff, *Baling with a Teaspoon*, John Long, 1953, quoted in Edward Horne, *A Job Well Done*, Palestine Police, 1982, p. 127.

5. Segev, *One Palestine, Complete*, pp. 334–5.

6. *Report of the Commission on the Palestine Disturbances* Cmd. 3530, HMSO, London, 1930, p. 45.

7. <http://www.adl.org/ISRAEL/Record/david_hacohen.asp>

8. Deeb and King (eds), *Hasib Sabbagh: From Palestinian Refugee to Citizen of the World*, p. 2.

9. Quoted in Segev, *One Palestine, Complete*, pp. 324–5.

10. Joseph Katz, 'Origins of the Arab–Jewish Conflict', in <http://www.eretzyisroel.org/~peters/depopulated.html>

11. Segev, *One Palestine, Complete*, pp. 325–6.

12. Maurice Samuel, *What Happened in Palestine*, The Stratford Company, 1929, pp. 205–7.

13. Ibid., p. 199.

14. Judah Magnes, Chancellor, Hebrew University, Jerusalem, 1929.

15. Presentation of Haim Kalvaryski entitled 'Relation with the Arab Neighbors', Central Zionist Archive (CZA) J1/8777.

16. <http://www.jqf-jerusalem.org/2004/jqf21/alternative.html>

17. Quoted in Aaron S. Klieman (ed.), *The Rise of Israel*, Vol. 17, Garland Publishing, 1987, p. 163.

18. Segev, *One Palestine, Complete*, p. 309.

19. Nur Masalha, *Expulsion of the Palestinians*, Institute for Palestine Studies, 1992, p. 20.

13 COMMISSIONS GALORE

1. Aaron S. Klieman (ed.), *The Rise of Israel*, Vol. 17, Garland Publishing, 1987, p. 179 ff.

2. Edward W. Said and Christopher Hitchens (eds), *Blaming the Victims*, Verso, 1988, p. 243.

3. *Palestine, Report on Immigration, Land Settlement and Development*, Sir John Hope Simpson, Cmd. 3686, HMSO, 1930, p. 141.

4. Tom Segev, *One Palestine, Complete*, Abacus, 2000, p. 333.

5. Nur Masalha, *Expulsion of the Palestinians*, Institute for Palestine Studies, 1992, p. 33.

6. Ibid., p. 37.

7. Lord Passfield, *White Paper* Cmd 3692, HMSO, 1930, p. 5.

8. J. M. N. Jeffries, *Palestine: The Reality*, Longmans, Green and Co., 1939, p. 631.

9. Minutes of a telephone conversation between the Prime Minister and Weizmann from the Zionist office at 9.30 p.m., quoted in N. A. Rose, *The Gentile Zionists*, Frank Cass, 1973, p. 26.

10. Rose, *The Gentile Zionists*, p. 42.

11. Ibid., pp. 63–4.

12. *Palestine Royal Commission, Report*, Cmd. 5479, HMSO, 1937, p. 92.

13. Rose, *The Gentile Zionists*, p. 62.

14. Ibid., pp. 63–4.

15. Nevill Barbour, *Nisi Dominus*, George G. Harrap, 1946, p. 161.

16. Ibid., p. 162.

17. Mary-Jane Deeb and Mary E. King (eds), *Hasib Sabbagh: From Palestinian Refugee to Citizen of the World*, Middle East Institute, University Press of America, 1996, p. 33.

14 PEEL AND PARTITION

1. Nur Masalha, *Expulsion of the Palestinians*, Institute for Palestine Studies, 1992, p. 19.
2. A. J. Sherman, *Mandate Days*, Thames and Hudson, 1997, p. 112.
3. Ibid., p. 114.
4. Ibid., p. 115–16.
5. *The Times*, 9 January 1939, quoted in O. S. Edwardes, *Palestine: Land of Broken Promises*, Dorothy Crisp & Co., 1946, p. 108.
6. Edwardes, *Palestine: Land of Broken Promises*, p. 109.
7. Ibid., p. 110.
8. N. A. Rose, *The Gentile Zionists*, Frank Cass, 1973, p. 124.
9. Nevill Barbour, *Nisi Dominus*, George G. Harrap, 1946, p. 179.
10. Azmi S. Audeh, *Carpenter from Nazareth*, Audeh Publishers, 1997, pp. 34–5.
11. Rose, *The Gentile Zionists*, p. 128.
12. Ibid., p. 134.
13. Ibid., p. 136.
14. *Palestine Royal Commission, Report*, Cmd. 5479, HMSO, 1937, p. 362.
15. Speech by Judah Magnes, during debate at the Session of the Council of the Jewish Agency, Zurich, 18 August 1937, Jud. Press Zentrale, Zurich, No. 956.
16. Rose, *The Gentile Zionists*, p. 140.
17. David Ben-Gurion, quoted in Noam Chomsky, *Fateful Triangle*, Pluto Press, 1983, pp. 91–2.
18. Shabtai Teveth, *Ben-Gurion: The Burning Ground, 1886–1948*, Houghton Mifflin, 1987, pp. 171–2.
19. *Palestine Royal Commission, Report*, Cmd. 5479, HMSO, 1937, p. 390.
20. Masalha, *Expulsion of the Palestinians*, p. 14.
21. Selig Eugen Soskin, memorandum to 20th Zionist Congress, quoted in Masalha, *Expulsion of the Palestinians*, p. 81.

22. Masalha, *Expulsion of the Palestinians*.
23. Berl Katznelson, quoted in Masalha, *Expulsion of the Palestinians*, p. 71.
24. Masalha, *Expulsion of the Palestinians*, p. 118.
25. Joseph Weitz, *My Diary and Letters to the Children*, Massada, Tel Aviv, 1965, Vol. II, pp. 181–2, quoted in Edward Said, *The Question of Palestine*, Vintage, 1992.

15 'LION-CUB OF ARABDOM'

1. Peter Partner, *Arab Voices*, BBC Publications, 1988, p. 18.
2. Quoted in Partner, *Arab Voices*, p. 18.
3. *Foreign Affairs Oral History Program*, Association for Diplomatic Studies and Training, c/o Bentley, 2814 N. Underwood St., Arlington, VA 22213, Box: 1 Fold: 411 Sabbagh, Isa K.
4. *Palestine: Statement of Policy*, Cmd. 6019, HMSO, 1939.
5. Richard Meinertzhagen, *Middle East Diary 1917–1956*, Thomas Yoseloff, 1959, p. 104.
6. *Palestine: Statement of Policy*, Cmd. 6019, 1939.
7. David Cesarini, *Eichmann: His Life and Crimes*, William Heinemann, 2004, p. 75.
8. Nur Masalha, *Expulsion of the Palestinians*, Institute for Palestine Studies, 1992, p. 30.
9. *Grundzüge des Vorschlages der Nationalen Militärischen Organisation in Palastina (Irgun Zewai Leumi) betreffend der Lösung der jüdischen Frage Europas und der aktiven Teilnahme der NMO am Kriege an der Seite Deutschlands*, David Yisraeli, *The Palestine Problem in German Politics 1889–1945*, Bar Ilan University (Ramat Gan, Israel), 1974, pp. 315–17.
10. Olive Renier and Vladimir Rubinstein, *Assigned to Listen*, BBC, 1986, p. 11.
11. Ibid., p. 57.

16 LOVE AND WAR

1. Alec Graydon, *The Details*, Ex Libris Books, 2003.
2. Olive Renier and Vladimir Rubinstein, *Assigned to Listen*, BBC, 1986, p. 146.

3. George Mansur to Lord Lloyd, Middle East Centre, St Antony's College, Oxford, Barbour Papers Box II, File 3.

4. *Foreign Affairs Oral History Program*, op. cit.

5. W. Roger Louis and Robert W. Stookey (eds), *The End of the Palestine Mandate*, University of Texas Press, 1988, p. 36.

6. Peter Partner, *Arab Voices*, BBC Publications, 1988, p. 61.

17 DISPLACED PERSONS

1. Proposal from Lessing J. Rosenwald to President Truman at their meeting in the White House, 4 December 1945, Truman Presidential Museum and Library <http://www.trumanlibrary.org/ whistlestop/study_collections/israel/large/ documents/ index.php?pagenumber=1&documentdate= 1945-1204&documentid=67&collectionid=ROI>

2. Shabtai Teveth, *Ben-Gurion: The Burning Ground,1886–1948*, Houghton Mifflin, Boston, 1987, pp. 855–6.

3. Peter Grose, *Israel in the Mind of America*, Alfred A. Knopf, 1983, pp. 209–10.

4. Ilan Pappe, *A History of Modern Palestine*, Cambridge University Press, 2004, p. 119.

5. W. Roger Louis and Robert W. Stookey (eds), *The End of the Palestine Mandate*, University of Texas Press, 1988, p. 42.

6. Ibid.

7. Grose, *Israel in the Mind of America*, p. 196.

8. Ibid.

9. Richard H. Curtiss, *A Changing Image*, American Educational Trust, 1982, p. 30.

10. A. J. Sherman, *Mandate Days*, Thames and Hudson, 1997, p. 177.

11. Menachem Begin, *The Revolt*, Henry Schuman, 1951, p. 215.

12. Sherman, *Mandate Days*, p. 178.

13. Ibid., p. 189.

14. United Nations Division for Palestinian Rights, *The Origins and Evolution of the Palestine Problem: 1917–1988, PART II 1947–1977*, Unispal website, <http://domino.un.org/unispal.nsf/>

15. Mary-Jane Deeb and Mary E. King (eds), *Hasib Sabbagh: From Palestinian Refugee to Citizen of the World*, Middle East Institute,

University Press of America, 1996, p. 34.

16. Martin Gilbert, *Exile and Return*, Weidenfeld and Nicolson, 1978, p. 286.

17. Edward W. Said and Christopher Hitchens (eds), *Blaming the Victims*, Verso, 1988, p. 120.

18 UNSCOP AND ROBBERS

1. United Nations Division for Palestinian Rights, *The Origins and Evolution of the Palestine Problem: 1917–1988, PART II 1947–1977*, Unispal website, <http://domino.un.org/unispal.nsf/>

2. Ibid.

3. Ibid.

4. Ibid.

5. Ibid.

6. Peter Grose, *Israel in the Mind of America*, Alfred A. Knopf, 1983, p. 238.

7. Jorge Garcia-Granados, *The Birth of Israel*, Alfred A. Knopf, 1949, p. 159.

8. Grose, *Israel in the Mind of America*, p. 235.

9. A. J. Sherman, *Mandate Days*, Thames and Hudson, 1997, p. 207.

10. Ibid., p. 208.

11. Ilan Pappe, *A History of Modern Palestine*, Cambridge University Press, 2004, p. 122.

12. Garcia-Granados, *The Birth of Israel*, p. 120.

13. Ibid., p. 149.

14. Ibid., p. 217.

15. Ibid., p. 218.

16. United Nations Division for Palestinian Rights, *The Origins and Evolution of the Palestine Problem: 1917–1988, PART II 1947–1977*, Unispal website, <http://domino.un.org/unispal.nsf/>

17. Garcia-Granados, *The Birth of Israel*, p. 244.

18. Ibid., p. 245.

19. Ibid., p. 93.

20. Nur Masalha, *Expulsion of the Palestinians*, Institute for Palestine Studies, 1992, p. 176.

19 THE UN VOTE, 29 NOVEMBER 1947

1. Peter Partner, *Arab Voices*, BBC Publications, 1988, pp. 84–5.
2. United Nations Division for Palestinian Rights, *The Origins and Evolution of the Palestine Problem: 1917–1988, PART II 1947–1977*, Unispal website, <http://domino.un.org/unispal.nsf/>
3. <http://www.ou.org/torah/tt/5760/yitro60/bhyom.htm>
4. Peter Grose, *Israel in the Mind of America*, Alfred A. Knopf, 1983, p. 250.
5. Ibid., p. 248.
6. Ibid.
7. Ibid., p. 251.
8. Ibid., p. 250.
9. Ibid., p. 242.
10. Letter from Michael Comay, Jewish Agency New York office, quoted in Michael J. Cohen, *Truman and Israel*, University of California Press, 1990, p. 164.
11. United Nations Division for Palestinian Rights, *The Origins and Evolution of the Palestine Problem: 1917–1988, PART II 1947–1977*, Unispal website, <http://domino.un.org/unispal.nsf/>
12. Peter Grose, *Israel in the Mind of America*, Alfred A. Knopf, 1983, p. 252.
13. Robert John and Sami Hadawi, *The Palestine Diary*, Vol. 2, New World Press, 1970, p. 250.
14. Grose, *Israel in the Mind of America*, p. 252.
15. Abraham Rabinovich, Jerusalem Post, 8 March 2002, quoted in <http://www.palestineremembered.com /Acre/ Palestine-Remembered/Story780.html>
16. Grose, *Israel in the Mind of America*, p. 252.
17. Ibid., p. 253.
18. Ibid., p. 251.
19. United Nations Division for Palestinian Rights, *The Origins and Evolution of the Palestine Problem: 1917–1988, PART II 1947–1977*, Unispal website, <http://domino.un.org/unispal.nsf/>
20. From summary of Robert John and Sami Hadawi, *The Palestine Diary*, 2 vols, New World Press, 1970, on <http://www.russgranata. com/palestine1.html>

21. Izzat Tannous, *The Palestinians*, I.G.T. Company, 1988, p. 431.

22. Ibid.

23. Jorge Garcia-Granados, *The Birth of Israel*, Alfred A. Knopf, 1949, pp. 263-4.

24. Rabinovich, *Jerusalem Post*, 8 March 2002, quoted in <http://www.palestineremembered.com /Acre/Palestine-Remembered/Story780.html>

25. Ibid.

26. Richard H. Curtiss, *A Changing Image*, American Educational Trust, 1982, p. 27.

27. Grose, *Israel in the Mind of America*, p. 256.

20 THE END OF HISTORY

1. <http://msanews.mynet.net/MSANEWS/199912/19991205.0.html>, An Interview with Ilan Pappe, by Baudouin Loos.

2. <http://sf.indymedia.org/news/2003/11/1662194.php>

3. Benny Morris, *The Birth of the Palestinian Refugee Problem Revisited*, Cambridge University Press, 2004, pp. 101-2.

4. Ibid., pp. 65-6.

5. Ibid., p. 72.

6. Ibid., p. 85.

7. Ibid., p. 75.

8. *The Times*, 18 May 1961, quoted in Edward W. Said and Christopher Hitchens (eds), *Blaming the Victims*, Verso, 1988, p. 81.

9. Joseph Katz, 'Origins of the Arab-Jewish Conflict', in <http://www.eretzyisroel.org/~peters/depopulated.html>

10. Simha Flapan, *The Birth of Israel*, Pantheon Books, 1987, p. 84.

11. <http://www.factsandlogic.org/>

12. Nur Masalha, *Expulsion of the Palestinians*, Institute for Palestine Studies, 1992, p. 175.

13. Walid Khalidi, *Before their Diaspora*, Institute for Palestine Studies, 1991, p. 252.

14. Morris, *The Birth of the Palestinian Refugee Problem Revisited*, p. 343.

15. Ibid., p. 69.

16. Ibid., p. 132.

17. Ibid., p. 237.

18. Ibid., p. 238.

19. Menachem Begin, *The Revolt*, Henry Schuman, 1951, p. 165.

20. Doris Katz, *The Lady was a Terrorist*, Shiloni Publishers, 1953, p. 96.

21. Ibid., pp. 132–3.

22. Morris, *The Birth of the Palestinian Refugee Problem Revisited*,
    pp. 237–40.

23. Quotes from Norman Finkelstein, *Image and Reality of the
    Israel–Palestine Conflict*, quoted in *The Origin of the Palestine–Israel
    Conflict*, 3rd edn (including Intifada 2000), published by Jews For
    Justice in the Middle East, <http://www.cactus48.com/truth.html>

24. Ibid.

25. Meron Benvenisti, *Sacred Landscape: The Buried History of the Holy
    Land since 1948*, University of California Press, 2000, pp. 152–3.

26. <http://msanews.mynet.net/MSANEWS/199912/
    19991205.0.html>, an Interview with Ilan Pappe by Baudouin
    Loos, Brussels, 29 November 1999.

27. Morris, *The Birth of the Palestinian Refugee Problem Revisited*, pp.
    263–5.

28. Henry Cattan, *Palestine, The Arabs and Israel*, 1969, quoted in *The
    Origin of the Palestine–Israel Conflict*, 3rd edn (including Intifada
    2000), published by Jews For Justice in the Middle East,
    <http://www.cactus48.com/truth.html>

29. Morris, *The Birth of the Palestinian Refugee Problem Revisited*,
    p. 183.

30. Ibid., p. 249.

31. Ibid.

32. Ibid., pp. 221–6.

33. Ibid., p. 316.

34. Ghada Karmi, *Guardian*, 19 October 2002.

35. Mary-Jane Deeb and Mary E. King (eds), *Hasib Sabbagh: From
    Palestinian Refugee to Citizen of the World*, Middle East Institute,
    University Press of America, 1996, pp. 34–6.

36. A. J. Sherman, *Mandate Days*, Thames and Hudson, 1997, p. 243.

21 PALESTINE LOST

1. Nur Masalha, *Expulsion of the Palestinians*, Institute for Palestine Studies, 1992, p. 191.

2. Ted Schwarz, *Walking with the Damned*, Paragon House, 1992, p. 284.

3. Kati Marton, *A Death in Jerusalem*, Arcade Publishing, 1996, p. 139.

4. Ibid., p. 148.

5. Bernardotte in letter of 23 July 1948, to brother Karl, quoted in Marton, *A Death in Jerusalem*, p. 160.

6. Marton, *A Death in Jerusalem*, p. 190.

7. Benny Morris, *The Birth of the Palestinian Refugee Problem Revisited*, Cambridge University Press, 2004, pp. 331–2.

8. Quoted in Marton, *A Death in Jerusalem*, p. 228.

9. Quoted in ibid., p. 162.

10. Quoted in Morris, *The Birth of the Palestinian Refugee Problem Revisited*, pp. 425–6.

11. Morris, *The Birth of the Palestinian Refugee Problem Revisited*, pp. 431–2.

12. Quoted in Marton, *A Death in Jerusalem*, p. 162.

13. Azmi S. Audeh, *Carpenter from Nazareth*, Audeh Publishers, 1997, pp. 106–11.

14. Ibid.

15. *Ha'aretz* magazine (www.haaretz.com), 9 January 2004.

16. Ibid.

17. Avi Shlaim, *The Iron Wall*, W.W. Norton, 2000, p. 35.

18. Avi Shlaim, private offprint.

19. Akiva Eldar, *Ha'aretz* magazine, 24 November 2003.

20. Arthur Koestler, *Promise and Fulfilment: Palestine 1917–1949*, Macmillan, 1949, pp. 199–200.

21. Doris Katz, *The Lady was a Terrorist*, Shiloni Publishers, 1953, p. 108.

22. Diary of Josef Weitz, quoted in Meron Benvenisti, *Sacred Landscape: The Buried History of the Holy Land since 1948*, University of California Press, 2000, pp. 155–6.

EPILOGUE

1. Avi Shlaim, *The Iron Wall*, W. W. Norton, 2000, p. 38.
2. Raymonda Hawa Taweel, *My Home, My Prison*, Holt, Rinehart and Winston, 1979, pp. 3–4.
3. Afif Safieh, *On Palestinian Diplomacy*, Palestinian Delegation to the UK and the Vatican, 2004, p. 21.
4. Paul Eisen,<http://www.nonprofitnet.ca/wao/wao.php?show&720>

INDEX

Declaration, 118; attends Paris
Peace Conference, 138–9, 142;
inaugurates Mandate, 149; meets
Arab delegation, 164–5
Balfour Declaration, 107–21, 180,
182; text of, 118; Arab response to,
124; American response to, 125;
enactment of, 129–31, 134–5, 143,
186, 191, 212; anniversaries of, 130,
188; incorporated into Mandate,
146, 149, 151, 158, 162, 165, 167,
221, 225, 255, 325; Zionist
justification of, 166–7; declared a
blunder, 175; 'anti-Balfour
Declaration', 221
Barbour, Nevill, 105
Baruch, Bernard, 271
Basle, 80–1
Baybars the Mameluke, 295
Bayreuth, 103
BBC Arabic Service, 2–4, 216–19,
225–8, 234–6, 239–40, 249, 264–5,
298
Bedouins, 25, 27–9, 34, 47, 73, 180
Be'ersheva (Beersheba), 67, 174
Begin, Menachem, 250–1, 256;
leads Deir Yassin massacre, 285
Beilinson, Moshe, 181
Beirut, 35, 135; earthquake, 61;
meeting with Nazis, 223;
American University, 234;
Sabbagh family members in,
291–3, 299–300, 323
Beisan, 288
Beit Jala, 317–18

Belem, 127–8
Belgium, 21
Bell, Gertrude, 140
Ben Gurion, David, 210, 255, 263;
heads Zionist movement, 221–2;
on concentration camps, 242–3;
terrorist activities, 246, 250; and
expulsion policy, 280, 282–3, 305;
covers for massacres, 312; plans
to seize West Bank, 318
Ben Shimon, David (Safad guide),
294–7
Beni Saqr tribe, 30
Benvenisti, Meron, 286
Berdichev, 16
Berlin, Isaiah, 163
Berlin, 106
Bernadotte, Count Folke, 301–4
Beth Akiba, 178
Bethel, 78
Bethlehem, 128, 177, 215
Bevin, Ernest, 244, 247, 251
Bible, 5, 53, 69; stories, 16–17,
83–96; truth and archaeology,
87–92; see also Genesis; Joshua,
Book of; Judges, Book of; New
Testament; Old Testament;
Samuel, Book of
Bir Zeit, 170
Biria, 71
Bishouti family, 56
Black Letter, 189
Blum, Léon, 271
Board of Deputies of British Jews,
104–5

INDEX | 363